WAR ECONOMICS OF PRIMARY PRODUCING COUNTRIES

WAR ECONOMICS OF PRIMARY PRODUCING COUNTRIES

By

A. R. PREST, M.A.

CAMBRIDGE
AT THE UNIVERSITY PRESS
1948

CAMBRIDGE
UNIVERSITY PRESS

University Printing House, Cambridge CB2 8BS, United Kingdom

Cambridge University Press is part of the University of Cambridge.

It furthers the University's mission by disseminating knowledge in the pursuit of education, learning and research at the highest international levels of excellence.

www.cambridge.org
Information on this title: www.cambridge.org/9781107452626

First published 1948
First paperback edition 2014

A catalogue record for this publication is available from the British Library

ISBN 978-1-107-45262-6 Paperback

PREFACE

I must first express my gratitude to the Master and Fellows of Christ's College, Cambridge, for it was their award of the Adelaide Stoll Research Studentship which rendered this work possible. A considerable proportion of the material is based on personal interview or correspondence with people either in this country or abroad, but it is impossible to mention them all by name. Mr W. B. Reddaway first suggested the scope of the enquiry to me and gave me most valuable advice and searching criticism on the manuscript at various stages. I have also had the benefit of various parts being read by Professor D. H. Robertson, Mr P. Sraffa and Professor J. H. Richardson. To all of these I owe a heavy debt for the alterations and improvements which they so kindly suggested. I must also thank the Editor of *The Banker* for his permission to reproduce material from an article in the issue for March 1946. Needless to say, the responsibility for the errors and faults that remain is entirely my own.

A. R. PREST

CAMBRIDGE

August 1947

INTRODUCTION

In the following chapters we shall be investigating the general economic problems of primary economies during the 1939–45 war. Our aim is to describe the war contribution of a number of primary producing countries, India, some of the countries of the Middle East, and two Crown Colonies, Nigeria and Trinidad, to see by what means this war contribution was achieved, and to show the principal reactions.

The concept of a war contribution is essentially vague, for not only are a number of different ideas bound up together, but many of the ideas themselves are often incapable of precise definition. We shall deal in this book with the direct utilization of man-power and resources for war, in the form of recruits, workers, or equipment and supplies for the Allied Forces; the more indirect but sometimes more important devotion of resources to exports of essential commodities; and the principal reductions in civilian consumption. This is a somewhat wide definition of war contribution, and clearly must involve a certain amount of arbitrary demarcation, particularly in deciding which exports are 'essential' commodities. Nevertheless, as will emerge later, it appears to be the most satisfactory indicator it is possible to adopt.

Discussion of the means of achieving the war contribution will largely revolve round the use of 'inflationary' methods of developing war output and the mainly unsuccessful attempts to control the consequences of these methods. Consideration of the principal reactions will be mainly a statistical picture of the general changes in prices, incomes, and capital assets. To some extent analysis of methods and results involves overlapping, for both are concerned with problems of large increases in prices and incomes, and these are both the means of securing productive resources for war and also the results of such diversion.

Some questions will no doubt spring to the mind. One will probably be—why such a selection of countries? And closely allied with this will be a second—are not the difficulties of applying economic and statistical analysis to 'backward' countries so great as to be almost insuperable? And thirdly—are not the differences between the countries selected so immense as to invalidate comparison?

The choice of countries was determined by several factors, such as the size of the war effort relatively to the resources of the country; the nature of the war effort; the price and income changes experienced; the amount of information available; immunity from enemy occupation. Clearly there are other countries that may fit any one of these categories better than those selected. A study of China or Greece will give more scope for considering problems of price and income changes, for instance, but, on the other hand, there are complications in those countries arising from enemy occupation. Of course, many more could have been included in this survey, but this would have taken more time, and it was judged better to write on these matters while they are still fresh in men's minds even if this did mean a narrowing of the field.

Perhaps it will be best to answer the second and third queries together. It is true that the countries dealt with do differ enormously in almost every conceivable way; in area, density of population, climate, geography, resources, economic structure and so on. Furthermore, the contributions they were called on to make in wartime were very different in character and degree. For some it was mainly a case of becoming self-sufficient in food; for others it was mainly one of supplying the Allied Armies with materials and man-power. It might well be said that the most obvious similarity between these countries is the lack of any satisfactory information about the ways in which their economic affairs are normally conducted.

The first answer to these objections lies in the nature of the fundamental economic problem of wartime which is broadly the same for all countries whatever differences there may be between them. This is dealt with more fully in Chapter I, but in essence it consists in directing economic resources to military uses, and although the form of the war contribution was so different in these countries, the same underlying problem remained for all. Furthermore, the methods actually adopted to deal with this contribution bring out the similarities of primary economies rather than the differences; difficulties of applying 'Western' controls or inducements to populations largely dependent on primitive agriculture were similar in all these countries. The phenomena of hoarding—and fear of hoarding—were common to all. There are, of course, great difficulties in gathering accurate statistics on these matters, but this difficulty is not nearly so great in the war period as it was in the past, as Colonial Governments and new regional authorities like the Middle East Supply Centre have intervened in trade and production to an unparalleled degree, and consequently much more information is available than before. Finally, analysis is in some ways simple because the number of industries is so small, and the staple articles of consumption are so few for the large majority of the population. It is in some ways easier to calculate the reductions in consumption of, say, an African negro, than of an English factory worker.

Our method of analysis will take the following form. The first chapter is a general summary of the wartime economic problems that had to be faced, and the principal difficulties encountered in dealing with them. The second, third, and fourth chapters contain detailed analyses of the problems in India, Palestine and Egypt, and they all follow the same method. Section 1 outlines the war contribution in real terms; Section 2 the main financial changes; Section 3 traces the link between the two; and Section 4 is a general critique of war organization. Chapters V–X are on the same general lines as Chapters II–IV but are less detailed. Chapter XI draws a few conclusions. It will be observed that the detailed chapters vary widely in length and scope. In particular, it would have been desirable to include a longer description of the economic controls in the Sudan; it will also be seen that some of the information on essential points such as money and price changes is very limited, especially in Chapters IX and X. These are, admittedly, undesirable defects, but in some cases analysis has been limited by the amount of information in existence, and in others by the amount available for publication. Despite these serious gaps it still seemed worth while to present the information that could be gathered in view of the paucity of material on primary countries which is normally available and accessible in this country.

CONTENTS

CHAPTER I

GENERAL SURVEY

The fundamental economic task of the Government of any country which takes part in war is to secure for the use of its own Armed Services, or those of the allies whom it supports, some portion of the gross annual flow of goods and services produced at home or imported from overseas. Whether the Government essays this task willingly or under coercion, whether the proportion of resources diverted to war needs is large or small, the essence of the problem remains the same. Now these goods and services needed for war purposes may in theory be acquired in two ways—they may be purchased for cash or they may be obtained by some form of requisitioning or voluntary contribution which does not involve any element of current payment. In practice there is an element of cash payment in the great majority of these transactions, for requisitioning without current payment is normally only possible under extreme conditions internally, even though it may be practised frequently by military commanders in conquered territories. Similarly, the proportion of the gross annual domestic output of goods and services which citizens will yield voluntarily is also very limited in practice, even if the carrot of future payment is dangled in front of their eyes. This point should not be confused with the fact that voluntary savings out of income can be, and often are, important. All that we need to establish at this stage is that people inside a country are not usually prepared to work for the State or supply goods to it without cash payment, even though there may be certain outstanding exceptions in external or inter-governmental transactions, such as the volume of Lend-Lease goods supplied by the U.S.A. from 1941 to 1945. Therefore our general proposition is that Governments engaging in war normally need to secure for their own use some part of the flow of currently produced goods and services, and that this need will usually involve cash payments.

Prima facie this means that there will be an addition to the volume of the overall flow of money demand for goods and services inside a country in any given period of time. Given the amount the Government wishes to spend, the *size* of this addition will clearly depend on the net amount by which private (i.e. non-Government) purchasers of goods and services curtail their money expenditure. This curtailment may be large or small, depending on the extent to which private purchasers reduce their demands voluntarily, and on the degree of success attached to such measures of compulsion as increased direct taxation, rationing, price control, limited production of normal consumption goods and so on. But, generally speaking, we may say that the net reduction in private money demand is not likely to be sufficiently large to outweigh the increase in Government money demand, and therefore some increase in the overall volume of money demand is inevitable in time of war. The main reason for this is the quite simple fact that it is much easier to secure goods and services, at any rate in the short run, by adding to the volume of total money demand than by only substituting Government for private demand. It is obviously much easier for a Government to debase a currency or print a few more notes than it is to devise administrative machinery for successfully introducing or increasing income taxes. Even apart from any question of administrative simplicity the first type of measure can be employed surreptitiously and stealthily, whereas the second will be done in the full glare of public opinion. After all, no Government can be expected to court unpopularity when it is unnecessary to do so. And not only is it better from administrative and political viewpoints to prefer additions to the volume of money demand, but in many cases this is the only means of obtaining goods and services quickly, which is often very necessary in war. It would hardly have been the height of wisdom in 1940 if the British Government had waited until the taxes were received in the following March to purchase the Spitfires necessary for the defence of the country. Furthermore, if the Government wishes to bring unemployed resources of labour, capacity or materials into use, this task is normally much more easily accomplished if expansion of the overall volume of money demand is allowed, in just the same way as the addition of a supercharger to a racing car enables it to obtain higher speeds more easily. Finally, it should be noticed that even if a Government's war expenditure is covered entirely by an increase in indirect taxation, there will still be a resultant increase in money demand as a whole unless suppliers of the taxed commodities do not raise prices at all.

The *effect* of any addition to the volume of money demand in any given period is clear in its outlines, even though many of the details may be complex. Broadly we may say that the effect on the general level of prices and incomes must depend on the extent to which it is possible to increase the supply of goods available for use. This increase in supply may be derived from a number of sources, such as an increase in current home production or imports, a reduction of current exports, releases from stocks or diversion of resources normally engaged on maintenance of capital equipment. This is the general position: the greater the increase in the overall volume of money demand and the smaller the increase in the flow of goods, the larger will be the rises in prices and incomes. But it must not be thought from this condensed sentence that there is, in practice, any very simple relationship between these three sets of variables. Even if the volume of money demand as a whole and the supply of goods and services available for use rise in equal proportion, this does not mean that there will be no changes in prices and incomes; for in wartime there are bound to be shifts in demand by the nature of the case, and the resources at a community's disposal may not be readily suitable to meet such changes. Reductions in stocks of whiskey, for instance, are not of much avail to a Government wishing to purchase tanks. Therefore, it may well be that technical bottlenecks will arise in some lines of production or that some entrepreneurs will be in a position to exploit purchasers. In either case there is likely to be a sharp divergence between prices and average prime costs,[1] and this is likely to force up the level of prices and incomes in some spheres of activity.

We may summarize our argument so far by saying that the exigencies of war normally mean some addition[2] to the overall volume of money demand in any given period of time, and that this quite frequently leads to some all-round increases in prices and incomes during that period. What is likely to happen in a series of periods? So long as the Government continues to spend in each successive period a greater amount than the reduction in private expenditure which it can secure or enforce, then the level of money demand must continue to increase. In the absence of any large increases in the supply of goods and services available there must clearly be successive rises in prices and incomes. Furthermore, if the Government aims at obtaining a certain volume of goods and services for war purposes, and not merely a certain value, the successive rises in prices reduce

[1] I.e. costs of all such current operating expenses as wages, raw materials, repairs and maintenance.

[2] This may, of course, be due to increased demands by other countries for exports as well as, or instead of, internal Government demands.

the real value of its purchases and will lead it to make even greater additions to the volume of money demand in pursuance of its aims. This would seem to indicate even further rises in prices and incomes, but in actual practice there are mitigating factors to be taken into account. In the first place the yield of taxation is likely to increase as prices and incomes rise, and this will help to reduce the volume of private money demand; secondly, it is also possible that there may be some redistribution of income in favour of the profit-earning classes,[1] and therefore there may be an increase in voluntary savings which will also help to restrain the growth in money demand. For these reasons, therefore, any process of expanding money demand normally contains elements which sooner or later tend to slow down the rate of increase.

We must now ask how the primary producing countries dealt with in this survey fit into the picture we have traced. In general, as will be shown in the individual chapters, their Governments obtained the economic resources needed for war by a process of adding to the volume of money demand, rather than substituting public demand for private. In the industrialized countries, on the other hand, this object was achieved by a much greater degree of substitution of public-money demand for private.[2] Of course, the distinction is one of degree and not of kind. No country was able to secure resources for war without an expansion of money demand; and none of the countries considered here was totally unable to restrain private-money demand in some way or other. The general contrast between industrial and primary economies is still clear however. Not only did the industrialized countries control the expansion of money demand more closely, but, as will soon become evident, they were also generally more successful in increasing the supply of goods available for use. Therefore, for both reasons, it might be expected from our analysis above that the changes in prices and incomes would be relatively greater in primary than in industrialized countries. Comparative statistics of price changes in different countries are shown in Table 1.

It is necessary to add a word of warning about this table, for comparisons between statistics in different countries, even when they are good statistics, are notoriously full of pitfalls. The changes shown

[1] This point is developed more fully on p. 24.

[2] Appendix I shows the comparative expansion of the stock of money in a number of countries.

by cost of living indices in wartime may not give a true picture of what really happened for two main reasons. In many cases consumption patterns were changed out of all recognition, either by consuming less of normal foods or other goods, or dispensing with them altogether, and therefore any comparison of prices based on a pre-war system of weighting is not likely to be an accurate indication of what happened to the cost of living. Then many commodities, even if obtainable, were only to be bought at free- or black-market prices, whereas the majority of indices only reflect official controlled prices. On the whole it is probable that these official indices underestimate the rise in the cost of living in primary *vis-à-vis* advanced countries, both because the change-over[1] to more expensive substitutes went further and because black-market prices were much more common.

TABLE I. *Cost of living indices*

Country	August 1939	June 1945	Country	August 1939	June 1945
India	100	223	Nigeria	100	176
Egypt	100	290	Trinidad	100	179
Palestine	100	257	Great Britain	100	135
Cyprus	100	233	U.S.A.	100	130
Sudan	100	166	Canada	100	120
Iraq	100	369	Australia	100	112
Syria and Lebanon	100	562			

Source. League of Nations, *Monthly Bulletin of Statistics.*
Note. India figure is for Bombay.

We shall now proceed to deal with the reasons why these primary countries were unable to prevent wide changes in prices and incomes, and this in turn will entail consideration of why the volume of money demand increased so much and the volume of goods and services so little. We shall tackle these related problems under three main headings:

(1) Size and nature of war demands.
(2) Characteristics of primary countries.
(3) Methods of organizing war contributions.

Before we start on this analysis, however, we must clear up a terminological difficulty, and that is the meaning we shall attach to the word 'inflation'.

[1] We are only dealing here with changes which were forced on the consumers and not voluntary changes connected with higher standards of living.

The senses in which the term 'inflation' is used are legion. The principal differences between them are, first, whether the verb 'to inflate' is to be taken to refer to *any* increase or only to an increase which is in some sense abnormal, and secondly, whether the words 'inflate' and 'inflation' are primarily associated with changes in the supply of money, the level of prices, the level of money wages, or the overall volume of money demand for all goods and services. Further difficulties of definition ensue if we try to specify exactly what we mean by the level of prices (wholesale or retail, subsidized or 'natural', controlled or black market) or by money wages (rates or earnings, efficiency wages or not). Yet another sense is to reserve the term for a situation where there is an abnormal diversion of resources to ends which are not in the best interests of the community, as conceived by some criteria of economic welfare. In the ensuing chapters inflation will usually be taken to indicate an expansion of the volume of overall money demand greater than that associated with normal swings in activity.[1] When dealing with specific aspects of this movement, such as incomes and prices, we shall speak of income-inflation or price-inflation. We may now return to the main path of our analysis.

1. Size and Nature of War Demands

Perhaps the most satisfactory way of analysing the diversion of economic resources which war entails is to draw up a budget of the supply and demand for real resources. On the supply side we have the gross national output and the imports of goods and services; on the demand side we have the military demand for resources, exports of goods and services, and home consumption and gross capital formation:

Resources available	*Resources required*
Gross national output	Military demands
Imports of goods and services	Exports of goods and services
	Domestic consumption and gross capital formation

In this section we shall only be concerned with military demands and with exports and imports. We shall deal with the question of gross national output and domestic consumption and capital

[1] To say that *any* expansion of the flow of money demand is inflationary would mean that inflation could occur at the bottom of a slump or when a Government substituted indirect taxes for direct.

formation in the next section. What should be noted at this point is that military demands and exports constitute a drain on a nation's resources, whilst imports represent an addition.

What form did military demands take in primary countries, and how important were they? In the first place many countries contributed recruits to the Armed Forces; as we shall see, some 2,500,000 Indians were recruited, and some 90,000 Nigerians. But, large as these figures are, it is extremely doubtful whether this was a major source of labour shortage. Whereas approximately 11% of the total population of Great Britain was in the Armed Forces, only 0·6% of the Indian population and 0·4% of the Nigerian were enlisted, and so it is hard to believe that this was important.

The second main form of contribution was satisfying the demands of the Allied Armies for goods and services. It is necessary to make a distinction here between those goods and services which were purchased by the military authorities, and those which were purchased by the local Governments. The importance of this distinction will be seen shortly.

Much the most important of the two, of course, was direct military purchase. This covered many categories of foodstuffs and equipment purchased for armies stationed both in the supplying country and elsewhere; the services performed by local labour employed as builders, fitters, dockers, labourers, and in a host of other jobs; and the consumption of goods and personal services by individual soldiers. These direct military purchases were, by and large, the most important war contribution of the countries dealt with here. This was particularly so in the case of Trinidad, where the construction of American defence bases diverted a large amount of local labour. Of the Middle East countries, perhaps it was most important in Palestine, where average annual military expenditure per head of the population from 1939 to 1944 was higher than in any other Middle East country, when due allowance is made for price changes.

Local Government purchases were usually not important compared with military demands. It is true that Government expenditure increased heavily in all countries, and in some cases more than proportionately to the rise in local prices. This was particularly so in India, where Government defence expenditure expanded from £37·2 million in 1939–40 to £343·7 million in 1944–5, but even here it was outweighed by Allied military expenditure over the whole period 1939–45.

To put military demands in their correct setting, it is necessary to take into account movements in volume of exports and imports. Then we shall be in a position to form some idea of the importance of the different claims on resources.

The part played by exports in consuming economic resources differed considerably from one country to another. In the early war period a large part of the export trade of practically all these countries was threatened by a sudden slump, owing to the restriction of shipping facilities, the closing of the European markets and the Mediterranean Sea route in 1940. Generally there was a fall, or at least a failure to increase, in price indices at this time, which was in marked contrast with the upward movement in Great Britain.

In India the acreage given to jute and cotton production was decreased; in Palestine ruin was threatened to the citrus growers, and the Government had to step in with advances and guarantees of bank loans; special arrangements were made for the British purchase of Egyptian cotton and Nigerian cocoa to prevent collapse; and relief works had to be opened in Cyprus to succour the unemployed. This dislocation of main export markets and exports was important, for it not only created the rather dangerous illusion that there was plenty of spare labour and resources in these countries, but it also helped to obscure the local Governments' eyes to the more fundamental economic problems of war. At this stage the major worry was how to prevent bankruptcy among their export trades rather than how to prepare for the coming shortages of goods of all kinds.

But many other commodities were not affected by this collapse, and their supply was vital to the Allies throughout the war. In some cases it was a continuance of peacetime trading on normal lines between private exporters and importers; in other cases bulk purchase by Government agencies, such as the Ministry of Food's purchases of Indian tea, or the Ministry of Supply's purchase of Nigerian tin and Indian jute, was the principal channel through which trade flowed.

Reductions in the volume of imports[1] were common to all countries, either because of lack of shipping space or because of scarcity of supply. In most cases it was the reduced supply of capital goods which was most important; but in some there were severe cuts in manufactured goods and semi-manufactures, and in others raw materials and foodstuffs. Furthermore, there were many changes of type and quality as well as overall reductions of particular categories;

[1] Excluding munitions and other supplies for the Allied Armies.

e.g. India had to import wheat instead of rice, and the Middle East countries had to import light manufactured goods from Egypt or Palestine instead of from Great Britain or the U.S.A. The ports which were used in wartime were often different from pre-war days, either because some had become unusable for strategic reasons or because the source of supply had changed. Such factors as these, we shall see, often threw a far greater strain on the economy of the country than a mere examination of global import reductions would suggest. Finally, some countries had to pay for imports prices which had risen much further than the general price level of home-produced goods.

We are now in a position to summarize the main problems of real resources which war brought to these primary economies. Broadly the difficulty was to meet vastly increased demands on military account, or, sometimes, export account, from resources that were suffering from decreased supplies of imports. And we shall see in § 2 that ability to increase production from home resources was for various reasons strictly limited. Furthermore, the new demands did not only take the form of increased consumption of old lines of production, but often involved the starting of completely new industries. India produced tea but she also built aircraft; Egypt produced cotton but also many manufactured goods; Nigeria produced cocoa but also columbite and wolfram.

The next point to note is that special problems were involved in the large military demands of the Allies for food, equipment and manpower, for this was a contrast with the main belligerent countries, where the principal war demand was that of the home Government for goods and services. Now this distinction is important. If the main war expenditure was incurred by the Allies, there was little reason why the local Government should be very concerned about the effects on prices and incomes, particularly if it was not actually at war. It is, after all, a far cry from piling up sterling balances as a neutral to piling up internal war debt. But even apart from this question of willingness to take action, ability to do so was often limited for several reasons. In the first place, military demands were sometimes not known, even within orders of magnitude, by the Governments concerned. Local contracts were arranged by military authorities, and there was little check on the resources which were diverted in this way. Secondly, military demands were not known by the population. A Government's current expenditure is always known from budget estimates, but the cloak of secrecy effectively hid any information about military expenditure by the Allies. Thirdly, military demands were usually incalculable. Throughout the war years it was never known exactly what part any individual country would have to play, and there were many local vicissitudes of military demand which were due to the changing requirements of military strategy. This was in contrast to Great Britain where Government expenditure was always known, and where it absorbed a fairly constant proportion of the national income after 1941.

These difficulties made it impossible to keep taxation and savings in step with current military requirements even if the will had been there. For if in the first place military expenditure is not known it is difficult for a Government to know at what level to set taxation or how far to encourage savings, and it is still more difficult to convince the public that it is necessary for them to make additional sacrifices. And even if military expenditure is known by the Government it is impossible to keep taxation in step if expenditure is liable to sudden fluctuations. The inevitable time lag between making a tax decision and reaping the results means that taxation *ex post* may be completely out of alinement with expenditure *ex post*. It was much easier to keep taxation and savings in step with expenditure in Great Britain where the rough level of future expenditure was known in advance, but even here the proportion of expenditure covered by taxation was not so great in 1940–1 as it was in the later war years when the taxation system was fully geared up to expenditure.

Thus in the primary countries the normal method of financing military expenditure was by credit creation. Of course the amount of this varied from country to country, depending on the size of military expenditure, and on such offsets as a surplus of imports over exports, gold sales, local savings, etc. In Palestine, for instance, it was damped down by a large import surplus; in the later stages of the war in India gold sales were not unimportant.

Therefore, we may say that the price-income changes in primary economies are to some extent explained by the nature, as well as the size of, the war effort they were called on to make, for this introduced problems different from those which the advanced countries had to face.

2. Characteristics of Primary Economies

In the table of resources available and required for war at the beginning of the last section, we deferred over for later consideration 'Gross national product' and 'Domestic consumption and gross capital formation'. There have been disputes in the past among economists over what items should be included under these headings, but now it is generally agreed that in any given period of time gross national product may be taken to be the total national output of all types of goods and services; domestic gross capital formation is the volume of new capital goods plus maintenance and repair of existing capital goods plus changes in stocks.[1] Domestic consumption is the value[2] of that portion of the gross national product of goods and services actually being consumed by the civilian population and national troops.[3]

Now in so far as a country is able to increase its gross national product or reduce its domestic gross capital formation, it is able to mitigate any repercussions on domestic consumption due to the increases in military demand and exports and the reduction in imports. In so far as it has to reduce domestic consumption, the more it is able to do this by controls of various kinds, the less necessary will be a large measure of inflation.

Our first query is to see how far primary economies were likely to be able to increase their national output and reduce their domestic capital formation. It would appear at first sight as if there should have been a considerable reserve of resources which could have been used for increasing the national output, for in the majority of primary countries in pre-1939 days under-employment of labour was a characteristic feature of the economy. In some cases this was due to the pressure of an expanding population on the limited quantity of land, as in India and Egypt, where the fragmentary strips of land due to successive division are a most serious problem. In other cases it was

[1] See *Impact of War on Civilian Consumption* for a more detailed discussion.

[2] The distinction between consumers' expenditure and actual consumption will usually be neglected throughout the following pages (but see p. 25).

[3] Strictly, domestic consumption should only include the goods and services actually consumed by the civil population and those which national soldiers would have consumed as civilians, i.e. any consumption due to their role as soldiers should come under 'war demands'. However, the magnitude of this factor could not easily be assessed; in any case the error involved by neglecting it must be very small. The important thing is to exclude individual purchases of goods and services by foreign troops.

due to the depressed state of the markets for primary products which had led to severe restriction of output. Yet despite this apparent reserve of resources the recorded increases in output in wartime were very irregular. In some countries it was found possible to initiate new industries or expand old ones. India became a producer of munitions of various sorts; Egypt and Palestine became manufacturers of many metal and textile goods which had previously been imported. In other countries there was a considerable expansion of staple products, e.g. Nigerian tin and timber, or Iraq petroleum. Attempts were made also by many countries to increase foodstuffs production, but although results varied from country to country and from crop to crop, success was rather limited in this respect as may be seen from the detailed chapters.

In some cases this was due to the depletion of the labour force. In Trinidad, for instance, the diversion of labour to defence bases robbed the sugar plantations of much of their labour force. But labour shortage, of unskilled agricultural labour at any rate, was never a problem in India and the Middle East countries.

The main explanation there is to be found in the structure of primitive grain economies. The routine of the small proprietor is much the same in all these countries. He tries to produce sufficient grain to satisfy five requirements:

(1) To feed himself, his family and his animals.
(2) To allow some seed for the next crop.
(3) To meet any liabilities, such as taxes or rent.
(4) To pay some interest and possibly some capital on his debts.
(5) To exchange his surplus, if any, for necessities, such as clothing, footwear and household goods, etc.

Now both the tastes and commitments of these peasants are usually fairly static, and so if grain prices rise their reaction may be to produce less instead of more.[1] The normal economic incentive to which we are so used in industrial countries does not apply in nearly such a straightforward manner to Eastern peasants. Furthermore, and this may be more important in the Middle East, this tendency is reinforced if household necessities are scarce and their prices so high that they are beyond their means, however much grain they sell. The argument often used in Britain since the war ended, that

[1] Even if production does not fall the surplus available for sale may decrease, either because they eat more or because they hold more.

to increase production it is necessary to have an increased supply of consumption goods available for purchase, applies with even greater force to primitive economies.

Of course it was not only a question of willingness of small proprietors to increase their production, but also one of ability. We have seen that in the Middle East and India the unskilled labour supply was not difficult, but even there the shortage of, for instance, skilled mechanics to repair agricultural machinery became more and more pronounced. Such machinery as there was needed repair badly in the later war years, for imports were very much restricted. But lack of machinery was not so important for the great majority of small proprietors who have never seen anything more elaborate than the primitive implements which are described in the Bible. With these methods—it should be remembered that in pre-war days capital per acre even in the Punjab averaged about 45*s*. compared with £15 in Great Britain[1]—it was impossible to hope for much increase in production. Nor was this situation made easier by the difficulty of reaching a large, illiterate and uneducated population by any of the normal methods of propaganda. It is not much use telling a poor peasant who is already working as much as possible that he must increase his production because of a war being waged by other countries many thousands of miles away. There were other reasons, too, which were specific to various countries; in Egypt a very important factor was the shortage of fertilizers; in India the difficulty of bringing more land under cultivation was immense. And in all the fickleness of climatic conditions played an important part in determining output in any one year.[2]

These are some of the reasons which explain why there were definite limits to the possible increases in agricultural production. The situation was often made worse by the impossibility of procuring the crops which were being produced. In some cases this was due to the physical impossibility of transportation. Communications were never good in the Middle East or India, and the strain imposed on them in war made even the carriage of essential foodstuffs difficult, more particularly where reorientation of sources or outlets altered the volume or direction of traffic.

Perhaps the most important factor of all was hoarding of supplies,

[1] *The Economist*, 30 January 1943.

[2] For an assessment of this factor in Cyprus, see Lanitis, *Rural Indebtedness and Agricultural Co-operation in Cyprus*, p. 36.

for this was a cumulative vice. The root cause is a fear or expectation of shortages, or even a fear of someone else thinking on the same lines, and if it is sufficiently widespread this in itself tends to cause a shortage which in turn leads to still more hoarding. Furthermore, it is a vice which permeates all classes of society, Government, merchant, dealer, producer and consumer. For instance, the inter-provincial barriers to free movement of grain in India were an important factor in the great famine of 1943. The peasant, however, is probably the greatest offender of all. The cunning devices which he will adopt to prevent his hoards being discovered are revealed by the experiences of the Office des Céréales Panifiables in Syria.[1] And the greedy merchant classes of the Middle East and India were always eager to exploit a situation of scarcity in peace or in war. A good example of this was the 1942 wheat crisis in Syria. Syria is normally a wheat-exporting country, but in 1942 scarcity developed owing to hoarding, and prices rose to about £50 a ton compared with world prices in the region of £20 a ton. Consequently, it was decided to import wheat in an attempt to break the ring of merchants who were primarily responsible. The imported wheat was sold at less than ruling market prices, but the merchants continued to hold their stocks, knowing, or guessing, that the imports could not continue for long. In fact only 100,000 tons were imported owing to lack of readily available supplies, and prices subsequently rose to their original figure.

Finally, smuggling of supplies is another age-old custom in the countries of the East. The long frontiers of the Middle East countries, and the disparities in price levels, made illegal traffic inevitable. Similar difficulties arose between British India and the Indian States.

Of course, many of the features detailed above applied to Nigeria and Trinidad as well, despite the different structure of agriculture. Not only were the same difficulties of economic incentives and the same lack of machinery and fertilizers present, but also shortages of labour played some part in limiting output in Trinidad.

We have seen that the success of some primary countries in producing some manufactured goods in wartime was appreciable, but it was in relation to pre-war output rather than in relation to wartime needs, and it did not prevent a shortage of nearly all types of manufactured goods in these countries. Industrial production was subject to a number of limiting factors, as there was frequently a shortage of

[1] See p. 237.

skilled labour, or even of men who could be trained to be skilled. This was apparent in Egypt and Palestine by 1942, for instance.

Probably the most important single factor was the lack of machinery, both mechanical and electrical, in all countries. Not only was it impossible to secure new machinery, but the necessary spare parts to patch up the old were not available either. In India, textile mills were frequently working 168 hours a week in order to utilize existing machinery to the full. In so far as any one cause can be singled out as the ultimate limiting factor on production, machinery must undoubtedly be placed first. Raw-material sources were often cut off and new methods had to be found. Coal was the worst trouble in this respect, as the countries dealt with here were all coal importers, with the exception of Nigeria, and thus suffered badly from the general shortage.

Finally, the lack of the background of external economies, so well developed in the Western countries over the nineteenth and twentieth centuries, was another handicap. It is not easy for a generation accustomed as we are to adequate facilities for marketing goods to appreciate the difficulties which occur in primary countries. We assume that if the peasant or the small producer can be induced to work harder the battle is won, but in reality it has hardly started. Storage facilities need to be better in tropical countries than in cool climates, but usually they are much worse. Docking arrangements and internal lines of communication were often a dangerous bottleneck in Great Britain during the war, but the much poorer facilities available in most primitive countries came into operation as a limiting factor at a very early stage. Labour exchanges and adequate credit institutions are taken for granted by us, but they are unknown in such countries as these. On the other hand, it should be noted that when local military demands were the main source of demands on man-power or factory production, some of these difficulties were not quite so acute as under normal conditions.

It is important to notice that the increases in industrial production were often achieved by methods which were inefficient by Western standards. This was particularly true of the expansion of light manufactures in the Middle East. Further, the delays in securing components or raw materials, so common in wartime, helped to push up costs of production.[1] Moreover, industrialists and entrepreneurs of some countries were able to extort from the Allied authorities very

[1] The sugar industry in Trinidad is a good example of this.

high rates of profit. In more than one Middle East land a net return of 12% on capital and provision for complete amortization in 3 years was not uncommon. Finally, high costs of raw material and other imports from overseas played an important part in some countries. All these factors helped to push up prices still further, adding momentum to the original impetus.

We must now turn to a different problem and ask what resources could be made available through reductions in gross capital formation. It is impossible to give any accurate statistical answer to this even in Palestine where national income information is available, but clearly the resources available from any reduction could not be large for the simple reason that there was so little industry in these countries before the war. Resources were released, however, through the contraction of building for domestic purposes and the inability to execute repairs and maintenance to plant. Stocks of goods, too, were reduced, but it is doubtful whether the proportion of stocks to turn-over is as high in primitive countries as in Western, and consequently whether even the relative scope for economy is so great.

It is now time to answer the other query we posed at the beginning of this section—how far is it possible to reduce consumption in an orderly manner in primary economies? Avoidance of a high degree of inflation must inevitably depend on this. In framing an answer, the first point to note is the low standard of living of the people of these countries. Even though accurate statistics of national income are not available, the general picture of the extreme poverty which is the lot of so many millions is too familiar to need illustration here.[1] The problem of reducing the consumption of such people in an orderly manner is vastly different from that encountered in Western countries. It is rather a barren argument to debate whether a 20% cut in luxury consumption, however defined, inflicts more hardship than a 2% cut in basic necessities, however defined, but the general truth of the proposition that an orderly reduction of luxury consumption presents less difficulties than a reduction in basic necessities is not seriously open to doubt.

Any attempt to reduce consumption rationally must involve State interference in economic life on a considerable scale, for controls over income and expenditure, distribution and rationing involve a large administrative effort if they are to be successfully applied. But in these countries the State had no strong tradition of dealing

[1] Some comparative statistics are reproduced in Appendix I.

with economic problems. It is true that in Great Britain the State on the whole kept out of the mechanism of production and exchange in pre-1939 days, but, nevertheless, its tentacles had been spreading over the British economy for a number of years. Income tax was an old-established institution, social insurance dealt with most sections of the community, and regulations dealing with labour conditions were wide and extensive. Furthermore, price or output regulation by Marketing Boards, usually Government sponsored, was a common feature by 1939.[1] But it is broadly true to say that, before the Colonial Welfare and Development Act of 1940, Colonial Governments acknowledged little responsibility for economic affairs. Nor was there any great tradition of State interference in industry or commerce in the non-colonial countries, India, Egypt, Iraq, Syria, where much the same attitude persisted. Furthermore, at the few points where the State necessarily came in contact with economic activity there was no tradition of compliance with official laws and decrees; it was much more a point of honour to dodge tax payments, for instance, than to comply with them. Perhaps even more important, the administrative staff necessary to impose and maintain adequate controls in these countries was simply not available. It is a salutary reminder to economic planners that the Ministry of Food in Great Britain employed some 39,000 people in 1943.[2] It is also easy to forget that the Board of Trade schedule of Utility clothing prices contained over 10,000 entries. It is true that the relatively simpler needs of primitive peoples would entail a smaller (proportionate) amount of work than the complex consumption patterns of advanced countries, but when it is realized that in the whole of India there were only 1400 members of the Indian Civil Service, and in Cyprus with a population of 400,000 the total staff engaged in income tax and estate duty assessment was only 16, the impossibility of contriving really adequate controls must be admitted. Moreover, the standards of honesty and efficiency were far from high in so many countries, a state of affairs which, regrettable as it is, almost inevitably follows from low wages and poor working conditions. Furthermore, there was little chance of recruiting additional staff, for the relatively small proportion of population engaged in commerce and finance, etc., in primitive countries means that when there is a sudden call for black-coated

[1] The importance of Marketing Board experience for wartime food administration in Great Britain has been stressed by a recent writer. See Hammond, *Econ. Hist. Rev.* vol. XVI, no. 1.

[2] Hansard (Commons), 18 March 1943.

workers there is very little reserve from which they can be drawn. This is in marked contrast to the industrialized countries where there was a large reserve of people already trained or willing and able to be trained. The situation was, of course, intensified by the very absence of adequate controls over labour, which meant that such talent as there was might be wasted in less useful activities. Perhaps the best illustration of the difficulties caused by the lack of adequate administration is afforded by the contrast between the Sudan and the other countries of the Middle East. The Sudan has a first-class administrative machine, and the controls imposed and maintained were such that the cost of living index in 1945 stood only 66% above the 1939 level. It is true that military expenditure per head never attained the same dimensions as in Egypt and Palestine, but, on the other hand, it might reasonably be argued that the huge size and diversity of population and conditions would have rendered controls more difficult. These handicaps were, nevertheless, surmounted.

In other countries a large land area and lack of uniformity often did impede the imposition of controls. Palestine, for instance, had frontiers with Transjordan and Syria, and in these countries prices were consistently higher than in Palestine itself and thus a constant inducement to smuggle out goods, making the supply position still more precarious. There were many complications due to the mixture of races in Palestine, as we shall see when we tackle that country in detail. In India, too, many of the problems that arose were due to the large size of the country and the many differences between British India and the more loosely administered Indian States.

The economic structure of primary economies makes it hard to control either the incomes of the population or their spending out of income. It is impossible even to assess the incomes of primitive producers, who do not keep records, and the shortage of staff made it difficult to devise special methods of collecting taxes on such incomes, even if there were no constitutional difficulties as in India. Thus increases in the rates of direct taxation took place, but the great majority of the agricultural population were untouched by them. Furthermore, it was only possible to increase rates of indirect taxes within fairly narrow limits, as the pre-war tax structure was regressive and bore hardly on the poorer sections of the populations. There were almost impossible difficulties to be overcome in imposing rationing. It was most essential to ration foodstuffs both on account of their basic nature and because they were often in very short supply, but when some 90% of the population lives by producing or trading in foodstuffs, a workable rationing scheme is not easy to devise. In fact, it may even be difficult to stop the peasant from increasing his own consumption when prices rise, or when labour which has been living off his output is drawn off the land on to road building or other wartime occupations. In India, where the land is grossly overcrowded, this latter difficulty was particularly formidable. In these respects the contrast with Western countries is obvious.[1] Further, even if the administrative machinery had been adequate, the heterogeneity of the population and the lack of any accurate statistics of populations or dealers would have hindered the running of a really successful rationing scheme in the towns. Certain successes were achieved, but in general it is fair to say that rationing never did more than secure better distribution of some items in short supply. It was hardly ever tied up with schemes (such as those for grain requisitioning) designed to increase the flow of supplies on to the market, and it was never comprehensive enough to act as a general check on expenditure. Similarly, price control was difficult to devise in countries where many transactions are habitually settled by a lengthy process of bargaining, and still more difficult to enforce when the administration was not conspicuous in size or ability.

Nor was it easy to reduce expenditure by encouragement of saving. Habits of holding money or bonds are not ingrained as they are in more industrialized countries. The majority of these people have no surplus over consumption requirements normally, but even when they have they invest in land, property, jewellery or precious metals. Prices of assets such as these tend to rise rapidly in wartime (it is extremely difficult to prevent such movements by administrative action even in Western countries) and therefore may well be regarded as a bullish symptom and create an expectation of rising prices all round, which may in turn very well lead to rising prices all round. The sensitivity of the masses of the East to price changes yields little to the more sophisticated organized markets of the West.

In brief, the deep-lying characteristics of primary economies made the realization of additional resources from expansion of output or reduction of gross capital formation extremely difficult. Equally, the possibilities of orderly reductions of consumption requirements were strictly limited.

[1] But the parallel with the argument (April 1946) that it was impossible to ration bread in the U.S.A. will not escape notice.

3. Methods of Organizing War Contributions

We have seen so far that a relatively large war contribution was demanded of the primary economies, and that the nature of their economic structure and background made it difficult to secure this contribution without a large expansion of money demand. We must now ask how far, given these facts, the methods actually pursued by Governments were responsible for the large rise in prices and incomes which actually took place. In other words, could more powerful and energetic methods of control have been imposed, and would they have held inflation in check?

A full answer to this obviously involves detailed accounts of the structure of wartime controls in each of the countries concerned, and these will be given in the following chapters. Nevertheless, it may not be without interest to glance at the broad outline of wartime controls in the primary countries, comparing them both with one another and with the methods adopted in the more advanced countries. At first sight it appears as if sufficient controls were adopted in all these countries to deal with all eventualities. There were substantial increases in taxation rates in all of them, and in most new taxes on income in the form of either income tax itself, surtax, or E.P.T., were imposed. Large-scale attempts on Western lines were made to increase savings at various stages, and a number of special methods to isolate purchasing power were adopted too. Gold was sold in the Middle East countries and India, in both bar and coin form, with the twin intentions of mopping up expenditure and reducing the rate of growth of sterling balances.[1] Premium Bonds were sold in Palestine, Cyprus, Iraq and India with varying degrees of success. The amount and form of rationing varied from country to country, but in most cases attempts were made to impose some form of rationing of basic necessities, at any rate in the towns. Closely associated with consumers' rationing schemes were the methods of controlling the distribution of commodities from the producer along the chain to retailers. For home-produced goods the most widely practised scheme was compulsory grain requisitioning from the small producer. Basic imported goods were subject to Government monopoly in most

[1] An additional motivating factor in the Middle East was the monetary agreement with Iran that 60% of her sterling and dollar holdings should be convertible into gold at the official parity. Therefore gold sales at market prices in Iran were actually a means of conserving Allied gold as well as preventing the growth of sterling balances.

Middle East countries, and various restrictions were imposed on dealers in other imported commodities. The system of price and profit controls was bound up with the Government control of distribution. Price-control enforcements were made from the very early days of the war. The first profit-control regulation of the Middle East was introduced in Palestine in 1942, and a comprehensive Profiteering and Hoarding Prevention ordinance was enacted in India in 1943. Subsidy programmes were also widely adopted to stabilize prices, and although there were many differences in the amounts paid out in subsidies and in the range of commodities covered, most Governments recognized their responsibility to keep down the prices of basic necessities. Another generally accepted principle was that of differential cost of living bonuses to lower paid employees.

Quite apart from these 'financial' controls numerous attempts were made to safeguard the flow of consumers' goods by 'physical' controls. In all countries import licensing was adopted to cut down imports of inessential commodities, and vital goods became the subject of bulk-purchase arrangements which were a really tremendous innovation for these countries. Regulations to prevent the export of commodities in short supply, like the embargo on food exports from India in 1943, were also imposed. Home production of goods was encouraged by a variety of methods. Food production was increased in Egypt and Trinidad by the compulsory reduction of the cotton and sugar areas respectively; Government Ordnance factories played an important part in Indian production; and in all countries innumerable devices of propaganda played their part in expanding output in both the agricultural and manufacturing sectors of the economy.

After reading this imposing array of Government measures one might well wonder whether an insufficiency of controls had anything to do with inflation in these countries. This is, indeed, the superficial impression, but it is no more than superficial, as we shall see if we examine them a little more closely.

In the first place a number of controls found to be vitally necessary in Western countries were never applied. Most important is the complete absence of any strict control over labour. It is true that some rather half-hearted measures were adopted late in the day for freezing labour in key jobs in, for instance, Palestine and the Sudan, but nowhere (except in the Nigerian tin mines) was there any conscription of labour, either industrial or military. In primary countries this was all the more essential, as appeals for volunteers could not be expected to have the same force as in the principal belligerent countries. In fact, labour movements were secured almost entirely by allowing wages to rise sufficiently in the key occupations. Nor was there much effort to limit producers' incomes by direct methods, for such anti-profiteering regulations as were imposed usually only dealt with limited sections of the community. On this matter it is significant that in the Sudan, where increases in prices paid to primary producers were kept *below* the increases in the cost of living index, inflation advanced neither so far nor so fast as it did in other Middle East countries. In Syria, where high prices were paid by the Office des Céréales Panifiables to the grain growers, inflation was at its worst in the Middle East. Not even in India, where control over the placing of military orders was closer than anywhere else, was there always anything to correspond to the intricate systems of contracting and costing employed by the Defence Departments in this country. Then again, although many rationing measures were evolved, they were never comprehensive enough or consistent enough to act as a general limitation on expenditure as they were in this country or in Germany. Finally, the normal method of financing the huge military expenditure (i.e. by credit creation) and the lack of adequate safeguards to confine the purchasing power so engendered were rather a gift offering to Providence. When such large additions were being made annually to the stock of money, more and not less stringent controls than in advanced countries were needed to restrain consumption expenditure.

Secondly, quite apart from the absence of some controls altogether, many others were not introduced until the latter stages of the war when inflation was already rampant. In Egypt, for instance, compulsory reduction of cotton growing and import licensing were not introduced until 1942, and there was never any savings drive at all to help finance military expenditure. In Palestine there was no real attempt to control prices until 1942. In India grain requisitioning from the peasants only started in earnest in 1943, nor was there any profiteering control or limitation of new issues of capital until that year. In Cyprus there was no real savings drive until the sale of Premium Bonds in 1943. These are only a few illustrations, but they do point to the indisputable fact that many of the controls that were adopted amounted to reinforcing the banks after the flood had already started. One lesson which the contrasting experience of two wars has driven home, in this country at any rate, is that it is necessary to nip inflation in the bud rather than to try to kill off the full-blown flower.

Thirdly, the fact that many of the controls imposed were a dead letter in practice must be considered. Price-control regulations never meant much in the Middle East countries in the early war years, and although they were tightened up later the lack of adequate supplies at controlled prices frequently made the black-market prices much more representative of what the average consumer had to pay. In India the same general picture holds good. Similarly, many rationing schemes only worked very imperfectly. We have seen that rationing was usually no more than an attempt to reduce inequitable distribution of key commodities, but in some cases it did not fulfil even this objective in principle, let alone in practice. It is difficult to believe that there was any really sound reason why an Egyptian pasha should receive a much larger ration of sugar than the fellaheen. Import licensing, too, was often only nominal in the early war years.

We have now completed our brief survey of wartime methods of control. Given the fact that a large drain was being imposed on the resources of these countries, and given the institutional difficulties of expanding output and reducing consumption in an orderly manner, is it still possible to argue that greater foresight and vigour could have mitigated the degree of inflation? It is possible to explain away the absence of some controls and the imperfect administration of others (i.e. the first and third of the points that we have just discussed) by the considerations examined in § 2, but excuses of this nature are not a valid explanation of the failure to impose controls *in time* to prevent uncontrolled inflation, for in most countries much more effective controls were imposed in 1943–4 than had been the case in the earlier war years. This, of course, was done under pressure from various sources; on the one hand the very extent of inflation was itself a driving force, and on the other hand there was pressure from a number of outside bodies, such as the Middle East Supply Centre in the Middle East, and the West African Supply Centre in West Africa. But if it was possible to limit the spread of inflation by controls in 1943–4 it seems difficult to argue that it would not have been possible to check its growth by more resolute action in 1940–1.

What were the reasons for this failure? There seems to be a number of answers to this: in some cases it was due to indifference and apathy; in others it was due to lack of experience and foresight or to false reasoning;[1] in others it was due to a genuine belief that stiff measures

[1] In particular, the conception of inflation as a purely monetary phenomenon associated with printing of notes to meet Government expenditure was a potent source of error.

were impracticable for political or other reasons. The detailed chapters will show the relative importance of these factors in each specific country.

We have now seen, albeit in brief and sketchy outline, the main reasons why the primary countries were generally unable to restrain the growth of money demand, why the supplies of goods available were not easily increased, and thus why there were large-scale changes in prices and incomes. It is now necessary to ask whether these great changes in any way diminished the war contribution it was possible to obtain from these countries. In other words, could the war effort have been greater if the degree of inflation had been less?

It is possible to produce sound reasons for arguing that in Western countries a large degree of inflation may hinder the war effort, and conversely, that careful planning may make it possible to exact a greater contribution from the population. For it is highly probable that a large expansion of the volume of money demand may cause undue hardships to some or even to most sections of the population. In the first place, as idle resources are absorbed during the period of working up to full employment, it is highly likely, as we saw,[1] that the normal relationship between average prime costs and prices will be disturbed. On this account there may be some redistribution of income in favour of the profit-earning classes at the expense of those whose incomes are relatively fixed. Although opinions differ among economists about the extent to which it is possible to attach any degree of precision to the concept of the economic welfare of a whole community, it would, nevertheless, be generally agreed that some unnecessary current hardships may be imposed by such a redistributive process, and that they are likely to depend on such factors as the distribution of income between the various income classes at the outset, the size of the different classes, the degree of redistribution and the length of time for which it lasts. Of course, there may be complicating factors, such as occur if one section of wage earners whose services are in heavy demand or whose organization is particularly strong, manage to obtain an increase in wage rates and thus tend to gain at the expense of other sections who suffer from a further rise in prices of goods produced by that section. But the general principles are still clear.

In the second place, we must examine what happens when

[1] See p. 3.

a country's resources are being fully utilized in the widest sense (i.e. when stocks and replacement of capital equipment have been reduced to a minimum level) and it then becomes necessary to direct more internal resources to war needs. This can only be done by cutting down domestic consumption expenditure, but the hardships imposed on the community will vary with the form and manner in which this cut is enforced. If the Government relies largely on the simple process of expanding the volume of money demand, then it is highly probable that resources will be diverted from the manufacture of necessaries, such as bread, to Government service, while the production of silk stockings continues unimpeded. It would generally be agreed that such an occurrence, where necessities but no luxuries are curtailed, does impose unnecessary hardships on the community. Similarly, if consumption expenditure is reduced largely by cuts in expenditure on non-durable products, the reduction in *consumption* which is imposed on the population is much greater than if the cut were mainly confined to durable goods. Further, if the necessary cut in consumption expenditure is spread through all classes of society, and if the disparities in income between different classes are very large, it is still more probable that current hardships are not being minimized. However much one may disagree about the degree of precision which can be attached to Professor Pigou's principle of *least aggregate sacrifice*,[1] the general nature of the argument that the current hardship imposed on the community is greater if consumption expenditure is reduced by cutting out the common necessities of the poor rather than the luxuries of the rich cannot seriously be questioned. Lastly, we must consider what will happen if the community is unwilling to save the income which it is no longer able to spend on the goods (or services of economic resources) requisitioned by the Government. By hypothesis, it is no longer possible to increase output as a whole, and therefore prices will tend to rise all round. The same reactions will then follow as those dealt with above when we discussed the course of events when all resources are gradually brought into use. The entrepreneur and merchant classes inevitably tend to gain, and the rentiers and wage earners to lose, although in the latter case it may only be a temporary loss, depending on the degree of organization and bargaining power.

Such are the bases of the argument that a large degree of inflation may hinder the war effort, for if undue hardships are imposed on the

[1] *A Study in Public Finance* (3rd ed.), pt. II, ch. I, passim.

community then it is very likely that social unrest may be prevalent, that strikes will take place, relations between entrepreneurs and employees will become embittered, with consequent adverse reactions on the national output and the volume of goods made available for war needs. There can be little doubt that there was a close and significant correlation between the greater degree of planning of economic resources in Britain in the Second World War (in comparison with 1914–18) and the greater proportion of resources which it was found possible to divert to war.[1]

Now does this argument hold in the case of the primary countries with which we are dealing? The main question to deal with is whether the large changes in prices and incomes which took place imposed undue hardships on the community. This is a tricky point, for it is fatally easy to point to such obvious contrasts as the fate of the poverty-stricken wretches who starved to death in the Bengal famine, and the gains of the new Indian multi-millionaires, or the glaring paradox between the Egyptian fellaheen living in their mud hovels and the new-found wealth of other sections of the community. From there one can easily progress to a long diatribe on the horrors of inflation.

We shall find as we proceed that it would be unwise to draw too many conclusions from these notorious contrasts, for the assumptions on which analysis of the effects of inflation in advanced economies is normally based do not apply, without careful modification, to primitive countries. Many individuals or families grow their own food or weave their own cloth and are thus self-supporting for their major needs. And even if individuals are not self-supporting many remote village communities of India and the Middle East are. Thus, any analysis concerned with the effects of changes in the value of money is a tool which is likely to snap in our hands when applied indiscriminately to isolated communities for whom transactions with the outside world have little importance. The normal analysis of the effects of inflation tells us that the rentier classes tend to suffer and the business classes to gain from the redistribution of wealth. Where the creditor classes form a very small and rich section of the community which is often engaged in current trading, and where the major debtors are the poorest sections of the peasantry, the social significance of inflation

[1] See Beveridge, *British Food Control*, ch. x, for a picture of the serious industrial unrest and disorganization of the economy, which were incipient in the winter of 1917–18, before adequate rationing measures were imposed.

is clearly very different. Where wages or rents are commonly paid in kind further complications arise. The very fact that inflation is so difficult to control in primary countries indicates that not many people are left behind on the spiral.

Even if it is not clear that there were any very wide changes in the distribution of income associated with the inflationary process in primary countries, it might well be argued that there were some very heavy reductions in consumption of staple items during the war years, and that obviously raises the question of whether a greater degree of planning and less reliance on expansion of the volume of money demand would have made it possible to concentrate more on reducing consumption of luxury or durable goods. There is clearly some force behind this argument, but its importance must not be exaggerated, for it will be found that reductions of supplies of many essential goods was not at all due to the diversion of internal resources to war needs, but simply to the curtailment of imports. This factor, much more than the expansion of money demand, was the key to the hardships experienced by the populations of many countries.

Thus it would be unwise to assume, without detailed examination, that the wide changes in prices and incomes in primary economies necessarily implied sharp falls in real income or haphazard curtailment of essential commodities for a very large section of the community. Further, it must be realized that the large expansion in money demand was a means of rapidly increasing the volume of national output and, *prima facie*, the quantity of resources devoted to war needs in countries where economic development normally proceeds at a notoriously slow speed. On all these grounds, therefore, we must be careful in arguing that the large degree of inflation was itself an important limitation on the war effort. This does not mean that there were no changes in the distribution of income—the enormous gains of some small cliques are sufficient to show that there were; it does not mean that the inflationary movements actually experienced would not have had much worse consequences from the point of view of the war effort if they had developed further; all that is implied is that in considering the problems involved by inflation in these countries it is perhaps more apposite to use the background of England in the days of Adam Smith—or, perhaps better, France in the days of Arthur Young—than the conditions of modern industrialized societies.

CHAPTER II

INDIA

§1. Physical Changes

Man-power

Any attempt to estimate the overall changes in the Indian man-power position during the war years would be extremely hazardous in view of the paucity of available statistics on the subject. Nevertheless, it is possible to form some idea of the more direct ways in which the war effort absorbed man-power by looking at the figures of recruits to the Armed Forces, the increase in the numbers in public employment and the changes in private employment. The numbers in the Indian Armed Forces may be seen from Table 1.

Table 1. *Indian Armed Forces*

Service	1939	1945
Army	189,000	2,500,000
Navy	2,300	30,000
Air Force	1,600	30,000
Women	Nil	10,000
Total	193,000	2,570,000

Source. India and the War (India Office pamphlet).

Note. These figures include personnel from Indian States, the numbers of which increased from 40,000 to 400,000.

It is not possible to be so precise about the increased numbers in public employment, but the estimates of Rao[1] are the best available. These show that between 1939 and 1945 the total number in public employment in British India (including the Armed Forces, auxiliary manual labour employed by the Forces or the Government, workers in Government factories and the Civil Service) increased by about 3·2 millions. Of these, we have already seen that the Armed Forces took about 2,100,000,[2] and so an overall figure to cover the other three categories is about 1,100,000. It is not possible to split these categories accurately, but the change in Government factory employment may

[1] *Economic Transition from War to Peace in India*, pp. 19-20.

[2] 2,100,000 is arrived at by correcting the difference between the 1939–45 totals shown in Table 1 for the change in the numbers recruited from the Indian States.

be seen from Table 2 to have been rather less than 300,000 between 1939 and 1944. Undoubtedly by far the larger part of the remainder was in the manual-labour category employed in operations connected closely with the war effort, such as the building of airfields, etc.

The increase in the numbers in private employment consisted of those engaged in factory production, those in small-scale industry, and those on constructional work of various sorts. Rao[1] estimates that the increase from 1939 to 1945 of workers in these categories was of the order of 5 millions in British India. Detailed information is available only on the changes in the volume of labour in factory employment which may be seen from Table 2.

TABLE 2. *British India—volume of factory employment* (000's)

Industry	1939	1944
Total no. employed	1751	2517
(*a*) Government and local fund factories	132	419
(*b*) All other factories	1619	2098
(i) Textiles	817	993
(ii) Engineering	148	265
(iii) Minerals and metals	55	94
(iv) Food, drink, tobacco	247	294
(v) Chemicals, dyes	58	90
(vi) Paper and printing	44	53
(vii) Wood, stone, glass	52	96
(viii) Hides, skins	13	35
(ix) Gins and presses	163	143
(x) Miscellaneous	22	35

Source. Indian Labour Gazette, Statistical Summary of Social and Economic Trends in India.

Notes. (1) Figures include both permanent and seasonal workers (the total of the latter in 1944 was 295,000, and they were almost wholly in private factory employment).

(2) The relative magnitude of factory employment in the Indian States may be seen from the fact that in 1939 the total number employed there was 300,000. No figures are available over the war years, but the proportionate increase is not thought to have been as great as in British India.

The recorded increase in private factory employment is only about 480,000, and while this is only a small fraction of the total increase in privately employed labour it is significant that the major part was in textiles and engineering in which, as we shall see, the main Indian industrial contribution to the war effort took place. Finally, the slow

[1] Ibid.

rate of increase of factory employment in India in the years before the war makes it reasonable to assume that much the greater part of this estimated increase in 5 millions employed was connected with military and export demand.

These rough estimates of wartime demands on Indian man-power show that increase in public and private employment probably absorbed some 8 million workers. Our next task is to fit this into the general picture of Indian labour supply. It is clear that when account is taken of the increasing population (the all-India population was about 380 millions in 1939, and assuming that the pre-war rate of increase of about 5 millions per year was maintained, this would mean that it would be about 410 millions in 1945), the overall wartime drain on Indian man-power was merely a drop in a bucket. In no general sense could India be said to have exhausted her labour reserves as we did in this country. Indeed, in view of the extreme unproductiveness of labour in agriculture, its inefficiency in many branches of industry and the wartime bottlenecks in machinery and equipment in India, it seems reasonable to argue that many more men could have been drawn into the Armed Forces or auxiliary services without affecting production seriously.[1] But this statement should not be taken to mean that man-power problems were not important, or that on occasions labour bottlenecks did not arise, for there were certainly bottlenecks of skilled and semi-skilled men, despite the technical training schemes[2] and general controls on skilled labour,[3] which often set a limit to production. Furthermore, in some districts there were even shortages of unskilled labour. In the Punjab, for instance, where recruiting was strong, the supply of agricultural labour was far from plentiful, and in the coal fields of Bihar there were shortages of both skilled and unskilled labour, due to such factors as the higher wages available to labour in building roads and airfields. In fact, the legislation prohibiting women from working underground in the mines had to be relaxed in the later war years as the labour situation was so bad. And the shortage of coal produced, combined with transport difficulties in making it available, was in itself a major factor in limiting output from some textile mills.[4] These modifications must be borne in mind in weighing up our general conclusion.

[1] See p. 79.

[2] These turned out some 62,000 trained men by February 1944 (*Indian Yearbook*, 1944).

[3] See p. 72.

[4] See p. 76.

Production

We now have to give some account of the size of the Indian war output and the relation it bears to the national income and output. The most satisfactory method would be a comparison mainly conducted in real terms, but the limitations of the statistical material available make this impossible, and therefore the picture outlined must necessarily be mainly delineated in money terms.

In assessing the Indian war contribution it will be most convenient to consider the direct contribution (in the sense of war expenditure) separately from the indirect contribution of exports. A general picture of the direct contributions of India may be seen most easily from the figures of defence expenditure as shown in Table 3.

TABLE 3. *Defence expenditure in India (£m.)*

Financial year	Recoverable	Indian	Total	Wholesale price index (19 Aug. 1939 = 100)
1939–40	3	37·2	40·2	125
1940–41	40	55·2	95·2	115
1941–42	145	78·0	223·0	137
1942–43	229·5	200·4	429·9	171
1943–44	283·4	296·9	580·3	236
1944–45	341·3	343·7	685·0	244

Sources. India Office; *Reserve Bank Statistical Summary.*

Notes. (1) Recoverable expenditure is expenditure made by the Indian Government but reclaimable from the U.K. Government under the Defence Plan of 1939. It relates to all British military expenditure (including personal expenditure of troops) but does not include expenditure of bulk-purchasing authorities such as the Ministry of Food and the Ministry of Supply.

(2) Indian expenditure includes capital expenditure on defence, Reverse Lend-Lease, and 'non-effective' charges (i.e. pensions and gratuities paid to ex-Army personnel). Some expenditure under this general heading was really on imports and not on Indian products (e.g. Supply Department contracts placed overseas reached a maximum of £11·7 million in 1942–3, and a capital sum of £15 million was paid to His Majesty's Government in 1944–5 to meet non-effective charges), but in general these sums may be neglected.

(3) U.S. military expenditure is not included, but it is understood that this was very small.

(4) Wholesale price figure for 1939–40 is for 7 months ended March 1940.

The value of contracts placed by the Supply Department in India on behalf of Allied military requirements is also illuminating, as may be seen from Table 4.

In order to place these figures of defence expenditure and value of contracts in the right perspective, it is essential to remember that the national income of British India was estimated at about £1250 million in 1931–2,[1] the last date for which a really detailed estimate exists. The national income must have risen since then both on account of increased prices and increased output. Various estimates have been made which usually agree on such figures as £1500 million in 1941[2] and £2570 million in 1943.[3] These estimates are clearly subject to wide margins of error and should be treated with the utmost caution. Nevertheless, they do show very roughly the background against which the military expenditure and Government contracts must be judged.

TABLE 4. *Value of contracts (£m.)*

Year	Value
1938–39	4
1939–40	16
1940–41	59
1941–42	147
1942–43	186

Source. Budget Speeches.

Notes. (1) Figure for 1943–4 was £100 million, but this is not comparable with figures for earlier years owing to the opening of new Departments in 1943 which took over some of the functions of the Supply Department.

(2) These contracts apply to indigenous organized industry only. Values of contracts placed with small industry were £3·75 million in 1941–2 and £4·6 million in 1942–3.

The wartime changes in the Indian economy due to this military expenditure were manifold. In the first place there was a considerable expansion of output in the munitions and near-munitions groups. Between 1939 and 1944 the number of ordnance factories (filling and engineering) was trebled, and the number of employees rose from 15,000 to 100,000;[4] whereas in 1939 only 600 workshops capable of supplying engineering components were available, by 1945 there were 1500 engaged on Government work. Output of guns and ammunition, for instance, rose many times above pre-war level.[5] By 1945 machine tools were being produced at the rate of 350–400 monthly, whereas in 1939 the annual production rate was less than 100.

[1] Rao, *National Income of British India*. [2] E.g. *The Times*, 6 August 1941.

[3] Rao, *Commerce*, 26 February 1944. [4] *Indian Information*, 1 June 1945.

[5] For the half-year September 1939–March 1940, 183,430 rounds of artillery ammunition were produced, and during the year 1944–5, 2,474,000 rounds; output of artillery equipments similarly expanded from 97 to 1376 (*Statistics Relating to India's War Effort*).

Furthermore, not only was there an extension of production, either by increased output from existing factories or by the building of new factories, in established lines, but many types of goods previously not manufactured in India were turned out. This was particularly true in the general engineering, aircraft, automobile, shipbuilding and electrical industries. For instance, aluminium alloy drop forgings and various high-speed and stainless steels were produced for the R.A.F. A shipbuilding industry with a labour force of 50,000 grew up and built and repaired many different types of ships. A noteworthy special contribution was the supply of railway equipment to Iran and the construction of the track between Iran and India in 1942.[1]

Secondly, military demands absorbed a large proportion of the output of other industries as well as the munitions groups. The textile industry was much the most important of these. The Supply Department, whose demands in peacetime were negligible, took about 3900 million yards of cloth from March 1939 to March 1945, out of a total output of about 26,000 million yards.[2] The value of contracts placed for tentage rose from about £750,000 in 1939–40 to £12 million in 1942–3.[3] The output of the fifteen main woollen mills which were all on Government work rose from 7·3 to 27 million lb. per annum between 1939 and 1944.[4] The Indian leather industry also played an important part. Between 1939 and 1945 the Government Harness and Saddlery factory expanded its labour force from 2000 to 20,000, and by 1945 there were some 700 contractors to the Supply Department employing some 25,000 men.[5] Whereas 100,000 pairs of boots and shoes were supplied to the Indian Army in 1938, some 6·6 million were supplied in 1943.[6] Timber purchases by the Supply Department rose from 242,000 tons in 1940–1 to 1,274,000 tons in 1943–4.[7] Between March 1939 and March 1945 some 5200 cwt. of paper and pasteboard (or 43% of total output) were absorbed by Government or defence requirements.[8] Output of chemicals and dyes for war purposes expanded enormously, and even penicillin was produced on an experimental scale.

[1] *The Economist*, 29 March 1943.
[2] *Capital*, 1945 Survey.
[3] *Indian Information*, 1 June 1945.
[4] I.L.O., *Wartime Labour Conditions and Reconstruction Planning in India*, p. 19.
[5] *Review of Commercial Conditions (India)*.
[6] *Eastern Economist*, 25 August 1944. *Statistics Relating to India's War Effort.*
[7] *Indian Information*, 1 June 1945.
[8] *Statistics Relating to India's War Effort.*

Perhaps the best indication of the impact of Supply Department purchases on the Indian economy may be seen from Table 5, which shows the distribution of contracts between different industries in the early war period. It will be seen from this table that engineering and various textile industries absorbed a very large proportion of the total value of contracts.

TABLE 5. *Supply Department purchases* (1 *Sept.* 1939 *to* 31 *Dec.* 1941)

Industry group	Value of purchases (£m.)
Engineering, hardware, miscellaneous	73
Cotton textiles	38
Woollens	13·2
Other textiles	21·6
Foodstuffs	12·1
Leather	7·6
Timber and wood	6·8
Total	172·3

Source. Report: Reserve Bank of India, 1941–2.

Note. Figures relate to contracts with indigenous industry only.

It will be observed from Table 5 that purchases of food by the Supply Department only amounted to some £12 million over that period. While this underestimates the amount of food purchased for the Army, as some was made under local arrangements (e.g. vegetables), the general statement that the feeding of the Allied Armies in India did not constitute a serious drain on Indian resources is valid.[1]

Finally, as we have seen, the considerable demands for local labour for building by the military and for many types of personal service, was another important form of war contribution.

We have now obtained some idea of the direct war contribution of India in satisfying military requirements, and so it is time to examine the magnitude of the indirect war contribution in the form of exports.

[1] See *Foodgrains Policy Committee Report*, 1943, where it was estimated that the 1943 intake of foodgrains by the Army would only be about 650,000 tons as against a total supply of over 50 million tons—and not all of this was a *net* requirement, in so far as Indian troops would consume a large proportion of this if they were civilians. Similarly, the maximum off-take of tea for the Armed Forces was 35 million lb. in 1943–4, when total production was 554 million lb. On the other hand, sugar demands seem to have been more appreciable, the peak demand of 1943–4 being 105,000 tons, or 9% of total output.

It is clearly somewhat arbitrary to classify all exports under the heading of 'war contribution', but in view of the logical and statistical difficulties of arriving at any satisfactory demarcation between war and non-war exports it seems best to take the widest definition and include all exports by private traders.

TABLE 6. *Principal exports*

Commodity	Quantity			Value f.o.b. (£m.)		
	1938–9	1941–2	1944–5	1938–9	1941–2	1944–5
Raw cotton (000's tons)	483	257	57	17·9	12·0	5·2
Cotton waste (000's cwt.)	550	792	326	0·6	1·2	0·57
Cotton piecegoods (m. yd.)	177	771	423	3·6	19·8	25·4
Cotton twist and yarn (m. lb.)	38	89	17	1·4	5·5	1·7
Raw jute (000's tons)	690	315	160	10·1	7·8	5·6
Gunny bags (millions)	598	491	387	9·3	13·5	18·5
Gunny cloth (m. yd.)	1549	1695	1303	10·0	25·6	25·8
Tea (m. lb.)	348	382	415	17·5	29·7	28·6
Groundnuts (000's tons)	835	395	214	7·4	3·7	4·7
Linseed (000's tons)	318	256	92	3·3	3·0	2·0
Lac (000's cwt.)	643	766	438	0·95	3·7	3·2
Rubber (m. lb.)	17·2	14·5	6·7	0·53	0·54	0·38
Manganese ore (000's tons)	456	722	156	0·8	1·8	0·4
Mica (000's cwt.)	162	241	77	0·86	2·3	2·2
Raw hides and skins (000's tons)	35	35	14	2·8	3·55	2·99
Value of exports	—	—	—	122	179	159
Average volume	100	93	56	—	—	—
Value of re-exports	—	—	—	4·8	11·5	12·5
Value of all exports	—	—	—	126·8	190·5	171·5

Source. Accounts for Seaborne Trade of British India.

Notes. (1) Figures exclude Government exports of all types including military stores, but include bulk purchases of consumer goods by foreign Government agencies (e.g. Ministry of Food purchases of food).
(2) Figures refer to British India only.

Table 6 shows us the main stores entering into Indian export trade and the relative fluctuations in volume and value over the war years. It should be noted that some goods supplied to the United States under Reverse Lend-Lease are included under these figures, and therefore if we aggregate these exports with the total value of defence expenditure we are to that extent double-counting, but the error involved is very small[1] and will be neglected in later discussion.

It may be observed from Table 5 that the Indian war effort on the export side was at its maximum in the early war years. Although the value of exports was higher in 1944–5 than in 1938–9, the volume had shrunk considerably. The major reason was the reduction in cotton and jute acreage which caused the volume of exports of raw cotton and jute to fall fairly consistently throughout the war years. Government restrictions of exports were also important. They caused the volume of cotton piecegoods to fall from 689 million yards in 1942–3 to 382 million yards in 1943–4.

To coordinate our results so far we may say that whereas in the early years of the war the main Indian contribution was in the volume of exports, in the later years the military demands on India imposed a much greater strain on real resources and contributed much more to the inflationary potential.

We must now ask how far the drain on Indian economic resources involved in the various ways of satisfying war demands was compensated by increases in overall output. To give a complete picture we need some idea of the changes in national income and output in real terms, but we have already seen the possible errors involved in such calculations in India. The estimate made by Dr Rao[2] in 1944 shows that the value of the 1943 national income in terms of 1939 prices would have been approximately £1550 million, and this must be compared with the commonly quoted figure of about £1300 million for the 1939 national income. This shows some increase in the volume of national output,[3] but the margin of error involved in such calculations is so wide as to render any such generalizations extremely precarious. Perhaps a more profitable line of approach will be to look at the production figures in some main industries.

It must be emphasized that the figures in Table 7 are far from being a complete picture of Indian industry in wartime as they do not include some war industries, nor do they allow for production from small-scale industry.

[1] The total value of Reverse Lend-Lease amounted to £150 million (*Government Press Communiqué*, 31 May 1946). A large portion of this was covered by goods and services supplied inside India (e.g. from 1942 to 1944 the construction of airfields alone amounted to £18 million) and another part was covered by Indian Government exports.

[2] See p. 32.

[3] The proportionate increase in national output per head is much less owing to the rapid increase in population.

Statistics are not available for all munitions outputs, but we have already seen that the expansion of private factory employment in many types of engineering and allied products was considerable, and in many war or quasi-war industries overall output expanded rapidly.

TABLE 7. *Industrial production*

Commodity	1938	1939	1940	1941	1942	1943	1944
Coal (m. tons)	28·3	—	29	29·2	28·9	25·5	26·5
Paper (000's cwt.)	1184	1416	1753	1871	1821	1752	2001
Pig iron (000's tons)	1576	—	1959	2015	1804	1687	1303
Steel ingots (000's tons)	977	—	1285	1363	1299	1366	1264
Cement (000's tons)	1512	—	1727	—	2183	2112	2044
Sugar (000's tons)	650	1241	1095	778	1070	1216	985
Jute manufactures (000's tons)	1221	1277	1108	1259	1052	947	975
Cotton piecegoods (m. yd.)	4269	4012	4269	4493	4109	4870	4695
Cotton yarn (m. lb.)	1303	1243	1349	1577	1533	1680	1620
Footwear (m. pairs)	—	—	—	7·6	16·2	13·2	6·0
Sulphuric acid (000's cwt.)	512	—	778	—	813	848	778

Source. Monthly Survey Business Conditions (and miscellaneous others); *Recent Social and Economic Trends in India.*

Notes. (1) Figures are for all India.
(2) Figures for jute manufactures include twist and yarn.
(3) Figures for sugar refer to factory-refined white sugar only.

Government factory production, too, must have expanded considerably in view of the trebling of the labour force on Government work. If included in Table 7 these war industries would undoubtedly make for a greater overall increase of output over the war years than the figures show. On the other hand, the small number of employees in Government factories in relation to all factory employment must be borne in mind in assessing the importance of their increased output in relation to the gross national output.

It is difficult to weigh up the importance of the omission of small-scale output. Production as a whole expanded during the war years, but although there clearly were increases in some trades closely connected with war, e.g. some metal and leather goods, there appear to have been decreases in others. Thus in cotton textiles it is estimated that whereas small-scale weaving annually turned out some 2000 million yards of cloth (or 33% of total output) before the war, the average production over the war years was only about 1500 million yards.[1]

[1] *Capital*, December 1945.

Probably an important limiting factor was the shortage of raw materials in many trades. An investigation in Poona in 1943[1] shows that the annual level of retained imports of brass and copper in the Poona municipality fell by some 39% from 1936–8 (average) to 1941–2. Similarly, the supply of cotton yarn fell by 67·5% over this period. It would be impossible to assume that these examples are typical of all India or of a large number of trades, but it would be equally unwise to neglect them altogether.

Bearing these points in mind, is it possible to make any definite pronouncements about the overall wartime expansion of Indian industrial output? It is clear that the peak limit appears to have been reached in 1942–3 rather than in the later war years. Some estimates place the overall expansion of output at about 60%[2] in real terms, which appears to be of the right order of magnitude when we remember the absolute importance[3] and the relatively smaller expansion of small-scale industry.

Discussion of the expansion in industrial output is unlikely to give us an adequate picture of the overall expansion in the national output, when such a large proportion of that is due to agricultural output of various sorts.[4] The figures in Table 8 show the changes that took place, although to anyone unacquainted with the notorious character of Indian agricultural statistics, due warning against attempts to deduce too much from them should be given.

To draw any dogmatic conclusions from this table would be hazardous, but broadly speaking the traditional conception of the inelasticity of supply of Indian agriculture seems to be supported.[5] It is true that the large increase in rice output in 1943–4 is an exception to this, but the general conclusion still seems valid. Despite all the various attempts of the 'Grow more Food' campaign which was inaugurated after the Food Production Conference of April 1942, the area of cultivated land, output per acre, and the extent of double

[1] Gadgil and Sovani, *War and Indian Economic Policy*.

[2] See Rao, *Commerce*, 26 February 1944. But lower figures are given by the *Eastern Economist* (11 August 1944), which gives figures of 25% increases for unorganized industry and 50% for organized.

[3] In 1931–2 about 20% of the national income was estimated to be due to industrial production, half of this being due to small-scale output (Rao, *National Income of British India*).

[4] 52% in 1931–2 (Rao, ibid.).

[5] It is true that this table only shows the trend of major crops, but there is no reason to assume that the output from, e.g., forestry expanded or contracted over this period to any marked extent.

cropping failed to show any very substantial increase. In the words of the Woodhead Commission 'the results achieved were not spectacular'. The reduction in raw cotton and jute production was, of course, a result of the deliberate policy of restricting acreage sown to each crop.

TABLE 8. *Indian agricultural output* (000's *tons*)

Commodity	1938–39	1940–41	1942–43	1943–44
Rice	26,069	23,838	26,594	32,393
Wheat	10,267	10,283	11,242	10,016
Jowar, bajra, maize	12,750	14,444	15,070	14,647
Linseed	442	434	411	395
Groundnuts	3,275	3,700	2,821	3,263
Other oil seeds	1,450	1,640	1,643	1,540
Sugar-cane	3,389	5,800	5,076	5,696
Cotton	4,990	6,080	4,554	5,060
Jute	9,690	5,460	—	5,430
Tea	452	464	564	554

Sources. Food Statistics of India, 1946; *Famine Enquiry Commission, Final Report*; International Tea Committee, *Bulletin of Statistics.*

Notes. (1) Figures refer to all India.
(2) Cotton and jute figures are in 000's bales (of 400 lb. each). Tea figures are in million lb.

Finally, there is the question of what happened to services and miscellaneous items whose value was estimated to be about £300 million or 25% of the national income in 1931–2. Clearly the requirements of the Army and the war effort generally must have increased output under this heading by drawing men from the villages where they were grossly under-employed to act as servants, etc. Rao[1] puts the increase at about 20% in real terms, but any such estimate is clearly subject to even wider margins of error than the others we have already quoted.

In summary we may say that the military and export contributions together drew heavily on Indian resources, but the evidence on the expansion of national output in real terms (or rather, national output per head of total population, which is the more relevant concept as population expanded considerably) does not point to a very marked increase, when due allowance is made for the overwhelming preponderance of agriculture in the Indian economy.

[1] *Commerce*, 26 February 1944.

Consumption

As military contribution and/or exports expand, a cut must be made in national consumption unless either home-produced national output or imports can be expanded, or gross domestic capital formation be reduced sufficiently. It has been shown that there is little reason to believe that the *overall* expansion of national output per head in India during the war years was very substantial. The next question which arises is what happened to gross domestic capital formation. We have seen that in poor countries the level of investment in capital goods of different sorts is normally not very high, and the margin which is likely to be available is therefore quite low. Broadly, this argument applies to India, though it is tempered by such facts as the amount of stocks on the hands of some manufacturers at the outbreak of war.[1] It is noteworthy that little attempt was made to restrain private investment before 1943, when an ordinance was passed (17 May 1943) restricting capital issues, although shortages of imported machinery inevitably kept down the level of investment activity over the war years both before and after the ordinance.[2] Whether the hoarding of grain by peasants and speculative dealers increased stocks as a whole it is difficult to tell, for the effect of this was to concentrate rather than to increase stocks. Generally, however, it is fair to say that any increased war contribution had to be met mainly by high imports or reduced consumption. Table 9 shows the changes in some of the principal imports over the war years.

It will be seen from Table 9 that imports were in fact reduced over the war years to a very low level. The importance of the overall change is best seen from the fact that in 1938–9 they formed about 9% of the national income, whereas in 1943–4 they only formed 2·5% of the national income, although it is true that a considerable improvement took place in 1944–5, when the total value climbed up to £157 million. The categories which suffered most were food, drink and tobacco, and manufactured goods, imports of which fell between 1938–9 and 1943–4 from £18·0 to £5·3 million, and from £69·5 to £33·8 million respectively. The changes which took place in some

[1] See *Indian Yearbook*, 1944: 'Prior to the second world war the main Indian industries—especially the textiles—were beginning to feel the slump. Stocks on the hands of the manufacturers were accumulating, night shifts were closing down.'

[2] Thus it was argued that machinery had been worked to a breakdown and civil building completely neglected over the war years (1946–7 Budget Speech). Railway maintenance was also very much reduced.

individual commodities, such as cotton piecegoods, foodgrains and metal ores and goods, give point to these generalizations, and the falls in kerosene, machinery and manures are significant in various contexts which will be examined later. Furthermore, even apart from changes in the total volume of a particular type or class of imports there were

TABLE 9. *Principal imports*

Commodity	Quantity			Value c.i.f. (£m.)		
	1938–9	1941–2	1943–4	1938–9	1941–2	1943–4
Total imports	—	—	—	115	130	89
Index of volume	100	74	40	—	—	—
Raw cotton (000's tons)	96	138	76	6·4	11·5	13·1
Cotton piecegoods (m. yd.)	647	182	3·7	7·6	3·3	0·18
Cotton twist and yarn (m. lb.)	34·5	8·2	0·63	2·2	0·94	0·088
Metals and ores (000's tons)	344	196	69	8·1	9·6	3·1
Brass and bronze (000's cwt.)	315	75	13	0·79	0·38	0·10
Iron and steel (000's tons)	223	118	25	4·4	4·5	1·2
All machinery	—	—	—	14·8	9·6	7·9
Textile machines	—	—	—	2·5	1·7	2·4
Electrical machines	—	—	—	2·8	1·8	1·65
Agricultural machines	—	—	—	0·10	0·22	0·015
Electrical instruments	—	—	—	2·5	1·8	1·13
Grain, pulse, flour (000's tons)	1602	1106	8·7	10·3	11·2	0·23
Spices (000's cwt.)	2069	1286	158	1·97	1·7	0·67
Kerosene (m. gal.)	182	152	80	4·8	5·5	4·2
Paper and pasteboard (m. cwt.)	3·0	1·3	0·45	2·4	2·6	1·3
Wood	—	—	—	2·15	2·15	0·12
Glassware	—	—	—	0·94	0·49	0·12
Hardware	—	—	—	1·9	1·6	0·70
Manures (000's tons)	99	10·7	5·5	0·79	0·12	0·078

Source. Accounts for Seaborne Trade.

Notes. (1) Figures exclude military and N.A.A.F.I. stores but include Lend-Lease civilian goods.
(2) Figures refer to British India only.

many changes in composition or quality which were often of the utmost importance. The best known example of this is the cessation of rice imports from Burma.[1] Then the fact that the east coast ports became virtually unusable in 1943—and as a result imports had to be brought into other ports—threw an immense strain on the transport facilities and general working of the Indian economy.[2]

[1] See p. 44. [2] See p. 75.

This evidence on the reduction of imports, combined with our previous demonstration of the wartime drain on resources, clearly shows that some falls in total consumption and even greater falls in consumption per head must have taken place. Equally clearly it is impossible to call in the evidence of statistics of national outlay as we are accustomed to do in the case of more advanced countries. Nevertheless, it may be possible to approach the problem of the impact of the war on general consumption by concentrating on a study of some principal items.

The main needs of the poor millions of India are food, cloth and kerosene, and by examining the available supply of these items during the war years it is possible to make some general deductions about changes in consumption. In the case of foodgrains it is not apparent that there was any great change in the total supply available for consumption as a result of war conditions. The amount of home production and excess of imports over exports varied in the manner shown in Table 10.

TABLE 10. *Major foodgrains available* (000's *tons*)

Year	Net production	Imports (less exports)	Total amount available
1937–39 (av.)	49,528	837	50,365
1939–40	50,088	2,221	52,309
1940–41	47,957	963	48,920
1941–42	49,481	432	49,912
1942–43	51,385	-292	51,093
1943–44	55,057	298	55,365

Source. Foodgrains Policy Committee Report; Food Statistics of India.
Note. Figures include rice, wheat, jowar, bajra, maize, barley and ragi production.

These figures do not allow for the effects of military demands, but these were estimated in 1942–3 to amount to about 650,000 tons (500,000 tons of wheat and flour and 150,000 tons of rice), and, of course, all of this did not represent a net drain on supplies in comparison with pre-war years, as Indian soldiers would have consumed grain in their capacity as civilians. On the other hand, it must be remembered that the population was expanding over this period at the rate of about 5 millions per annum, making an increase of 6·5% in 5 years, and for that reason alone the supply of foodgrains per head was not up to pre-war standard. And this position was made worse in 1942 by the influx of refugees from Burma. But as far as these statistics go (and their notorious character has already been pointed out),[1] it does not appear that military demands and the cessation of imports contributed substantially to a *general* shortage of foodgrains, although, as we shall see, there were particular shortages due to these causes in different types of foodgrains, different provinces, and different income classes.

In the case of clothing, it is more apparent that war conditions did lead to a decrease in available supplies per head. In pre-war years the annual mill output of cloth in India was about 4000 million yards and handloom output about 2000 million yards; the net imported balance of piecegoods was about 400 million yards and defence requirements were negligible, which meant that a total of about 6400 million yards was available for consumption annually.[2] Over the war years (March 1939–March 1945) mill output averaged 4408 million yards and handloom output was reduced to about 1500 million yards, which meant a total home supply of roughly 5900 million yards. The average of imports of piecegoods over the war years was 205 million yards and the average of exports (including re-exports) was 540 million yards per annum, leaving an annual net export balance of 335 million yards. Defence purchases amounted to an average of 650 million yards over these years. Thus the average available supply for civilian consumption may be deduced from these figures, i.e. 5900 − 335 − 650 = 4915 million yards, or approximately 23% less than in pre-war years.[3] Clearly these figures are not precise, the estimates of handloom weaving being a particularly weak link in the chain. Furthermore, they take no account of changes in stocks which are believed to have been high in 1938–9,[4] and by giving estimates of average consumption they hide the tremendous shortage which occurred in 1942–3 when mill production was only 4109 million yards, imports had fallen to 13 million yards, exports (including re-exports) were at their peak level of 835 million yards, and Supply Department requirements reached about 800 million yards. Finally, they mask the effect of

[1] See *Foodgrains Policy Committee Report*, p. 9, for a list of the known defects of these statistics.

[2] See *Eastern Economist*, 29 March 1946, where it is calculated that the average supply available over the years 1934–9 was 6260 million yards. See also *Memorandum of the Federation of Indian Commerce and Industry*, December 1942, which puts the 1938–9 figures at 4634 million yards (excluding hand-loom output).

[3] See *Capital*, 1945 Survey, and *Commerce*, December 1945, for further details. Information which has come to hand since in *Indian Cotton Textile Industry* 1945–6 *Annual* (p. viii) confirms these figures.

[4] See p. 40.

population increases, for whereas supplies available per head averaged 17 yards in 1939, they only averaged 12 yards in the war years.

Kerosene supplies for the civilian population were undoubtedly much less than in pre-war years. Imports in 1938–9 were 182 million gallons, but in 1942–3 they were 94 million and in 1943–4 80 million gallons. Figures of home production were 38·7 million gallons in 1938 but only 15·9 million gallons in 1944–5. Rationing of kerosene, by restricting distribution to a fraction of previous levels, was, in fact, widely adopted over India.

These pointers indicate the reductions in consumption which were brought about in India. Perhaps another indication could be seen in the tremendous shortage of metals which occurred. We have already seen how imports fell from 344,000 tons in 1938–9 to 69,000 tons in 1943–4, and also how the retained imports of metals in Poona municipality were reduced.[1] The Supply Department also took a large part of indigenous steel output, and thus it became increasingly difficult to effect any small repairs to primitive farm implements and similar equipment.

So far we have kept to very general considerations about the reduction in consumption. It is now time to consider some of the more detailed ways in which this reduction was effected. We have said that war conditions did not materially affect the total supply of foodgrains available, but they certainly affected the type of foodgrains supplied to the population. The most obvious instance of this is the cessation of the annual 1½ million tons of rice imports from Burma in 1942 which, combined with such other factors as the 1942 cyclone in Bengal, and the difficulties of procurement and distribution, meant that a large number of consumers had to be prepared to eat wheat instead of rice in 1943.[2] The character of the cut in consumption of cloth was somewhat similar. The reduction in imports cut out the finer varieties, and the standard cloth produced after 1943 (60% of capacity was reserved for Supply Department and standard clothing requirements) was both coarse and unpopular. In 1942–3 the supply of dhotis and chadars was only about 50% of the 1938–9 level.[3]

Furthermore, the overall figures of consumption conceal the

[1] See p. 38.

[2] See *Indian J. Econ.* July 1945, p. 116, for a description of the problems involved in Madras by this change-over.

[3] *Review of Trade of India*, 1942–3.

enormous differences between the various provinces, and even between districts in the same province. To some extent these discrepancies link up with the distribution between the rural and urban populations (see infra p. 46), but not entirely so. For instance, the Bengal famine of 1943 cannot be explained in any such simple way, and this was the most glaring example of inequity in the changes in food consumption. Local military demands also were important in this connexion, as although the bulk of military food was purchased centrally, local shortages, particularly in north-east India, were in no small part due to their demands.[1]

It is not easy to generalize about the spread of consumption reduction between the different income classes, apart from the large industrialists, landowners, and merchant classes about whose war-income increases there is no doubt whatever. It is not, for instance, possible to say that the real income of the poor people in the towns definitely tended to fall more or less than that of the poor people in the country, even in any one district or area. The extent of the relative gain or loss in the country depended to a large extent on whether a man was cultivating his own land, or whether he was a labourer, and this distinction is often blurred and imprecise in India. Such investigations as have been made seem to show that those who owned their own land secured the largest reduction in indebtedness during the war,[2] but the extent to which wages of labourers rose varied enormously from one area to another.[3] The largest gains must clearly have been made by those who paid money rents and did not employ wage-earning labourers, and, of course, the relative gain was still greater if debts were high. In the towns, too, there were enormous disparities in the changes of real income. The inquiry by Geren shows that in his sample investigation in the Punjab, the lowest classes of menials and servants tended to lose most. Despite the system of dearness allowances and bonuses on earnings to employees, earnings lagged a long way behind the rise in the cost of living. In the R.I.N. Dockyard, Bombay, the wages of unskilled labour (including dearness allowances and the concession from a cheap grain shop) had risen from 32 Rs. 8a. per month to 56 Rs. per month between August 1939 and September 1944 (i.e. an increase of 75%), whereas the cost of living index had

[1] See *Eastern Economist*, 2 July 1944.

[2] See Geren, *Impact of Rising Prices on Various Social Strata in Punjab*, and Patel, 'Inquiry into agricultural indebtedness in wartime', *Indian J. Econ.* April 1945.

[3] See p. 52.

risen from 105 to 231 over the same period.[1] Similarly, the real wages of underground miners in Jharia showed a decline between 1938 and 1942.[2]

A general investigation in Bombay city indicated that average monthly earnings rose from 31 Rs. 12a. in August 1939 to 65 Rs. 10a. in November 1943 (i.e. an increase of 107%), excluding the benefits of earnings, bonuses and sales of cheap grains. Over the same period the cost of living rose by 135%.[3] If any weight can be placed on these investigations, it seems that even the greater regularity of work reflected by the increases in earnings was not sufficient to compensate for price increases.

Perhaps the best general index of the position of the agricultural cultivator, *vis-à-vis* the rest of the community, is gained by an examination of the movements of wheat and rice prices compared with kerosene and cotton piecegoods prices as shown in Table 11. In so far as the wheat-rice price level moved upwards relatively to the kerosene-piecegoods level, agriculturalists tended to gain at the expense of townspeople.

TABLE 11. *Relative price movements*

Date	Rice	Wheat	Cotton manufactures	Kerosene
Aug. 1939	100	100	100	100
Dec. 1941	172	212	196	140
Dec. 1942	218	232	414	194
June 1943	951	330	501	201
Dec. 1944	333	381	285	175

Sources. Review of Trade of India, 1942–3; Explanatory Memorandum to Budget Speech, 1945.

Note. Prices are averages for all India.

Up to the end of 1941 it is broadly true to say that these price levels moved in favour of the cultivator, but whereas over 1942–3 the rice cultivator still gained, the wheat cultivator was less happily placed owing to the rise in prices of piecegoods. The 1944 position seems to indicate that the cultivators still had a preponderant advantage.

These comparisons between different income groups are only indicative of changes in real income and therefore not necessarily of reductions in real consumption. The physical allocation of goods

[1] See *Bombay Labour Gazette*, September 1944.
[2] See Bose, *Indian J. Econ.* January 1944.
[3] See *Indian Labour Gazette*, April 1944.

between different areas and between town and village is an important determinant as well as changes in ability to purchase them. Foodstuffs were clearly more likely to be available in the country than in the town both on account of transport difficulties and withholding of supplies by the cultivators. These two influences together certainly resulted in a concentration of the shortages in the towns. Nevertheless, there were enormous variations between different country districts. Sugar and kerosene were short in the Punjab, for instance.[1] It is difficult to generalize about cloth, as although the major part of production took place in the mills of the towns they were also responsible for the major decrease in available supplies, production from handlooms being fairly well maintained. Thus cloth was not available in the Jharia area in the early part of 1943. At the same time, it is broadly fair to conclude that in the light of the wretched poverty of India's millions, relative changes in overall consumption between different classes must have been roughly correlated with changes in real income.

In conclusion, we may say that war demands and the reduction of imports inevitably meant cuts in general consumption of cloth, kerosene, and metal goods, even if not of foodgrains. There were many changes in consumption, apart from overall decreases, owing to changes in the types of goods available, the allocation between different provinces and districts, and the increases and decreases in real income which took place. On the whole it is probable that the towns suffered most. The absolute reductions in consumption were certainly heavier there as, with a normally wider range of purchases than the peasants, they suffered many more inconveniences; and so in all probability the relative reductions were greater too. However, even if it can be argued in this way that the poorest section of the community (the rural element) were not hit most hardly, it should not be thought that any section of the population was in a strong position to endure these cuts. National income per head was, after all, only about £4. 10*s*. in 1939, and any cut in consumption in such circumstances is a vastly different proposition from the wartime cuts which occurred in industrialized countries.

[1] See Geren, op. cit.

§ 2. Financial Changes

In this section it is necessary to look at the changes which took place in the supply of money, the level of prices, incomes of different classes, and the accumulation of sterling balances.

Supply of money

Table 12. *Supply of money*

Date	Notes in circulation Rs. (m.)	Index notes in circulation	Bank deposits (demand) Rs. (m.)	Bank deposits (time) Rs. (m.)	Bank deposits (total) Rs. (m.)	Index all bank deposits	Index notes and bank deposits
Aug. 1939	1,703	100	1,355	1,026	2,381	100	100
Dec. 1939	2,190	129	1,380	990	2,370	99	112
June 1940	2,373	139	1,369	1,060	2,429	102	115
Dec. 1940	2,257	133	1,668	971	2,639	111	117
June 1941	2,596	152	1,822	1,029	2,851	120	133
Dec. 1941	3,042	179	2,167	1,083	3,250	136	154
June 1942	4,392	258	2,610	966	3,576	151	195
Dec. 1942	5,606	329	3,397	1,100	4,497	189	247
June 1943	7,202	423	4,112	1,298	5,410	217	309
Dec. 1943	8,219	483	4,989	1,523	6,512	272	361
June 1944	9,260	544	5,651	1,823	7,474	312	410
Dec. 1944	9,943	584	6,161	2,028	8,189	344	444
June 1945	11,335	666	6,244	2,354	8,598	361	488

Source. Reserve Bank Reports.

Notes. (1) Figures exclude Burma.
(2) Notes do not include 1 rupee notes.
(3) Bank deposits refer to scheduled banks only.

It will be seen from Table 12 that the note circulation expanded much further than did the total of bank deposits. Time deposits did not show any tendency to expand at all until the start of the general anti-inflationary campaign in 1943.

Prices

Wholesale- and retail-price indices are shown in Table 13.

Before we can attempt any comparison of movements in the supply of money and changes in the price levels, the exact significance of the price indices shown must be understood. The wholesale price indices are calculated by the Economic Adviser's Office, and may be taken as being representative of India as any one price level could be in war-time. It is significant to note that food prices rose most and that prices of manufactured goods showed higher increases than did those of raw materials. The retail prices indices are based on the local cost of living indices and suffer from all the usual faults of such statistics; the prices used are usually local-controlled prices which are sometimes relevant, but quite frequently not. The weighting used was somewhat out of date before 1939, and, of course, owing to enforced changes in the pattern of consumption expenditure has been still more so since that date.

TABLE 13

Date	Wholesale prices					Retail prices		
	Raw materials	Food	All primary commodities	Manufactured goods	General	Bombay	Madras	Cawnpore
Aug. 1939	100	100	100	100	100	100	100	100
Dec. 1939	129	127	136	145	138	108	110	112
June 1940	112	103	108	117	114	106	109	108
Dec. 1940	124	108	113	119	115	110	112	111
June 1941	139	115	126	147	126	116	111	114
Dec. 1941	150	127	137	154	143	123	123	151
June 1942	161	152	152	166	155	145	131	175
Dec. 1942	172	178	176	221	185	179	161	224
June 1943	182	303	237	257	242	223	182	336
Dec. 1943	189	292	232	252	236	236	193	334
June 1944	204	283	236	260	241	224	208	315
Dec. 1944	211	274	248	258	250	224	213	297
June 1945	208	263	240	245	241	223	226	298

Sources. Wholesale prices: *Economic Adviser's Index*; retail prices: *Cost of Living Indices.*

It is difficult to obtain any statistics of black-market prices, but Table 14 gives some idea of the conditions in the Bihar coal fields in February 1943.

TABLE 14. *Controlled and free prices*

Date	Dal	Atta (wheat flour)	Salt	Mustard oil	Ghee
	Rs. a. p.	Rs. a. p.	Rs. a. p.	Rs. a. p.	Rs. a. p.
Sept. 1939	0 2 3	0 2 0	0 1 6	0 7 0	1 4 0
Feb. 1943					
Controlled	0 5 0	0 4 0	0 2 6	0 12 0	—
Free	0 8 0	0 8 0	0 3 0	0 12 0	2 8 0
Ratio free/controlled	1·6	2·0	1·2	1·0	—

Source. Communicated by Professor D. T. Jack.

Note. No cloth prices are included as cloth was unobtainable in this area in February 1943.

These figures are, of course, of limited application as they only relate to one area in February 1943, which was before the acute food crisis of 1943 came to a head, and the ratio between free and controlled prices of foodstuffs is probably less than it was later in the year. How impossible it was to secure goods, except at free prices, may be seen from the fact that even Government departments paid them on occasions.[1]

The other main point to note about the retail-price indices is their enormous dispersion between different areas. To some extent this is revealed in Table 13, but if a wider selection of towns is included it will be seen that the dispersion is underestimated. For instance, a comparison of retail price levels in July 1943 shows that if August 1939 is taken as 100, prices had moved as follows:

Madras	185	Cawnpore	341
Bombay	225	Nagpur	361
Lahore	275	Jamshedpur	429

However, with the limitations of possible analysis firmly fixed in our minds, we may make some comparison between the increased supply of money and the increased price level. It may be seen that throughout the war period the supply of money increased faster than prices with the sole exception of Cawnpore prices in June 1943. To some extent more money must have been used in normal private and business transactions, but a considerable amount must have been hoarded too. In no sense can the rise in prices in India in the war period be compared with the great German inflation or the classic conception of the subject. Even when the high level of black-market prices is taken into account there is no evidence of a widespread flight from the currency, except possibly in Bengal in 1943. The contrast between the permanent 'lead' of money on prices in India with the more variable conditions in the Middle East will be elaborated later.[2]

Incomes

Profits. Accurate indices of changes in profits are difficult to compile in advanced countries, but in India hardly any figures exist at all. The only general indication is the index of the Economic Adviser, which shows that with 1938 as 100, the declared profits of some 350 companies had risen to about 250 by 1942. This may mean much or little, depending on the representative nature of the companies

[1] See *Commerce*, 7 January 1943. [2] See pp. 207, 229.

concerned. It is idle to speculate on the significance of this change, and it will be more worth our while to concentrate on wage changes.

Wages. No general indices of wage changes are available for India, and the only way of tackling the problem is to take the results of a number of selected observations.

For agricultural wages the most comprehensive statistics are to be found in the Appendix to the *Woodhead Commission Report*, where figures elicited from a number of different Provincial Governments are produced. In Bengal wages lagged consistently behind foodgrain prices in the early war years, but by 1944 appear to have largely overtaken them as shown by Table 15.

TABLE 15. *Agricultural wages and foodgrain prices (Bengal)*

Date	Wages index	Date	Average prices foodgrains (index)
1939–40	100	1939	93
1940–41	110	1940	100
1941–42	115	1941	109
1942–43	125	1942	160
1943–44			
1st 6 months	130	1943	385
2nd 6 months	200–300		
1944–45			
1st 6 months	400–500	1944	280

Source. Woodhead Famine Inquiry Commission (Final Report).

In the Punjab unskilled wages did not lag far behind prices, although the overall position was not as favourable (see Table 16).

TABLE 16. *Agricultural wages and foodgrain prices (Punjab)*

Year	Average wages index		Food prices index
	Skilled	Unskilled	
1938–39	100	100	100
1943–44	250	300	330

Source. Woodhead Famine Inquiry Commission (Final Report).

The representative character of these statistics may be doubted for two reasons. First, the methods by which the figures were compiled and the claim that they do give a true picture of changes in these provinces is open to suspicion. Secondly, even if we take the order of magnitude of these changes as correct, it is not legitimate to assume that these figures are representative of all British India and still less of the States. On the basis of what we know about the effects of the war on the economy of the different provinces (e.g. the large absorption of man-power from the Punjab by the Defence Forces and the concentration of industry and defence works in Bengal and neighbouring areas), it would be reasonable to assume that agricultural labour would be rather less plentiful in these Provinces than others, and therefore would account for the rise in wages relatively to prices. This hypothesis does seem to be borne out by the information obtained by the Woodhead Commission from other Provinces, even though it is not as detailed as the statistics quoted above. For instance, it was considered that in Madras wages of field labourers had risen some 100% above pre-war figures by 1943, whereas food prices had risen some 150%; in Orissa and Assam too wages had on the whole lagged behind prices. In the Central Provinces and Bengal, wages and prices had more or less risen side by side, although in Bombay Province, where again, significantly, the demand for labour had been heavy, wages had generally risen faster than prices. Where agricultural wages are more often paid in kind, as in Sind, it is interesting to note that the share of the labourer's reward in total output had remained about the same.

Evidence on wage changes of plantation labour is available from the annual returns of earnings of workers in the Assam tea gardens (Table 17).

TABLE 17. *Assam tea gardens. Average monthly cash earnings*

Year	Men	Women	Children
	Rs. a. p.	Rs. a. p.	Rs. a. p.
1938–39	7 15 3	6 7 5	4 9 2
1939–40	7 14 1	6 3 8	4 7 9
1940–41	8 2 1	6 8 4	4 10 11
1941–42	8 11 5	7 2 10	5 4 4
1942–43	8 10 4	6 15 4	5 4 2
1943–44	9 10 3	7 13 1	5 14 10

Source. Indian Labour Gazette.

To rely on changes in earnings as indicative of changes in wage rates would indeed be foolish. Although earnings did not increase in the same proportion as wage rates paid to farm labour there are several factors to be taken into account. First, the amount of work done by male labour was less because they tended to spend an increasing amount of time in rice cultivation. Secondly, the perquisites available on the plantations—cheap rice, cloth, housing and medical attendance—were not normally available to other types of agricultural labour.

Can we draw any conclusion from this evidence? It is tempting to play safe and say that the different experiences vary so much as to invalidate any general conclusion, but on the whole it does not seem unreasonable to conclude that, by and large, agricultural farm labour did not suffer a very severe fall in real income as the result of war expenditure. At the outset of a general price rise such as occurs in wartime wages do lag behind prices, but as time goes on this lag is eliminated. Although there was some tendency for commutation of payments in kind into money payments, this on the whole was a disadvantage for individual workers; the effects on families were masked by setting more members to work. Finally, as we have already seen,[1] cultivators as a class were in a better position than labourers as a class, and therefore men who worked both as cultivators and labourers suffered even less than the above analysis suggests.

The lack of any wage index relating to labour in organized industry in India makes easy assessment of wage changes impossible. In many cases changes in basic rates did not occur, but the system of granting dearness allowances and bonuses on earnings, and opening grain shops at the factories (frequently selling grain at less than controlled prices) was beneficial to labour. In general wages appear to have lagged behind prices during most of the war period, although it is not possible to be at all precise about the margin. We have seen[2] that in the dispute at the R.I.N. Dockyard, Bombay, it was claimed that the cost of living had risen 120% between August 1939 and September 1944, whereas the wages of unskilled labour (including allowances, etc.) had only risen by 75%. And in Bombay City earnings rose by some 107% and the cost of living by some 135% between August 1939 and November 1943.

Continuous statistics do exist on the average daily earnings of underground and other workers in the Indian coal fields. These changes are shown in Table 18.

[1] See p. 45. Another investigation made in the Gujarat in February 1945 showed that the overall reduction in debt between 1938 and 1944 of some 178 farmers was about 38% (cf. *Indian J. Econ.* July 1945, p. 10).

[2] See p. 45.

TABLE 18. *Average daily earnings of underground miners (Bihar)*

Year (Dec.)	Average earnings per day	Index
	Rs. a. p.	
1938	0 9 7	100
1939	0 9 9	101
1940	0 9 6	99
1941	0 10 0	104
1942	0 12 4	128
1943	0 14 2	147
1944	0 15 6	162
1945	1 0 2	169

Source. Department of Mines Reports.

Note. These figures do not allow for cheap rice concessions. In 1943 rice was supplied by employers at the rate of 5½ seers for 1 rupee.

Although exactly parallel statistics on the cost of living are not available, it does seem quite clear that earnings lagged behind the cost of living, for in 1943 this was reckoned to have risen 135% above 1939 levels. Whether wage rates (including cost of living bonuses) lagged behind the cost of living so appreciably is more doubtful, as there appears to have been more absenteeism and irregular attendance in the pits in the war years.

On the other hand, it was estimated that by 1945 railway workers in the lowest wage ranges had been completely compensated for the rise in the cost of living by dearness allowances and cheap grain.[1] The Select Committee on National Expenditure[2] also found that wages cost per unit of output in textile manufactures had increased by 125% between February 1941 and May 1944, which appears to indicate a rise in earnings reasonably commensurate with the changes in the cost of living.[3]

This somewhat scrappy evidence is clearly not sufficient to tell us with any accuracy how much real incomes of town dwellers fell. But when we remember the importance of black-market prices,[4] and the rather doubtful workings of the controls over foodgrains and cloth, even in the later war years, it is probable that many workers must

[1] Railway Budget Speech, 1945.

[2] *4th Report*, Session 1944–5.

[3] This conclusion seems to be borne out by figures quoted in I.L.O., *Wartime Labour Conditions and Reconstruction Planning in India*, p. 56, which show that average annual earnings per worker in the textile industry increased from 293·6 Rs. in 1939 to 571·2 Rs. in 1943.

[4] See p. 49.

have had considerable falls in real wage rates, persisting at least until 1944–5. Although no statistical evidence is available, it seems fairly clear that, as in so many countries, some of the worst hit classes of all were the lower paid clerks, postmen, policemen and the like.

Sterling assets

Table 19 sets out the fall in sterling debts and the accumulation of sterling assets. During six years an external debt which had been accumulated over the course of decades disappeared and a strong position as an international creditor was attained instead.

TABLE 19. *Sterling debts and assets (£m.)*

(1) Date	(2) Sterling debt	(3) Sterling assets	(4) Net assets	(5) Annual change in sterling debt and assets	(6) Annual change including other Indian payments
31. iii. 39	333	48	− 285	—	—
31. iii. 40	310	107	− 203	+ 82	+ 82
31. iii. 41	227	108	− 119	+ 84	+ 84
31. iii. 42	126·5	213	+ 86·5	+205·5	+205·5
31. iii. 43	35·5	385	+ 349·5	+263	+301·5
31. iii. 44	21·5	713	+ 691·5	+342	+342
31. iii. 45	11·5	1023	+1011·5	+320	+335

Sources. Budget Speeches; *Reserve Bank Reports.*

Notes. (1) Figures of sterling debt include Government of India debt and railway stocks and debentures. Annual figures of debt reduction are based primarily on Budget Speeches which show a slightly higher rate of repatriation than do *Reserve Bank Reports.*

(2) Difference between column 6 and column 5 is explained by repayment of Chatfield Debt (£8·5 million) and Railway Annuities agreement (£30 million) in 1942–3 and non-effectives agreement (£15 million) in 1944–5.

(3) Sterling assets do not include holdings of commercial banks, but it is understood that these movements have not been significant.

§ 3. INFLATION AND CONTROLS

Our task in this section is to estimate how far the Indian war contribution described in § 1 may be regarded as the prime cause of the price-inflation over the war years. We shall start by examining the relative importance of the different causal factors in the situation, and then proceed to explain why such a degree of price-inflation as that described in § 2 took place.

It is possible to isolate four major factors as motivating causes of wartime inflation in India; Allied military expenditure, Indian defence expenditure, receipts from exports of merchandise, and 'other external items'. The relative importance of these factors will be seen in Table 24, but before we can do this, it is necessary to build up some of the figures.

First, we have to adjust the figures of Allied military expenditure as it was partly financed by sales of gold, and to this extent cannot be regarded as a primary reason for price inflation. This adjustment is made in Table 20. It will be noted that only British military expenditure is detailed, as American military expenditure was almost entirely financed by gold sales,[1] and therefore need not be taken into account at this point.

TABLE 20. *British military expenditure (£m.)*

Year	Gross figure	Gold sales	Net figure
1939–40	3	—	3
1940–41	40	—	40
1941–42	145	—	145
1942–43	229·5	—	229·5
1943–44	283·4	50·6	232·8
1944–45	341·3	54·1	287·2

Sources. Budget Speeches; Shenoy, *Sterling Assets of Reserve Bank of India.*
Note. Gold sales valued at actual selling price and not official parity.

Secondly, we have to adjust Indian defence expenditure figures, as all that we need are Indian Central Government budget deficit figures. In so far as the extra defence expenditure was covered by higher taxation, it clearly was not instrumental in adding to the expenditure stream. These figures are shown in Table 21.

TABLE 21. *Indian Central Government receipts and expenditure (£m.)*

Year	Receipts	Defence expenditure	Civil expenditure	Total expenditure	Deficit
1939–40	71·2	37·2	34·0	71·2	Nil
1940–41	80·7	55·2	30·4	85·6	4·9
1941–42	101·0	78·0	32·5	110·5	9·5
1942–43	132·7	200·4	56·2	256·6	123·9
1943–44	189·0	296·9	62·7	359·6	170·6
1944–45	251·7	343·7	75·9	419·6	167·9

Source. India Office.

Note. Receipts are net of any taxes received by Central Government on behalf of Provinces but include other miscellaneous receipts (though railway receipts are adjusted for railway expenditure). Expenditure figures include defence capital items as well as current account.

[1] Special information. The total amount involved over the war period was very small.

Thirdly, in so far as receipts from exports of merchandise are balanced by expenditure on imports, they do not usually add to outlay. The figure we are really interested in is the balance of trade from year to year as shown in Table 22.

TABLE 22. *Balance of trade (£m.)*

Year	Value of imports	Index of volume 1938–39 =100	Value of exports (including re-exports)	Index of volume 1938–39 =100	Balance
1939–40	127	102	161	104·5	+34
1940–41	121	81	153	88	+32
1941–42	131	74	191	93	+60
1942–43	86	37·6	147	62·5	+61
1943–44	100	40	159	54	+59
1944–45	144	67	172	56	+28

Source. Accounts for Seaborne Trade.

Notes. (1) Figures include Government (non-defence) imports and exports as well as private trade. Lend-lease civilian goods are included.

(2) 1944–5 figures have been adjusted, as published figures include a large amount of petrol intended for military use.

Finally, we have to make an estimate of 'other external items', which is an omnibus heading to cover transactions on invisible current account and capital account. It is impossible to make any separate estimate of these as complete figures are unknown or unavailable. Nevertheless, as published figures of Indian sterling holdings are a reasonably accurate guide to changes in all Indian sterling holdings, and also to holdings of all foreign assets, it is possible to derive figures from these which may be regarded as a fair approximation to the true position. Before any deductions can be drawn from changes in sterling holdings, however, it is necessary to correct these for movements of treasure (apart from gold movements allowed for in Table 16 supra), for clearly any exports of treasure are a deduction from, and any imports of treasure an increment to, capital assets. These adjustments and the subsequent inferences about changes in 'other capital items' are made in Table 23.

We may now combine the results of Tables 20–23. In Table 24 the relative importance of the various factors is clearly brought out.

Pride of place has to be given to British military expenditure, even though exports proceeds were important in the early war years, and the internal budget deficit played some considerable part in 1942–5. The derived figures of 'other external items' (apart from the rather mysterious figure for 1943–4) seem to follow the general trend of such changes in invisible payments as are known. Clearly the repatriation of sterling debt, and the 1942 agreement over the Railway Annuities, which provided for a single payment to His Majesty's Government in lieu of the normal annual payments, must have reduced invisible imports over the war period.

TABLE 23. *Indian external transactions (£m.)*

(1) Year	(2) Annual growth of sterling assets	(3) Net movement of private treasure (+import) (−export)	(4) Total (col. 2 −col. 3)	(5) Net British Government expenditure	(6) Balance of trade	(7) 'Other external items' (derived) (col. 4−(col. 5 +col. 6))
1939–40	+ 82	−22·7	+ 59·3	3	+34	+22·3
1940–41	+ 84	− 8·6	+ 75·4	40	+32	+ 3·4
1941–42	+205·5	− 1·3	+204·2	145	+60	− 0·8
1942–43	+301·5	− 1·6	+299·9	229·5	+61	+ 9·4
1943–44	+342	− 2·3	+339·7	232·8	+59	+47·9
1944–45	+335	− 3·4	+331·6	287·2	+28	+16·4

Sources. Previous tables; *Accounts for Seaborne Trade.*

Note. +in column 7 indicates that, on balance, invisible exports were greater than imports or capital imports were greater than exports.

TABLE 24. *Inflationary factors in India (£m.)*

Year	Net British military expenditure	Indian budget deficit	Balance of trade	'Other external items'
1939–40	3	Nil	+34	+22·3
1940–41	40	4·9	+32	+ 3·4
1941–42	145	9·5	+60	− 0·8
1942–43	229·5	123·9	+61	+ 9·4
1943–44	232·8	170·6	+59	+47·9
1944–45	287·2	167·9	+28	+16·4

Source. Previous tables.

Note. The importance of the budget deficit is overestimated in so far as it is due to any payments made overseas (e.g. non-effective charges paid to people outside India), but the error involved is not large so far as defence expenditure is concerned. (See Table 3, note (2).) It has not been possible to obtain complete figures of civil expenditure outside India for all years, but in 1938–9 annual interest and pension payments were about £15 million; by 1943–4 they were about £4 million.

Although British military expenditure was more important than the Indian budget deficit on the whole, it is reasonable to consider the effects of the two combined together. From the point of view of administrative machinery and internal economic results they were identical, and there is no point in treating them as separate influences when analysing the nature of income and price-inflation in India during the war years. The major part of this section will therefore be spent in tracing the methods and consequences of defence expenditure, and this term must be understood to include these two separate elements. At the end of the section we shall deal briefly with some special circumstances associated with exports and imports of goods and with 'other external items'.

To understand the nature of the impact of defence expenditure on the Indian economy, it is necessary first of all to glance at the provisions of the 1939 Defence Financial Agreement between India and the United Kingdom. The nature of this plan has been the subject of a good deal of misrepresentation and acrimonious discussion in both countries. It may be said to fill an old bottle with new wine. The old bottle was the principle that expenditure for the purposes of India's own defence fell on India, and the rest fell on the United Kingdom; the new wine was that the Indian Government paid the cost of all forces in India (Indian and European) and the cost of all equipment and supplies needed for them so long as they did not exceed the level fixed as being necessary for Indian defence, and with certain small exceptions, the United Kingdom Government paid for any forces or supplies needed in India above this level and for all Indian troops and Indian military supplies used outside India.[1] The mechanism of financing British military expenditure was simple, as the Indian Government itself, and not the local British military authorities, as in most other countries, made the various contracts and purchases, and was subsequently recouped by the British Government. As British acquisition of rupees from ordinary trading in merchandise was insufficient to pay for normal British imports, and as sales of sterling securities and gold only covered a small part of expenditure, the normal method was to credit the Reserve Bank of India with sterling assets, which allowed the necessary expansion of credit. Similarly, Indian defence expenditure not covered by taxation or long-term loans was financed by creation of rupees against short-term assets.

Thus the main effect of British military expenditure was, as in the other countries studied in this survey, a large increase in the supply of money. But we have seen there was no direct correlation between

[1] For exact details see Select Committee on National Expenditure, op. cit.

money and prices. The initial effect on the price level in fact depended on the ways in which the additional expenditure was organized. If demands on a country's resources are haphazard and uncoordinated, bottlenecks are going to appear quickly, whereas if the defence demands can be dovetailed in with normal demands, it is possible to adjust the economy to war with a minimum rise of wages and prices.

The Indian Government achieved some success in this direction, as the advantages of centralization were secured by having a Supply Department common to Indian and British requirements and placing the great majority of purchases through it. Attempts were also made, at any rate after 1941,[1] to apply sound pricing principles to contracts, the normal methods being to fix prices in accordance with the ascertained costs, allowing a fixed profit per unit of output,[2] or to base prices on previous experience in the type of output concerned. Thus it was claimed in the Select Committee Report[3] that prices paid by the Indian Supply Department for cloth only rose about 70% between 1939 and 1944, whereas the (controlled) price to the consumer had risen by 160%. Similarly, the Foodgrains Committee reported that the majority of Army purchases of foodstuffs were centrally purchased, and as the main demand was for wheat (500,000 tons out of a total of 650,000), this did not impinge so much on the deficit areas which were suffering mainly from a rice shortage. At the same time centralization of purchases was not a panacea for all ills. It is doubtful whether contracts, and more particularly small contracts,[4] were always placed with the source most easily able to satisfy them without affecting production for civilian needs. Local Army purchases of such perishable foods as vegetables were often made without regard to supply conditions or controlled prices.[5] Furthermore, of course, there was no check on personal spending by individual Allied soldiers accustomed to much higher standards of living than local populations, which was an aggravating factor in pushing up the prices of consumption goods and personal services in many towns. Probably the most important way in which the defence expenditure

[1] Contracts in the earlier war years seem to have normally been by competitive tender.

[2] This, of course, meant that profits were high when the ratio of turn-over to capital was high. Little attempt seems to have been made to deal with this.

[3] Op. cit. [4] Ibid.

[5] *Eastern Economist*, 24 July 1944. See also *Foodgrains Policy Committee Report*, p. 13, where it was reported that military demands in Assam had led to shortage of milk, eggs and poultry.

was uncoordinated, however, was in local demands for labour. We have already seen[1] how the man-power shortage in the coal fields can be largely explained on these lines. It is worth noting on this point that military rates of pay for unskilled labour were sufficiently high to attract skilled miners from the pits. In June 1942 the Civil Defence Department promoted a scheme for Provincial registration, and the control of movement of civilian drivers; at the same time the War Transport Department was trying to establish a system whereby lorry drivers could earn 75 rupees a month with free rations, and the Adjutant-General was trying to recruit drivers at 60 rupees a month without rations. This is merely an example of the lack of coordination between different departments of the Central Government. When the Provincial Governments, the States and the local Army authorities are also brought into the scene, it is not difficult to see why wages and incomes rose in India.[2]

In the early war years there appear to have been few attempts of any sort to limit or control incomes. Not only did wages rise haphazardly according to local demand conditions for labour, but even dearness allowances varied enormously between different firms in the same area. Thus in the Bihar coal fields in 1943, dearness allowances ranged from 12½ to 25% additions to basic wages at different pits. To some extent there was after 1942 a tendency for employers to set up cheap grain shops and freeze dearness allowances at the existing levels (e.g. Tata adopted this principle from March 1943),[3] but even then some employers paid cash bonuses on earnings. A cynic might well say that the surest way to increase money earnings of labour in any country is to impose a high E.P.T. In general, there was little semblance of a wages policy in India during the war. It is true that wages policy in Great Britain was never very clear, but it might well be argued that in a country where collective bargaining is virtually non-existent, a Central Government wages policy is more and not less necessary. Finally, there were no direct limitations on profits, which, in view of the deficiencies of the contract system alone, often attained very high levels.

Our discussion of income controls would obviously not be complete without reference to agriculture. This matter is closely allied with

[1] See p. 30.

[2] A greater degree of co-ordination was achieved in the later war years, e.g. attempts were made to regulate building of airfields in accordance with local supplies of labour (*The Times*, 28 July 1943).

[3] *Commerce*, 4 April 1943.

price control of agricultural products, and will therefore be covered later, but we may point out at this stage that the control over agricultural prices was largely ineffective in the early war years, and therefore incomes rose just as haphazardly as in industrial work.

If war expenditure leads to higher incomes for these various reasons, consumption expenditure clearly tends to increase. The extent is dependent on the authorities' power to restrict it by taxation or other means, and the consumers' willingness to increase their savings during the war years. Table 25 shows the major changes in Central Government taxation over the war years.

TABLE 25. *Central Government receipts*

Year	Total receipts £m.	Tax receipts £m.	% of Indian defence and civil expenditure		% of all Indian expenditure plus recoverable defence expenditure	
			Total receipts	Tax receipts	Total receipts	Tax receipts
1939–40	71·2	59·5	100	84	96	80
1940–41	80·7	56·7	94	66	64	42
1941–42	101·0	71·5	91	64	39	28
1942–43	132·7	92·5	52	36	27	19
1943–44	189·0	127·7	52	36	29	20
1944–45	251·7	189·6	60	45	33	25

Source. Explanatory Memoranda to Budgets.

Notes. (1) Tax receipts are net of any sums paid to Provinces.
(2) Net revenue only of railways included.

It is clear from these figures that from 1939 to 1944 Central Government receipts and taxation came to bear a progressively smaller ratio to Indian expenditure, and played no part whatever in offsetting British expenditure. The position did improve somewhat in 1944–5, and certainly contributed to the general stabilization of price levels which was achieved. The main change in yields of different taxes was the large rise in the receipts from the various types of income tax and corporation tax, which rose from £12·45 million in 1939–40 to £124 million in 1944–5, almost exactly a tenfold increase. This was due to a variety of measures such as the introduction of E.P.T. in 1940, and successive increases in income tax, corporation tax, surtax, and E.P.T. itself, either by increasing the tax rates or by reducing allowances and exemption limits. Customs duties failed to increase from their pre-war level of about £30 million per annum owing to the reduction of imports, but central excise duty expanded from £4·9 million in 1939–40 to £28·7 million in 1944–5. Railway and postal receipts also showed substantial increases.

The main reasons limiting possible taxation were constitutional. In the first place, the Central Government had no power to tax agricultural incomes; income tax, for instance, does not apply. In the second place, Provincial and State taxation was very slow to increase. The major reason for this was that the Provinces relied mainly on land taxes which are traditionally fixed for a long period of time, but in some cases it is undoubtedly true that the strong agricultural interests in the Government opposed further taxation.[1] Agricultural income tax was imposed in some Provinces, Bihar (1939), Assam (1940) and Bengal (1943), but there were complications of land tenure due to Permanent Settlements which strictly limited taxation powers. All in all, the total revenue of the Provinces rose from £63 million in 1938–9 to £126 million in 1943–4,[2] and this is partly to be explained by the increased share of taxes collected by the Central Government. Land revenue itself showed little change. There was, of course, no Central Government direction of State taxation of incomes, and although this varied widely, in no case was it as heavy as Central Government income taxes. Finally, there was an ultimate limiting factor, even apart from such legal difficulties, for a tremendous outcry would have arisen throughout India if any attempt had been made to tax incomes sufficiently highly to offset British expenditure.

For these reasons taxation was not a very powerful weapon to counteract the effects of defence expenditure. Nor were people easily cajoled into saving more. We have already seen that the backward peasant does not readily hold his assets in the form of cash or bonds of any sort. This was particularly true in India, as the supply of silver to mint rupee coins was much less in wartime owing to heavy exports to the United Kingdom for munitions purposes, and the difficulty of obtaining any from the U.S.A.[3] Thus the Government was compelled to issue 1 rupee notes instead which the peasants were more reluctant to hold, fearing physical deterioration as well as

[1] This was particularly true in the Punjab.

[2] Expenditure rose slightly less (from £64 to £116 million), but in general Provincial surpluses and deficits may be neglected.

[3] 226 m. oz. were actually obtained on Lend-Lease.

financial depreciation. The figures of total 'small savings'[1] declined progressively from a total of £106 million in March 1939 to £69 million in March 1943. A National Savings Committee was appointed in 1943, but it was only in March 1945 that the 1939 total was overtaken. A number of loans were floated by the Government for the purposes of both financing Indian expenditure and repatriating the sterling debt, but no marked success was achieved until the later war years. Nor were the Premium Bonds issues started in 1943 as successful as they were in the Middle Eastern countries. Two lotteries, one with bonds of 100 rupees, and the other with bonds of 10 rupees, were issued,[2] but sales to small savers were never very important. What did happen was that the wealthy sections attempted to buy up whole blocks of these to get a tax-free investment, and therefore the outright sale of issues to the banks as practised in Cyprus was not feasible. By March 1945 total sales had reached 40 million rupees (£3 million).

Clearly the reluctance of cultivators to hold securities is a major explanation of these facts, but whether it is the whole explanation is open to doubt. Such evidence as there is goes to show that agricultural indebtedness was reduced in wartime.[3] Therefore, some peasants must have saved to pay off these debts, and the real question is whether the village moneylenders held their expanded cash assets idle, or whether their consumption expenditure increased. Furthermore, the vigour of the Indian Government in pressing home the need for savings was not unimpeachable. We have already seen,[4] for instance, that there was no restraint on capital issues until 1943. The concept of deferred savings does not seem to have been appreciated, although an exception must be made in the case of the Bihar Government, who tried to make the sugar-cane growers put receipts in defence savings.[5]

At this point we may refer to the anti-inflationary aspects of the repatriation of sterling securities. Different opinions[6] have been expressed about this, and it seems as well to straighten out the arguments. The normal technique was that the Reserve Bank was commissioned by the Government of India to purchase sterling securities with its sterling assets. The sterling securities were then

[1] Including Post Office Savings Bank, Defence Savings Bank, Cash Certificates, Defence Savings Certificates and National Savings Certificates.

[2] See *The Economist*, 18 December 1943.

[3] Patel, loc. cit. Also *Indian J. Econ.* July 1945. Geren, op. cit.

[4] See p. 40.

[5] Bose, *Indian J. Econ.* January 1944.

[6] See discussion in Budget Speech, 1943.

cancelled, and subsequently the Reserve Bank received short-term bills as assets. Thus, of itself, the repatriation did nothing to expand or contract the supply of credit, or to increase or decrease the inflationary potential. In so far as the Government or Reserve Bank was able to persuade the public to hold more long-term securities, of course, it was possible to decrease the supply of money, and, *prima facie*, the inflationary potential.

Finally, the use of gold and silver sales as a means of reducing consumption expenditure must be mentioned. Gold sales started in August 1943, and as we have already seen[1] some £50·6 million were sold by March 1944, and some £54·1 million from March 1944 to March 1945 on behalf of the British Government. In addition, American gold was sold to finance the American military expenditure. The normal method of sale was for the Reserve Bank to offer gold at a fixed price[2] which attracted buyers as soon as market prices tended to move higher. Although the amounts sold were not large in comparison with British military expenditure, these sales took place at a critical time in 1943–4, and probably played a not unimportant part in stabilizing prices. For although it is not possible to trace any direct connexion between the price of gold and the level of wholesale prices,[3] and although some gold was absorbed by people holding bonds or notes,[4] it is undoubtedly true that some was bought by people who reduced their hoards of commodities or consumption expenditure, and in this way it acted as a counter-inflationary factor. The volume of silver sales is not known exactly, but it cannot have absorbed more than a few million pounds. On the other hand, it is probable that a large proportion of the silver reached the small cultivators who were, after all, the main target of these weapons.

We have now seen that incomes tended to increase as a result both of the size of military expenditure, and of the methods by which it was organized and financed. We have also seen that taxation and savings inducements did not achieve outstanding success in limiting expenditure out of income. It is now time to examine the ways in which the various rationing schemes and distributing arrangements restricted consumption. It is impossible to separate out completely

[1] P. 56.

[2] Usually between 72 and 78 rupees per tola (i.e. £15–16 per fine oz.). See *The Economist*, 13 November 1943.

[3] See Mikesell, *Review of Economic Statistics*, May 1946.

[4] In this case there was clearly no additional saving by the community as a result of buying gold.

the different problems involved in consumers' rationing, control of distribution, price control, procurement and supplies, but so far as possible we shall deal with consumers' rationing only at this stage, and then later we shall consider problems of procurement, distribution, and price control.

In foodstuffs consumers were not rationed until May 1943, when rationing of foodgrains first started in Bombay City. This was extended to other towns of over 100,000 inhabitants, and by March 1945 it was claimed[1] that rationing of foodgrains covered some 42 million people (or rather more than one-tenth of the total population) in a large number of different localities. In addition to this 'full rationing' by means of cards, informal rationing covered a large number of villages,[2] and arrangements were made for 'provisioning' (i.e. allocation of subsidized supplies) to the poorest sections of the population in the United Provinces.[3] The normal rations fixed were 1 lb. of foodgrains per day for an adult male, but frequently consumers had to be persuaded to eat wheat instead of rice by such methods as appropriate taxes and subsidies. But even in 1945 rationing was not comprehensive for all large towns, as there were, for instance, four large towns in the Punjab alone unrationed.

Previous to 1943 there had been a large number of pious resolutions from conferences, and a few measures, such as the Foodgrains Control Order of 1942, which ordered that transactions in foodgrains could only be carried on by licence, but little had been done to lay the essentials of any rationing scheme by establishing real control of distribution.

Consumers' rationing, as we know it in this country, was mainly confined to foodgrains, but supplies of other consumer goods were restricted in various ways. Sugar was rationed in a number of towns and areas, although the exact amounts allowed and principles of rationing differed widely; e.g. in Jubbulpore, the size of the ration varied with income.[4] The control of the textile industry introduced in June 1943 was an attempt to increase production by rationalization of production and to bring down prices, both by direct price regulation and by forcing supplies on to the market. Although standard cloth appeared in considerable quantity after that time there were few

[1] Budget Speech, 1945.

[2] There were in Bombay Province, for instance, some 4000 fair-price shops in the villages (*Eastern Economist*, 12 April 1946).

[3] Woodhead Commission, op. cit.

[4] *Commerce*, 10 November 1945.

attempts at genuine clothing rationing.[1] Kerosene, as we have already seen, was distributed to traders and from traders to consumers in proportion to previous requirements. In July 1944 a general ordinance (The Consumer Goods (Control of Distribution) Order) was issued to regulate the supply, distribution and prices of consumer goods.

Is it possible to make any deductions from this brief survey of rationing? The details enumerated will have made it clear that rationing in India was of very limited scope. It applied only to a small number of commodities, to a limited number of areas, and a small proportion of the population, and frequently it does not appear to have worked successfully, even within these confines. Thus, although distribution of these commodities was made more equitable, in no sense can rationing be said to have acted as an anti-inflationary factor. The very people whose expenditure had to be kept in check, i.e. the prosperous sections of the peasantry, were not touched by a rationing system that applied very largely to urban populations; and if rationing schemes only touch a limited number of commodities, consumers have more and not less to spend on other commodities. It is only when rationing covers a wider range of goods and services that it can play an important part in restricting consumption expenditure.[2] Finally, there was no attempt to link up such rationing of rural populations as there was with inducements to produce more.

Direct methods of price control had a very mixed success in India. Broadly, it may be said that despite the series of six Price Control Conferences between October 1939 and September 1942 which considered the problems involved but did little to implement their considerations, no real success in controlling prices was reached until late 1943. The fundamental difficulty of the 1939–43 period was that the whole problem was tackled on a piecemeal basis. The facts that effective price control is impossible without Provincial control over supply and distribution, and Provincial control over supply and distribution impossible without central direction, even if realized, were not embodied in practical administration. There were many difficulties in Provincial control over supply, for this meant that

[1] For instance, cloth rationing was not introduced in Bombay until June 1945 or Calcutta until September 1945 (*Commerce*, December 1945).

[2] On the other hand, if rationing does restrict the consumption and price of one or two important commodities this may lead to greater willingness to work or greater confidence in the value of money, and either of these is a powerful anti-inflationary factor.

surpluses had to be assessed, purchased and collected from the cultivator; this was extraordinarily difficult, as the cultivators frequently wanted to conserve surpluses over previous consumption levels themselves, and even if not, they often held on to their stocks when prices were rising or were thought likely to rise. It was a true vicious circle, for if supplies could not be made available, such price controls as there were became inoperative, and if prices rose, cultivators became all the more loath to part with their stocks. The position was often made worse, too, by the shortage of acceptable media with which the cultivators could be paid. The Foodgrains Policy Committee found that the shortage of appropriate currency or consumer's goods had often increased the difficulties of procurement.[1] Even when surpluses had been extracted from growers there were many difficulties in distribution to be overcome in ensuring that supplies were not spirited away to intermediary speculative hoarders and black-market dealers, or to high-price areas. The methods adopted by Provincial Governments to fulfil these objectives varied considerably, but it is roughly true to say that it was the gradual spread of the principle of 'full monopoly' (i.e. Government responsibility for collection and distribution including transport priorities) which made any semblance of price control feasible,[2] for the various measures in 1942 fixing maximum prices and restricting movements and forward operations in wheat, and the establishment of regional committees for coordinating supply and regulating prices of foodgrains, were quite ineffective without adequate procurement machinery. The supply situation, in fact, became so bad in the North-Eastern Provinces that the experiment of allowing uncontrolled prices and free movement of grains had to be tried in the early months of 1943, with the hope of attracting stocks on to the market. Some supplies were brought to the most necessitous areas, but prices soared to enormous heights, e.g. in Calcutta the price rose by more than 300% between March 1942 and March 1943; wheat prices in Bengal ranged from 15 to 20 Rs. per maund in June 1943, compared with an average pre-war price of 3 Rs. per maund. Such were the results of the shortlived free-trade policy.

Gradually it was realized that price control could not work

[1] Op. cit. p. 46.

[2] The extent to which Provincial Governments intervened varied enormously. Some (e.g. the Punjab) only used their power to ensure a monopoly of export over grain which the cultivators brought to market voluntarily, whereas others, such as Bombay, had compulsory requisitioning of all surpluses over previous consumption (see *The Times*, 5 March 1946).

effectively on a Provincial Government level, and that much more active intervention by the Central Government was necessary. In the first place, a Department dealing solely with food supplies had to be established. Secondly, some coordinating machinery had to be devised to decide how supplies should be taken from surplus Provinces and transferred to deficit Provinces (the so-called 'Basic Plan'). Thirdly, the necessary pressure had to be brought to bear to force recalcitrant Provinces to collect and disgorge their surpluses. In the Punjab, for instance, the Minister in charge of agriculture had actually encouraged growers not to part with crops at current prices,[1] and in the United Provinces, Central Provinces and Bihar substantial stocks of grain were accumulating when Bengal was starving.[2] Possibly this erection of inter-Provincial barriers might be described as the most important single cause of the great Bengal famine of 1943.[3] Until they could be broken down even attempts at local price control could hardly be successful, let alone all-India price control. Fourthly, exports had to be controlled and distribution of imports over the country had to be planned according to wartime needs, and measures had to be taken to prevent excessive distributors' margins. Fifthly, general regulations to enforce all-India price control, either by ceiling prices or statutory maximum prices, had to be taken. These various aims were implemented in 1943 and 1944 by a series of measures such as the prohibition of forward trading and advances against commodities; the decisions after the Food Conferences of 1943 that procurement must be done by the Provincial Governments or agencies, and that statutory prices must be enforced for all major foods; the opening of model shops and other propaganda measures; and the various steps to fix maximum prices (e.g. for jowar and bajra) on an all-India basis. Export of foodgrains was forbidden from March 1943, and in the case of imports it was laid down as a general rule that selling prices must not exceed landed costs by more than 20%, even if no maximum prices were fixed.

Some time has been spent outlining the major aspects of price-control policy for foodgrains as they play such a large part in the Indian economy. Controls of other prices did not meet with so many difficulties, but they were still only partially successful. It was

[1] *The Times*, 28 July 1943. [2] Ibid.

[3] The relative state of rice supplies in different Provinces in 1943 may be seen from the fact that at one time rice prices in Calcutta were *five* times as high as those in Orissa.

reported, for instance, that prices had been fixed for such goods as kerosene, medicine, matches, rubber, newsprint, iron and steel, but neither Central Government nor Provincial Government price fixing had proved at all satisfactory, except in the case of purchases made by the Government themselves.[1] Another example of the ineffectiveness of price control was sugar. In April 1942 control of prices and distribution was instituted, but the prompt result was that nearly all supplies were driven into the black market.[2] In 1943, as we have seen, the textile control scheme was introduced with provision for ceiling prices. Many other regulations were passed in 1943 and 1944 controlling prices. The Profiteering and Hoarding Prevention Ordinance of October 1943 was an attempt to force supplies on to the market and effect price reductions of all consumer goods not subject to specific controls. Typical of the specific controls was the Drug Control Order of November 1943, which dealt with the distribution and prices of drugs and medicines. In general the same conclusion applies as in the case of foodgrains prices—that price control never was at all successful until the later war years.

It may be noted at this point that no extensive use was made of an official subsidy policy in India. There were some attempts to subsidize food prices in the United Provinces,[3] but these were on a small scale. The main reason appears to have been that the indirect inflationary effects of subsidies were considered to be more dangerous than the direct anti-inflationary aspects in a country where there was already a heavy budget deficit, and where there was no 'automatic' relationship between wages and cost of living indices. How far the absence of any such or similar wages policy was an important difficulty in operating price controls is a matter where opinions in India may differ; but experience in other countries does not.

In summary, it must be said that the attempts at price control did not show any real success until 1943, for at that time the very goods, foodgrains and textiles, for which control was most essential, had risen most in price.[4] The elementary principle that a District Officer cannot fix prices at some arbitrary level[5] and then leave them there

[1] *Economist*, 26 December 1942.

[2] The sugar control was described as 'probably the most outstanding failure of all Government's control schemes', *Capital*, 1942 Survey.

[3] See *Council of State Debates*, 16 February 1945.

[4] See Table 11.

[5] See Bhargava, *Price Control and Rationing*, p. 19: 'Local district officers have in some cases fixed prices of meat, milk, eggs, fowls, etc., irrespective of costs, with the result that control measures had often to be amended.'

in the hope that they will remain there, had to be learnt through bitter experience. Even if Central Government monopoly of purchases was not a matter of practical politics or administration (and it is not easy to decide which was the most important consideration), it was found that overall Central Government control and local monopoly purchasing were an essential prerequisite of enforcement of either statutory maximum or ceiling prices.

In a country where supplies are subject to the irrational and highly volatile fears of ignorant peasant producers and the unscrupulous deals of greedy merchant classes, adequate controls over supply are more and not less necessary than in industrialized countries. Furthermore, the essential relationships of the price structure seem to have been inadequately recognized. To control the price of wheat or rice it is not only necessary to have effective control over supply, procurement and distribution of wheat or rice but also control over the prices of cash crops, as otherwise if cash crop prices show a tendency to rise, cultivators will obviously tend to switch over production. Similarly, if there is a shortage of one foodgrain and prices are high, consumers may switch to another and controls may be quite powerless to prevent price rises. Thus, the fact that rice prices were rising in 1942, whereas wheat prices were subject to statutory control, meant that wheat growers held back supplies in anticipation of higher prices.

Official prices were stabilized reasonably well after 1943,[1] but the grim shadow of black-market prices overcast the lives of many people. The principal difficulty was controlling the activities and margins of merchants[2] rather than the prices ex-works or ex-cultivator, for although it was possible to impose a good deal of State trading into the procurement mechanism, distribution had largely to be left to normal traders, the main control being a mixture of threats and promises. It we take the four major consumer goods, textiles, foodgrains, hardware, and kerosene, it is fairly true to summarize by saying that control of kerosene and some of the more important hardware prices was fairly effective, but black-market operations in foodgrains and textiles were far too common to enable all, or even most consumers, to obtain their basic supplies at official prices.

If a large volume of purchasing power is created by military expenditure, and if the various possible ways of checking consumption expenditure are far from perfect, prices are bound to rise. The extent

[1] See Table 13.

[2] The same argument applies to rationing (Bhargava, op. cit. p. 47).

to which prices rise in such a situation, however, depends on the volume of supplies available to meet demand. We have already seen in § 1 that there were large reductions in imports, that imports as a whole, and in particular machinery and manufactured goods, play a vital part in the Indian economy, and that the success in expanding home output was rather mixed. We must now examine the attempts made to lighten these burdens.

There was no control over imports (except from enemy countries) until May 1940, and even by May 1941 only 117 commodities were under control, and it was only by June 1942 that import licensing was at all comprehensive. Restriction of imports was not very imaginative in the early war years. The tendency was to cut down all goods in much the same proportions and not to cut out luxuries and unnecessary articles completely.[1] In the later war years world supplies were the limiting factor to imports, but up to 1942–3 shipping was the real bottleneck. There seems to be no real reason for the failure to lay in stocks of grains except that the atmosphere of 'business as usual' permeated the air too strongly for such a revolutionary departure from traditional policy at that time. In the later war years active steps were taken to increase the imports of essential goods, e.g. imported grain, pulse and flour rose to 301,000 tons in 1944 from a mere 8700 tons in the previous year.

The master key to the successful working of any policy to expand output quickly in either agriculture or industry is some control over man-power. Without conscription in its military or industrial forms, the principal war belligerents would have been unable to secure any full utilization of economic resources, or the diversion of these resources to the most urgent ends. It cannot be argued that a man-power policy involving control over unskilled labour on an all-India basis was either practicable or desirable, but it can be reasonably maintained that some control was necessary at some times in some places, and it can be confidently asserted that a policy to control the allocation of skilled labour was essential, indeed vital, in the absence of any wages policy. In actual fact, a number of measures were adopted to deal with labour problems. National Service for skilled tradesmen was started in June 1940; a technical training scheme was instituted which turned out some 62,000 men by February 1944; Essential Services Orders on the lines of our Essential Works Order and National Service Labour Tribunals were inaugurated for skilled men.

[1] *Commerce*, 7 January 1943.

In some places (Jubbulpore was the first) Labour Supply Committees to settle conflicting claims for unskilled labour were set up. But these were frequently abortive, as the facilities were not available to observe whether regulations were being obeyed, or to do anything if they were not. We have already seen how skilled coal-miners were drawn into unskilled work on airfield construction and on road building. Another reason for labour shortage in the north-eastern Provinces was the uncontrolled movement of a rather panicstricken population when the threat of Japanese invasion was imminent. Finally, there was a complete absence of any controls, such as labour priorities, to prevent Government departments or private undertakings from competing with one another. It would not be unfair to compare the role of the Central Government Labour Department with the position of the old Board of Trade Labour Department in this country in the years before 1914, except that the latter was not hamstrung by considerations of dealing with a number of Provincial Governments unable, or in some cases unwilling, to pursue any adequate labour policy.

We must now examine why it was not found possible to expand agricultural output to any great extent over the war years; all that we shall be concerned with are the attempts to increase actual output, and not the difficulties of procurement. The main problems of primary production in the early war years were, as in so many countries, the cessation of the export trade. Markets which had previously absorbed, for instance, 56% of raw jute exports disappeared after the military defeats of 1940. Similar troubles were experienced by raw cotton, more particularly after the closing of the Japanese market in 1941. Extremely good yields and the fact that after the high prices in 1939 and the early months of 1940 some producers had switched over to cash crops made the position worse, and consequently drastic reductions in acreage had to be made in 1941–2. Bengal was perhaps the most seriously affected by these changes. These were the main problems of the early war years, and it was not until after the Food Production Conference of April 1942, or some 2½ years after the start of the war, that any measures were taken to expand output of food crops. The 'Grow more Food' campaign, which aimed at increasing the area of land under cultivation, diverting some land from cash to food crops, and increasing the annual yield from existing food acreage, then started. Numerous devices, such as propaganda, advances of loans, remission of taxes and rates, guaranteed prices, cheap seeds, and the provision of emergency irrigation facilities, were tried. Some success was achieved, but on the whole the results were disappointing.[1] For this it is possible to establish three major reasons. First, the peasants were possibly tempted by higher prices to produce rather less than before. This is a well-known economic characteristic of primitive economies, and although, as we shall see, it did not apply to Middle East countries in such a straightforward manner, it does appear to have been more influential in India. And even if they did produce as much they frequently consumed more themselves. Secondly, the opportunities for agricultural expansion are notoriously small in India. All but the most barren and unfertile stretches of land have been brought into cultivation years ago by the pressure of population, and irrigation is a long-term but hardly a short-term cure. And the means to cultivate more intensively were limited not only by the minute subdivisions of land and the ancient rites surrounding Indian agricultural methods, but also by the shortages of tractors[2] and fertilizers[3] which, never plentiful in peacetime, were reduced to extremely small proportions in war. Nor must it be forgotten that poor climatic conditions may add to these difficulties and counteract any attempts to increase output quickly. Finally, it is open to doubt whether the food-production campaign was pressed home as hard as it might have been. The total amount sanctioned in loans and grants from revenue or from the cotton fund and handed over from the Central Government to the Provinces and States was only £4·25 million from 1943 to 1945.[4] As such loans and grants were normally made on a 50/50 basis the total sums involved must have been extremely small.

What methods were adopted to expand industrial output during the war and what difficulties were encountered? At first the War

[1] In Bombay Province, for instance, the area under food crops expanded from 19·9 million acres in 1941–2 to 21·8 million in 1944–5, owing to the reductions in cash crops acreage. Nevertheless, food output failed to expand appreciably (output of rice, wheat and millets, which averaged 2·86 million tons in pre-war years, was only 3·01 million tons in 1944–5) (*Eastern Economist*, 12 April 1940). Irrigation brought some 300,000–400,000 acres under cultivation in the Punjab between 1941 and 1945 (Woodhead Commission, op. cit.).

[2] In 1943 it was estimated that 151 tractors ought to be imported in 1944 to meet the most essential needs, but, in fact, only nineteen were received (ibid.).

[3] The Foodgrains Policy Committee (op. cit.) estimated that average annual supplies of imported and home-produced fertilizers before the war were about 84,000 and 28,000 tons respectively. The total available supply in 1943–4 was put at 10,500 tons. Table 9 shows the reductions in imports of manures.

[4] Woodhead Commission (op. cit.).

Supply Board and later the War Resources Committee with their executive agency, the Supply Department, directed the industrial war effort (in collaboration with the Eastern Group Supply Council of course). The Director-General of Supply was at first responsible for all supplies from ordnance factories and purchases from private industry, but some of his functions were later diverted to other directorates. The general method used by these agencies until 1941 was the peacetime one of competitive tendering, but later this disappeared and contracts were placed with industry on ascertained costs and profits margins.[1] Competitive tendering with small-scale industry remained, however. The Department of Commerce was gradually developed during the war and from it grew two offshoots—the Food Department dealing (*inter alia*) with Army food requirements and the Department of Industries and Civil Supplies dealing with the allocation and supply of consumer goods, such as textiles, between war and civilian needs.

Despite this evolution of more specialized administrative machinery, the attendant series of controls for individual industries and the general tendency to coordinate the different sections of the economy more thoroughly, output in many lines of production did not respond as one might have expected. For instance, in 1943, cotton piecegoods, jute and paper manufacture all showed a decline in production which was not planned or premeditated like the decline in consumer goods output in England. There were a number of reasons for this, and among the most important were the shortage of coal and transport. The troubles in transport were, first, that a railway system with fewer facilities (railway stock had been despatched to the Middle East) had to carry a much larger volume of goods and passenger traffic (from 1938–9 to 1943–4 net ton mileage increased by 28% and net passenger mileage, excluding military specials, by 74%).[2] Secondly, the railway system of India was subject to a strain not unlike that which overburdened the European inland transport system during the war. The impossibility of using certain ports or a large volume of coastal shipping meant that the burden on some parts of the railway system was all the heavier, in just the same way as the strategic bombing of internal waterways and the disappearance of coastal shipping threw intolerable strains on the economy of 'fortress Europe'. In some ways the problem was worse in India, for the lack of adequate storage facilities in the villages raised many difficulties. In 1942, for instance,

[1] See p. 60.

[2] Railway Budget Speech, 1944.

the difficulties of transporting the jute crop to Calcutta led to a slump in jute prices in the country districts and a very high level of prices in Calcutta.[1] In some cases crops rotted altogether. Shortage of coal often accounted for engine failures, and the piling up of tubs and waggons at the pits meant that many hours were wasted in walking longer distances to load the coal. The shortages in coal output and the many problems of transport were often cumulative. As a result of these two great problems of transport and coal, textile factories, for instance, were often compelled to go on to short-time working and in some cases to close altogether. Even when these difficulties did not occur the shortage of textile machinery was very real, as imports were only of the same value (£2·5 million) in 1943–4 as they had been in 1938–9, and consequently the greater part of cotton textile machinery was normally working a 168-hour week. There were many labour troubles, such as the panic evacuations from the east coast, the high rate of absenteeism (this was particularly important in coal) and the political disturbances and associated hartals. Shortages of skilled labour often developed which could have been avoided if recruitment and training schemes had been properly coordinated with the expanding requirements of industry. For instance, a shortage of platers arose in the R.I.N. Dockyard in Bombay in 1943, due to the fact that demand for ship-repair labour had enormously expanded, but there was no control over the allocation and movement of skilled shipyard labour and no training facilities for platers at Government centres. Finally, it was only in the later war years that effective controls and priorities for use of scarce materials, such as iron and steel and rubber, were established.

We have now completed the major part of our inquiry in this section. We have seen that, by and large, defence expenditure was responsible for the additional drain on Indian economic resources, and we have seen the many reasons why it was not found possible to prevent a large price-inflation as a result.

All that we have to do now is to glance at the other major additional demands, receipts of exporters and the net receipts for 'other external items' and see if there were any special features or peculiar difficulties associated with these.

On the special aspects of exports two main points must be considered. The first is whether the goods which went overseas were in

[1] *Commerce*, 1942 Survey.

particularly short supply. The second is whether exporters' incomes were raised unduly by high prices for exports. On the first it must be pointed out that despite the licensing system, private export trade was not thoroughly controlled until 1942–3, when it was realized that the exports of cotton piecegoods and foodgrains were causing a serious drain on internal civilian supplies already depleted as a result of the rapidly rising population. Perhaps the best way of appreciating the expansion of cotton piecegoods exports from 177 million yd. in 1938–9 to 819 million yd. in 1942–3 is to recall that the total volume of exports remained almost constant up to 1942, despite the loss of export markets, for many staple products such as raw cotton, jute and oilseeds. On the second point there is little evidence to show that export prices increased much faster than internal price levels, as may be seen from Table 26.

TABLE 26. *Export and wholesale prices*

Year	Export quantum	Export price index	Wholesale price index (19 Aug. 1939 = 100)
1938–39	100	100	—
1939–40	104·5	120	125
1940–41	88	130	115
1941–42	93	156	137
1942–43	62·5	185	171
1943–44	54	227	236
1944–45	56	240	244

Source. Accounts for Seaborne Trade.

Note. Exports are private exports only, i.e. re-exports and Indian Government transactions excluded, but bulk purchases by British Ministry of Food are included.

This evidence is corroborated by the findings of the Select Committee,[1] which reported that there was no indication that bulk purchases by the Ministry of Supply or the Ministry of Food had been made at prices equivalent to or above normal market or controlled prices. Prices paid for tea were, in fact, well below other prices received by tea growers.

On the subject of 'other external items' it is possible to say little about the absolute magnitudes of the various items because so little is known. The total effect cannot have been great, and in so far as any of these receipts were due to capital transactions, there is no reason to assume that they went to swell the expenditure stream.

[1] Op. cit.

Finally, another point must be mentioned, not because it was important in India at all—that is why it was not brought into the discussion at an earlier stage—but because it is necessary to set out the data involved in order to facilitate comparisons with other countries at a later stage. The point in question is that of high import prices which in some countries played an important part in pushing up prices and incomes. In India there is no reason to assume that this factor had any great importance, as Table 27 shows.

TABLE 27. *Import and wholesale prices*

Year	Import quantum	Import price index	Wholesale price index (19 Aug. 1939=100)
1938–39	100	100	—
1939–40	102	106	125
1940–41	81	127	115
1941–42	74	153	137
1942–43	37·6	193	171
1943–44	40	195	236
1944–45	67	188	244

Source. Accounts for Seaborne Trade.

Note. Imports by Indian Government of military stores or normal Government equipment (e.g. office equipment) excluded, but civilian Lend-Lease goods included.

§ 4. CRITIQUE OF WAR ORGANIZATION

In this section we shall be concerned with the problem of whether the degree of price-inflation which took place in India was unavoidable or not. We shall start by considering some of the basic reasons which made a substantial rise in prices inevitable, and then we shall proceed to ask whether these reasons are in themselves sufficient to account for the rise that actually took place, or whether there were other less basic contributing factors.

The basic reasons which made some price-inflation inevitable may be grouped under the headings of the size of the war effort, the nature of the war effort and the special characteristics of the Indian economy. On the first it is not necessary to say very much. We have already seen that an expansion of prices and incomes is a necessary condition of expanding national output and diverting a considerable proportion of resources to war. This experience was common to all countries in the recent war, quite independently of the nature of the war effort. In India the fact that the major war demands at first consisted of

British military requirements and exports of merchandise made the creation of money against sterling assets necessary, and in the later war years the substantial internal budget deficit led to ordinary deficit financing. In view of the inelasticity of supply of factors of production and commodities, the accompanying increased outlay was bound to cause prices and incomes to rise.

The nature of the Indian war effort, however, was responsible for aggravating the degree of price rise. The first point is that India was called on for a 'mixed' war effort. She had to put an Army into the field; manufacture munitions and supplies for that Army; feed and clothe an expanding population and try to manage without or produce substitutes for some of the many imports which were cut off altogether or reduced to vanishing point. Now the overwhelming characteristic of the Indian economy is the under-employment of labour on the land; in economists' language, the marginal productivity of labour is extremely low or possibly even negative.[1] Further, in many branches of industry work is performed by thousands of labourers with very crude and primitive implements and often little machinery at all. In other words, the resources which are normally plentiful are not land as in the Argentine or machinery[2] as in the United States, but man-power. It seems perfectly clear that any attempt to utilize Indian resources in the best possible way should have aimed at recruiting a large Army but equipping it and possibly even feeding it from overseas. Instead, India was called on to produce more manufactured goods and grow more food despite the wartime lack of raw materials, fertilizers, and machinery which inevitably made these tasks even more difficult than they had been before. There seems little doubt that if, for instance, a million less British had been conscripted to Armed Service and a million more Indians, the overall effort of the two countries could have been greater. It is certain that the superiority of a British soldier over an Indian as a fighter, if there is any at all, cannot be nearly as great as the difference in efficiency between a British and an Indian in industry *given* the much more plentiful supply of machinery and industrial skill in this country.[3] Yet British industry was starved of man-power to enlarge the Armed Forces, while at the same time an Army of only $2\frac{1}{2}$ millions was recruited

[1] In the sense of not producing sufficient to keep itself.

[2] There was some spare capacity in 1939 (cf. p. 40), but this was quickly absorbed.

[3] It might be objected, of course, that British vulnerability to air raids was a partial offsetting factor.

from a country which literally has so large a population that it does not know how to employ it. Whether the ultimate reason is to be found in political intransigeance or military vanity, history alone will show.

Quite apart from this general point, it should be noted that of the Indian industrial expansion the major part was accounted for by a few industries, engineering, iron and steel, textiles and chemicals. Now some of these industries are highly localized in India. For instance, in 1939 some 400 out of 800 engineering works, 37 out of 157 foundries and rolling mills, 17 out of 26 chemical works, were to be found in the Bay of Bengal area.[1] In coal mining, too, Bihar and Bengal contain a very large proportion of the pits. The heavy concentration on a few industries meant that skilled labour reserves of the requisite types were soon likely to be exhausted; the heavy concentration on a few areas meant that in some places even shortages of unskilled labour were likely to arise.[2] Furthermore, other war factors, apart from the demand for industrial products, intensified the situation. The presence of the Japanese on the eastern borders of India led to mass evacuation in 1942–3, and the heavy drafts on man-power for road and airfield construction in these areas still further curtailed available labour supplies.

The tremendous reduction of imports (and it must be emphasized that in 1943 the volume of imports was only 40% of 1938–9, and the value only 3·5% instead of 9% of the national income) was another really fundamental difficulty, more particularly in view of the constantly increasing population. Many individual consumer goods (e.g. cotton piecegoods) were reduced to a far greater extent than that, and many commodities vital for Indian industry were in extremely short supply. The value of machinery imports was, for instance, only £7·9 million in 1943–4 as against £14·8 million in 1938–9, and the reduction in volume must have been far greater than this comparison suggests. Furthermore, the changes in source of supply and port of delivery made very heavy demands on an already overburdened transport system.

Despite these wartime difficulties in industry, however, the general all-India price indices (see Table 13) show that prices of foodstuffs rose more than the prices of manufactures, and they in turn more than raw-material prices. Can it be said that the nature of the war effort was responsible in any way for these discrepancies? Direct

[1] *The Economist*, 2 May 1942.

[2] Cf. p. 73.

Army demands, as we have seen,[1] were not important, although their incidence undoubtedly bore more heavily on some areas, particularly the north-east, than others. On the whole it is doubtful whether changes in supply and demand purely associated with the war effort were crucial, although the cessation of rice supplies from Burma in 1942–3 undeniably was an important aggravating factor.

Another aspect of the effect of war on the Indian economy was the way in which events crowded in on one another in 1943. This was the period of the war when military expenditure reached a high level, yet imports were at their lowest ebb, pre-war stocks were nearing exhaustion, the Japanese were on the borders of Assam, and there was a short fall in crops owing to natural causes. There can be little doubt that the Indian Government was extraordinarily unlucky in this conglomeration of economic tribulations.

Broadly, it may be argued that the acute expansion of demand on a narrow front and reduction of key imports undoubtedly were influential in creating bottlenecks. The situation was intensified because there was little advance warning of exactly what contributions India would have to make. If the nature of the additional demands had been known at an early stage of the war it would have been possible to expand training and recruitment in advance of production and therefore avoid or at least mitigate some serious bottlenecks.

On the question of how far the degree of inflation which took place can be accounted for by the special characteristics of the Indian economy, it would be possible to digress at great length. Here we must content ourselves with pointing out the major features which must be grasped before any conclusions can be made.

First, the fundamental weaknesses of the Indian economy must be realized. The Indian economy mainly consists of two imperfectly welded sections, an international economy superimposed on a primitive subsistence economy. What enabled the delicate mechanism of internal production and trade to carry on from year to year in pre-war days was the assurance of imports of machinery and consumer goods in sufficient quantity. When these imports were no longer available the whole economy was threatened with collapse. This is an instance of a case in which it is most misleading to judge matters by Western standards; industrialized economies are fundamentally more resilient than primitive agricultural systems. The difference is really like that between a four-engined and a single-engined aircraft;

[1] See p. 42.

mechanical trouble is disastrous for the latter but is only likely to slow down the speed of the former. We have already seen the physical transport and storage problems created by the switching of imports to fewer ports. Apart from purely physical problems there were many psychological difficulties which were exacerbated by the wartime 'shocks' to the economy. What assured supplies of foodgrains in peacetime was the existence of fairly steady prices and a sufficient supply of acceptable exchange media. When these normal relationships were disturbed, or even when it was thought that they might be disturbed,[1] the whole economy was threatened with breakdown, for any reduction in supply due to these causes is, *ipso facto*, concentrated on the urban areas. And India was not lacking in a merchant class prepared to exploit these difficulties.

Secondly, it is important to recognize the constitutional difficulties in India. The quasi-autonomous powers granted to the Provinces under the 1935 Act and the lack of any adequate central power over the States meant that it was impossible to have any uniform system of enactments applicable to all India. We have seen how income taxes differed between the Central Government and the States, and how difficult it was to persuade the Provinces to increase taxation. Price-control regulations, too, differed to an enormous extent. In August 1943, for instance, there were still no statutory maximum or ceiling prices fixed for any commodities at all in Orissa or the North-West Frontier Province, despite the fact that enabling legislation had been first passed by the Central Government in 1939. It was impossible to control the distribution of commodities and prevent smuggling from low- to high-price areas in such circumstances. The hesitations of the Provinces over the introduction of the standard cloth scheme are another example.

Thirdly, it must be realized that India has never been governed in detail in the same way as Western countries. The total membership of the Indian Civil Service in 1939 was only 1400, and out of these only 600 were British. The chronic shortage of administrators is quickly apparent when the size of the country and its population is taken into account. Furthermore, the quality of the administration, at least in regard to economic affairs, is open to doubt, as the knowledge of such matters by many officials in responsible positions appears to have been minute. Possibly the best comment on the normal methods

[1] It is doubtful whether many Indian peasants even stop at the 'sixth sense' which Lord Keynes imputed to the paragons of Wall Street.

of administering India is the lack of any official continuous statistics at all on many subjects (e.g. wage rates and earnings) and the many imperfections of most of those that do exist.[1]

Fourthly, political troubles have been a running sore in India for many years. The civil disturbances of 1942 were in no small part responsible for the falls in production in that year, and it is unnecessary to comment on the unwillingness of industrialists in Bengal to prepare for a scorched earth policy in the event of a Japanese invasion.

Such were the main features of the Indian economy which aggravated the degree of inflation. Before we discuss whether they justify the degree of inflation which did occur, we must glance at some of the palliatives which have been suggested at various times. First, it has been suggested that, although a cheap-money policy can be sustained in wartime in a well-controlled economy, a policy of high interest rates would encourage voluntary savings in a country like India.[2] In actual fact, the long-term rate on Government securities remained at approximately 3% throughout the war years, but all the same there is little reason to believe that higher rates would have had much effect. In the first place the people who must do the voluntary savings are the peasants, and there is no cause to think that their unwillingness to hold bonds or securities of any sort would be tempered by a mere change in interest rates from say 3 to 8%. Secondly, any increase in interest rates offered by the Government might well have killed the market in just the same way as the Bengal Government's attempt to secure more grain by raising prices led to more hoarding in anticipation of further rises. Thirdly, over many rural sectors of India long-term rates on Government securities mean little when many loans are transacted at rates of 20, 30 or even 40% per annum. Even if peasants are on balance reducing their indebtedness the village moneylender prefers to hold his assets in cash in the hope of lending to the peasants again rather than purchase Government bonds.[3] It is unlikely that any conceivable change in Government rates would affect this mentality.

It has also been suggested that the Reserve Bank's power to create credit against sterling assets should have been more strictly limited, and if the Allied authorities needed rupee finance beyond this limit

[1] Cf. Foodgrains Policy Committee, op. cit.
[2] Ghosh, *Indian J. Econ.* July 1943.
[3] Cf. Patel, loc. cit.

they should have obtained it by floating loans in India.[1] In effect, this seems to be merely another way of saying that the real demands on India's resources should have been reduced, for we have already seen the indifferent success of the Government of India in floating loans, and there is no reason to believe that the British Government would have had any better success at comparable rates of interest. Indeed, there is every reason to believe that it would have had less. And we have dealt with the reasons why any reasonable rise in interest rates would probably not have been successful. Given the level of war demand for India's resources this policy was simply not practicable.

Then there is the question of whether any change in exchange rate would have been helpful.[2] Appreciation of the rupee would not have had many advantages in relieving the inflationary pressure, for on the one hand the demand for exports (including British military expenditure) was very inelastic and on the other hand India was never troubled by high import prices. The probable effect would have been to reduce the total value of imports and therefore to increase the inflationary potential. Depreciation of the currency would have done more harm than good from India's viewpoint, as the sterling balances would not have risen so quickly and there might well have been a tendency for prices of such indispensable goods as kerosene, raw cotton and hardware to rise.

If the policy of selling gold had been started earlier or extended further it might well have been possible to mitigate the rise in prices. The effective limit to the policy seems to have been the United Kingdom stocks of gold, however. Clearly, such a policy would have been impossible before the Lend-Lease Act of 1941, and it is significant that it ceased in August 1945 with the end of Lend-Lease. When the considerable amount of gold used for official sales in the Middle East, as well as normal trade transactions, are taken into account, the limitations of the policy are apparent.

Nevertheless, despite all the factors peculiar to the Indian war effort and the Indian economy, and despite the impracticability of some alleged palliatives, it is still pertinent to ask whether inflation could not have been more restrained in India. In the absence of any adequate national income statistics no dogmatic statement can be made about the ratio of war demands to resources, but the degree of burden on India is open to doubt. In common with other primary countries the depressed state of the economy before 1939 meant that

[1] Vakil, *The Falling Rupee*. [2] *Eastern Economist*, 27 October 1944.

there were many spare resources. Not only was there the normal large reserve of under-employed labour on the land, but in some industries there was some spare capacity too.[1] The loss of export markets in 1940[2] and 1942 should have made still more resources available. The only years in which it could be argued that a heavy burden was imposed on India were really 1942 and 1943, for various alleviating measures were introduced in 1944–5 to reduce military demands for munitions and man-power and to increase the flow of imports. And even in 1943 it was said: 'India's war effort has clearly not yet reached the ceiling of the maximum utilization of available man-power and resources'[3]. In the light of this categorical statement the explanations given so far of the high price rises which had already occurred by that date seem to need further elucidation.

If we examine more closely the ways in which military demands were made on India, it can be seen that some of the difficulties experienced in other countries did not arise. The Indian Government itself, through its various departments and the Reserve Bank, was responsible for feeding, clothing, supplying and paying the Armies in India in accordance with the provisions of the Defence Plan, and making any necessary financial adjustments afterwards. There was never any question of the local Government not knowing the rate of expenditure of the Armies. Furthermore, as India was a provider of munitions and supplies and a base rather than an active centre of operations, there was never the same difficulty as in some Middle East countries of not knowing roughly whether the current demand on resources was merely a passing phase or one that was likely to be sustained. Finally, the provisions of the Defence Plan made it clear that the supply of a good deal of the heavy and specialized equipment needed was to be the responsibility of Britain and not of India.

When these factors are taken into account and weighed up, it must be agreed that some measure of responsibility for the degree of inflation experienced can be assigned to the methods of organizing the war effort and the controls imposed. We have seen that many controls were not imposed in any effective form until late in the day; there was no proper food rationing in India until May 1943, and price control was not known at all in some Provinces as late as August 1943. But the fact that these controls did work to some extent in the later

[1] Cf. p. 40.

[2] The magnitude of this can be gauged from the fact that it was thought necessary to send a special mission to the U.S. to explore potential trade outlets.

[3] Budget Speech, 1943.

years does indicate, *prima facie*, that if they had been imposed at an earlier stage of the war it might have been possible to curb the growth of inflation, despite all the attendant difficulties of bringing the Provinces and the States to heel. The controls over man-power found to be so essential in Western countries could not have been transposed to India in the same form, but the virtual lack of any man-power policy whatever was responsible for some bottlenecks that might have been avoided. The example of conflicting wages policies (see p. 61) is an indication of the lack of coordination between different Government departments, a defect which appears less excusable when the small size of the administration is taken into account. Perhaps the best illustration of the failure to enforce controls is the example (p. 50) of the Government itself making purchases from the black market.

To some extent these lacunae can be explained by lack of foresight. It was reported in 1942[1] that it was thought by the Government in the first year of war that the maximum force for which India could supply full equipment was about 100,000; an Air Force of nine aeroplanes with Indian pilots was thought ambitious, and the production of ships, automobiles and aircraft was dubbed impossible. It is only fair to say that in many other countries similar ideas were frequently held about war needs and possibilities, and that in India the Government was not stirred by any clear-cut decisions from His Majesty's Government on the part she would have to play. Nevertheless, the dilatoriness in imposing controls becomes more easy to understand in the light of this background. Not only was there some lack of foresight but also on some occasions reasoning was not altogether sound. Many of the discussions which took place in 1942–3[2] centred round the unimportant question of whether the war effort was being financed by credit-inflation in the sense of additions to the money stock against the security of Treasury bills. It is not easy to tell whether the authorities paid as much attention to this question as they so anxiously affirmed to their critics; if they did, a considerable amount of time was wasted. The real problem which was growing more and more urgent was a simple one of money demand outrunning supply; the security held against the new money created was of itself irrelevant to that problem. Then again, mountains were sometimes made out of molehills. Card rationing was declared

[1] *The Economist*, 10 October 1942.
[2] Cf. Vakil, op. cit., and Budget Speech, 1943.

impossible in the early war years because of the illiteracy of the population; in actual practice this was not such a very formidable obstacle. Finally, it is not easy to decide whether it was realized from the first that attempts to restrain inflation need an all-out attack on many fronts at once. To employ the heavy guns on price control and at the same time allow the distributors freedom to manœuvre is quite useless. All controls, whether financial or physical, must swim together or sink one by one.

CHAPTER III

PALESTINE

§ 1. Physical Changes

Man-power

Although comprehensive statistics on the employment and allocation of labour are, as usual, not available, it is nevertheless possible to form a rather better idea of the wartime man-power changes in Palestine than in the case of most countries.

Our first task is to assess Palestine's man-power contribution to the war. The direct contribution in the form of man-power for the Armed Forces may be seen from Table 1.

Table 1. *Numbers in Armed Forces*

1939	1,500	1945	39,500

Source. Anglo-American Committee of Inquiry, Cmd. 6808.

Notes. (1) Includes combatant and non-combatant elements in Transjordan Frontier Force, Palestine Regiment, Jewish Brigade, Arab Legion, and miscellaneous special detachments. Women are also included.

(2) Of these 39,500 enlisted approximately 27,000 were Jews and 12,500 Arabs.

In 1942 some 60,000 men and women were full-time workers for the Allied Forces, either producing manufactured goods or performing services;[1] of these 15,000 were employed by contractors in factories, 15,000 were building camps and performing various services in Army workshops and 5000 were on transport work.

It is known that these figures were somewhat greater in 1943,[2] and roughly the peak figure may be estimated to be about 70,000. All in all the Palestine direct man-power peak contribution to war was about 100,000.[3] This figure, of course, excludes man-power engaged in the export industries, which played an important part in supplying the civilian populations of the Middle East with goods which Great Britain and the U.S.A. had neither the shipping nor resources to provide.

[1] *The Economist*, 'Commercial History of 1942', 13 March 1943.

[2] It is reported in *Survey of Palestine*, vol. II, ch. XIII, that there was an increase of 5000 in the number directly employed by the Army from 1942 to 1943.

[3] As recruits for the services only numbered 21,200 in 1942 (see Table 2), but 39,500 in 1945 (see Table 1), it is assumed that they were about 30,000 by 1943.

There were two possible sources of this labour supply:

(1) Increase in the total number of workers employed.

(2) Decrease in the number of employed on non-war work.

It is apparent from Table 2 that there was an increase of about 50% in the number of wage earners in Palestine during the war years.

TABLE 2. *Wage earners and Army recruits* (000's)

Industrial group	1939	1942
Agriculture (hired labour)	35	20
Mining	3	3·2
Manufacture	37·2	52
Building and contracting	25	61·5
War Department civil employees	1·7	24·6
Transport and communications	18	20
Commerce and finance	21	22
Government and municipal	21	31·5
Hotels, restaurants, services	27	31·5
Other services	15	17·7
Palestine soldiers	1·5	21·2
Total	205·4	305·2

Source. Survey of Palestine, vol. II, ch. XVIII.

Notes. (1) Figures refer to male and female, and include unemployed.
(2) Seasonal workers such as farmers on constructional work are included.

To determine the increase in the number of workers employed it is necessary to adjust these figures for unemployment. Figures of Arab unemployment are not available but are not believed to have been high. Jewish unemployment averaged about 45,000 in 1939 and 10,000 in 1943. It can be seen that the employed labour force rose from some 160,000 in 1939 to 295,000 in 1942, and this increase is clearly more than sufficient to account for the supply of man-power for war purposes. There were several reasons for this great increase. In the first place the population expanded both because of the high Arab birth-rate and Jewish immigration, as Table 3 shows.

TABLE 3. *Palestine population*

Year (Dec.)	Jews	Moslems	Others	Total (millions)
1939	445,000	927,000	129,000	1·50
1942	484,000	995,000	140,000	1·62
1944	528,000	1,061,000	149,000	1·74

Source. General Monthly Bulletin of Statistics. *Note.* Nomads included.

In the second place many more workers were absorbed into industry. To some extent the figures of Table 2 are not a true indication of the net additional labour available for work, as some workers previously classed as 'unproductive' or self-employed were now regarded as wage earners, but the general picture remains true nevertheless. Finally, as we have seen, unemployment was very much reduced.

Although the increase in labour employed is sufficient to account for the overall wartime changes, it is not a complete explanation. The decrease in numbers occupied in agriculture from 35,000 in 1939 to 20,000 in 1942 must clearly have been due to military demands for labour in country districts as well as the general decline of citriculture. This is, however, the only example of any fall in labour employed[1] during these years, and therefore we may conclude by saying that the war man-power contribution was met from a large increase in the employed labour force. But even if there was no general reduction of labour available for civil purposes, there were certainly shortages which varied from district to district, from trade to trade, and as between skilled and unskilled.[2]

Production

We have two main problems to elucidate under this heading:

(1) What was the size of the war output in real terms?

(2) How far did national output increase in real terms?

This will lead us to the next section on reductions in civilian consumption.

(1) It is clearly not possible to give a complete answer to this, simply because the war output took so many forms; not merely was there a direct war output for the Forces, but there was also an indirect output for the civil sectors of the Middle East countries; not merely did the output for the military consist of goods, but also of services. There is no means of aggregating these various outputs physically, and therefore we shall have to be content with measurements which are partly physical and partly financial.

[1] It is possible to argue, of course, that other industry groups should have been employing more in 1943 on account of the increased population, and therefore in so far as they did not this represents a diversion from non-war to war work.

[2] The survey of skilled personnel in 1943 enumerated 41,000 (male and female) people. Of these 8700 were working in Services workshops (*Survey of Palestine*, vol. II, ch. XIII).

Let us consider the direct war output first, and by that we shall mean the goods and services purchased by the Allied Forces. The only comprehensive measure of this must be in value terms, and the obvious one to select is the total military expenditure. This is shown in Table 4, from which it may be seen that military expenditure absorbed a large proportion of national income in 1943.

TABLE 4. *Net military expenditure in Palestine (estimated)*

Year	Net military expenditure (£000's)	National income (£000's)	% military expenditure/ national income	Military expenditure per head of the population (£)
1939	2,600	32,740	8·0	1·7
1940	8,500	—	—	5·6
1941	20,700	—	—	13·2
1942	25,400	78,490	32·4	15·9
1943	31,500	92,400	34·0	18·9
1944	25,000	122,300	20·4	14·4

Source. Special estimate; Loftus, *National Income of Palestine.*

Notes. (1) Military expenditure includes all expenditure of Allied Authorities, and private expenditure of individual soldiers.

(2) Gross military expenditure figures are larger than the above by the amount of receipts of N.A.A.F.I. and officers' shops (excluding any local expenditure), and by the amount of various refunds from contractors.

(3) National income is net home-produced, valued at market prices. See Table 11 and notes.

Figures of Army contracts for goods tell much the same story as may be seen from Table 5.

TABLE 5. *Value of Army contracts (estimated)*

Year	£000's	Net value of industrial, agricultural and building output (£000's)	Percentage
1940	1,000	14,000	7·1
1941	4,000	—	—
1942	9,000	37,000	24·3
1943	13,000	44,700	29·0

Sources. The Economist, 15 Aug. 1942; *Review of Commercial Conditions* (Palestine); *General Monthly Bulletin of Statistics,* Aug. 1944.

Note. Foodstuffs expenditure included.

It may be seen from this table that by 1943 the Armed Forces were appropriating about 29% of the net output of agricultural and industrial and building production. In the case of industry alone the ratio was undoubtedly much higher.

What actual form did this provision of military supplies take? The main contributions were in light manufactures; many hundred thousands of uniforms, boots, water bottles, mess tins, camouflage nets, nuts and bolts, dry batteries, preserved foods, etc., were provided for the Armies in the Middle East. Foodstuffs were provided for locally stationed troops, and much local labour was employed on vehicle repairs and building constructional work, and on varied personal services. Many transport services were put at the disposal of the Allied Authorities, and in July 1943, for instance, one-tenth of all the omnibuses in Palestine were being used solely for military purposes.

A final element which must be mentioned in the direct war contribution is the Palestine Government's own expenditure on war measures. This was not large, or important in comparison with the other sums involved, but it should be mentioned for the sake of completeness. In addition to sums on civil defence and the Trans-jordan Frontier Force (this contribution was fixed at £42,796 in the later war years), there were a number of items such as expenditure on the various wartime controls. Total expenditure under these heads rose from £318,000 in 1939 to £1·2 million in 1944.[1]

The indirect war contribution of Palestine may be gauged from the principal export figures, which are reproduced in Table 6. Before the war Palestine relied very largely on citrus exports (they formed 77% of the total value), and only 12% of her exports went to other Middle East countries. By 1944 a number of industrial products had become more important than citrus fruits, and 56% of the total value of exports went to Middle East countries.

Apart from the principal exports shown below, many diverse commodities, such as leather goods, plate glass, pharmaceutical products, optical instruments, dental burs, soap, etc., were exported to many different countries. It should be remembered also that these expanded exports were not only due to increased output in industries,

[1] These estimates have been arrived at by abstracting the appropriate figures from the annual accounts, but owing to the way in which these are presented and a change in methods of allocating expenditure to the different headings in 1942, it is not easy to calculate the correct figure. Expenditure on high cost of living allowances and subsidies is not included in these estimates, nor in those on p. 96.

such as metal work and textiles, which were well established before the war, but also to some industries which were completely new. Diamond cutting and polishing only employed 200 men in 1939, but by 1945[1] 3000 men were employed. This industry was particularly important, as it was a valuable source of dollars to the sterling area.

TABLE 6. *Principal exports*

Commodity	Quantity		Value f.o.b. (£000's)	
	1939	1944	1939	1944
Citrus (000's cases)	13,359	2,707	3,769	1,568
Potash (000's tons)	63	98	400	887
Polished diamonds	Nil	—	Nil	3,235
Wearing apparel	—	—	38	1,100
Motor spirit (000's litres)	Nil	358	Nil	1,860
Gas oil and fuel oil (000's tons)	Nil	357	Nil	1,684
Total value	—	—	5,100	14,600
Total value (including re-exports)	—	—	5,400	15,600

Sources. General Monthly Bulletin of Statistics; *Statistical Handbook of the Middle East.*

Notes. (1) Re-exports of individual items excluded; military stores excluded.
(2) 1939 figures do not include exports to Transjordan.
(3) It is difficult to calculate an index of volume owing to the major changes in the character of the export trade but Nathan, *Palestine: Problems and Promise*, calculates that exports rose 79% in volume between 1939 and 1943 (excluding citrus and petroleum products).

We have now established some measures of war contribution and we can therefore turn to our second problem.

(2) How far did national output increase in real terms? Reliable estimates of national output exist and they are reproduced in Table 7.

TABLE 7. *Value of net national output* (*£000's*)

Item	1939	1942	1943
Agriculture	5·59	17·71	19·0
Manufacturing industries (including handicrafts and private utility companies)	5·37	13·62	20·0
Commerce and finance	4·79	8·53	10·0
Transport and communications	1·78	6·97	6·8
Others	12·71	29·06	34·2
Total	30·24	75·89	90·0
Total at 1939 prices	30·24	39·0	40·0

Source. General Monthly Bulletin of Statistics (August 1944).

Note. Figures are at factor cost. They include an estimate of the value of farmers' subsistence production.

[1] *Review of Commercial Conditions* (Palestine).

From these figures it would appear at first sight as if agricultural output kept pace with industrial, but this is only a superficial impression, as the real explanation is the increased concentration on higher priced products such as milk and vegetables.[1] It has, in fact, been calculated that some 75% of the increase in real income occurred in industry and transport.[2]

The basis of these statements may be seen from Table 8, which shows how production increased in the early war years in the most important industries.

TABLE 8. *Indices of production*

Date	Textiles	Metals	Machinery	Chemicals	Electrical appliances
Aug. 1939	100	100	100	100	100
Feb. 1942	202	213	191	153	314

Source. Wages Committee Report, 1943 (from figures supplied by Jewish Agency).

A comparison of the 1939 and 1942 Census figures gives us the picture shown in Table 9.

TABLE 9. *Industrial establishments*

Item	1939	1942 (Dec.)
No. of establishments	1,217	3,470
Persons engaged	20,414	49,977
Net output	£3·8 m.	£14·8 m.
Net output at 1939 prices	£3·8 m.	£7·0 m.

Sources. Census of Industry, 1939 *and* 1942.

Notes. (1) The two censuses had slightly different scope and are therefore not an exact basis for comparison.

(2) From December 1942 to December 1944 some 4000–5000 more workers went into industry.

(3) 1942 value of output is deflated by index of retail prices.

All in all it may be estimated that the pre-war volume of industrial output was doubled by 1942–3, and as we have seen when considering the increase in exports, this was not merely due to increased activity in the old-established industries, but also to rapid growth of new ones. Furthermore, it was achieved despite the impossibility of securing new industrial plant or of adequately maintaining the old,[3] and despite the fact that Palestine is singularly deficient in basic supplies of coal and iron.

[1] See Table 10. [2] *The Economist,* 30 December 1944. [3] See p. 97.

The expansion in industry was the most important constituent of the increase in national output, but it must not be assumed that agricultural output failed to increase at all. Although the statistics of output from primitive agriculture are not very reliable, those of production on modern mixed farms are accurate, and the overall figures shown in Table 10 may be assumed to indicate the trend of output of the main items reasonably well.

TABLE 10. *Agricultural production* (000's *metric tons*)

Crop	1939	1940	1941	1942	1943	1944
Wheat	89	136	90	104	66	57
Barley	86	102	68	114	62	41
Maize	6	9	8	7·7	4	3
Durra	43	58	65	58	31	25
Potatoes	10	21	21	23	15	51
Tomatoes	36	58	51	55	67	57
All vegetables	129	198	190	194	228	162
Eggs (000's)	58,816	63,055	58,792	59,991	65,293	73,848
Milk (000's litres)	35,061	37,009	41,364	49,429	56,050	61,486
Olives	35	45	13	63	75	10
Citrus (exports) (000's cases)	13,359	5,755	92	532	1,059	2,707

Source. General Monthly Bulletin of Statistics.

Note. Citrus export figures are not an exact indication of production, as other outlets were found for the fruit in the later war years.

It may be seen that the major increases in output were in vegetables and dairy produce. This was to some extent at the expense of other products, such as citrus fruit; indeed, the area available for crops was increased by the enforced contraction of the citrus groves. But it was also increased by the extension of irrigation to a considerable area of new land, and it should be remembered that this agricultural output was achieved with a smaller employed labour force than in 1939[1] and with machinery which gradually deteriorated owing to lack of spare parts, etc., as the war went on.

Finally, another index of increased activity is in railway transportation, expressed in ton-kilometrage. Whereas this was 103,000,000 in 1938–9, it reached a peak of 470,000,000 in 1943–4.[2] Similarly, sales of electricity increased from 91,475,000 kwh. in 1939 to 184,000,000 kwh. in 1944.[3]

[1] See p. 89. [2] *General Monthly Bulletin of Statistics*, June 1945.
[3] Nathan, op. cit. p. 179.

We have now seen that the war contribution of Palestine was considerable, and also that the increase in national income and output was considerable. This naturally leads to our next topic of civilian consumption.

Consumption

We shall here make some attempt to assess whether there was a fall in consumption of the civilian sector of the economy and, if so, how great it was. This involves bringing together the threads of our argument in the last section.

We have seen how the war contribution consisting of the output on military account, the output on Government account, and the output on export account, increased. We have also seen how the national output increased. Therefore, if we add to the national output the value of imported goods[1] and then compare the two totals, it will give us some idea of the relative changes of the resources available and the demands on these resources. This is done in Table 11.

TABLE 11. *War output and national resources (£000's)*

(1) Year	(2) Allied expenditure	(3) Government defence expenditure	(4) Exports (including re-exports)	(5) Total (cols. 2, 3 and 4)	(6) National output	(7) Imports	(8) Total (cols. 6 and 7)	(9) % ratio col. 5 to col. 8
1939	2,600	320	5,400	8,320	32,740	14,600	47,340	18
1942	25,400	760	9,200	35,360	78,490	21,300	99,790	35
1943	31,500	940	13,200	45,640	92,400	29,100	121,500	38
1944	25,000	1,200	15,600	41,800	122,300	37,200	159,500	26

Sources. General Monthly Bulletin of Statistics; Annual Accounts; Special information.

Notes. (1) See p. 92, n. 1, on constituents of Government defence expenditure.
(2) Imports for 1943 and 1944 include official gold imports.
(3) Exports and imports include all oil. This is strictly inaccurate but makes little difference to the results in col. (9).
(4) National output is valued at market prices.

[1] We need a measure of physical resources available, and therefore any items such as gifts of money or interest payments from overseas should not be counted in national output. Payments or receipts corresponding to such items as insurance or tourist expenditure should be counted, but as figures of these are incomplete they have been neglected. The only item of any importance at all was tourist receipts (the net receipts for 1942 were £800,000). It may be noted in passing that military expenditure figures in individual Middle East countries should really be reduced by the amount of soldiers' pay which was disbursed on tours in other countries, but the error involved in neglecting this correction cannot be large.

It will be noted that exports and imports are counted separately, rather than the net balance of the two being taken and added to (or subtracted from) the direct war contribution. This seems justified in the circumstances, for the two were not really related in wartime as they were in peacetime by consideration of the balance of payments. Physical limitations of shipping or supply were the limiting factors. When considering problems of physical resources the two items have really very little to do with one another.

The above figures show that the war sector took up a much greater share of the resources available in 1942 and 1943 than in 1939. This had to come out of domestic consumption or capital formation. Reliable statistics are not available on capital formation, but new issues were forbidden, inventories and stocks declined and machines fell into disrepair. Civilian building activity was reduced to a very low level, for according to the index of the *General Monthly Bulletin* it was in 1943 a tenth of what it had been in 1939. It is probable that these changes did little to cushion the fall in civilian consumption, simply because domestic capital formation was at a very low level to start with. What happened to domestic consumption may be seen from the rough figures of national outlay in Table 12.

TABLE 12. *National outlay (£m.)*

Item	1939	1942	1943
Home-produced goods plus net imports	21·0	38·0	44·0
Civilian consumption of services	13·0	17·0	22·0
Total	34·0	55·0	66·0
Total at 1939 prices	34·0	29·0	28·6
Index of total at 1939 prices	100	85	84

Source. General Monthly Bulletin of Statistics, August 1944.

Notes. (1) Government expenditure on goods and services excluded. (2) Figures are at factor cost.

It appears that the reduction in civilian consumption was about 16% between 1939 and 1943. But this underestimates the true reduction, as the figures of outlay given above include purchases by individuals in the Allied Armies. It may be noted that in 1944 the Government statistician made an estimate that consumption had been reduced 23%[1] from the 1939 level. It is not far wrong to estimate

[1] *The Economist*, 30 December 1944.

that the overall reduction in civilian consumption by 1943 was about 20%.[1]

Examples of the way in which this reduction in consumption materialized may be found in the amount of rationing introduced in Palestine, and in the reduction of imports. Rationing first started in April 1941 with a rather crude form of restriction of sugar sales, but subsequently far more sophisticated schemes of coupon and points rationing for a number of commodities were introduced. Durable consumer goods, too, were heavily curtailed. All imports for civilian consumption were restricted, and in some cases completely vetoed. Table 13 shows the decrease in imports between 1939 and 1943.

TABLE 13. *Principal imports*

Commodity	Quantity		Value c.i.f. (£000's)	
	1939	1943	1939	1943
Total imports	—	—	14,600	27,200
Index of volume	100	41	—	—
Barley (including maize and durra) (000's tons)	13	18	62	411
Rice (000's tons)	25	4·3	250	142
Millet and rye (000's tons)	13	23·6	69	509
Wheat and wheat flour (000's tons)	100	108	788	3,225
Sugar (000's tons)	28	23	333	631
Wood (000's cu.m.)	134	3·5	429	93
Cement (tons)	37,000	1·5	72	0·075
Coal (000's tons)	72	11	102	63
Iron bars, pipes, sheets (000's tons)	45	2·2	824	69
Raw and waste cotton (tons)	961	2,966	48	331
Cotton piecegoods (tons)	3,200	900	390	937
Fertilizers (tons)	10,191	6,300	88	156
All machinery	—	—	916	335
(1) Industrial and manufacturing	—	—	463	43
(2) Agricultural	—	—	30·6	31·5
(3) Electrical	—	—	33·0	12·0

Source. General Monthly Bulletin of Statistics.

Notes. (1) 1943 is chosen as year of largest reduction in volume.

(2) High figure of total value for 1943 is explained by imports of crude petroleum and unworked stones which were both nil in 1939 but formed the basis of Palestine export trade by 1943 (see Table 6). Values of these were £6·9 and £1·1 million respectively in 1943.

(3) Military and N.A.A.F.I. stores excluded (N.A.A.F.I. must be excluded as military expenditure figures are net of N.A.A.F.I. receipts). Civilian Lend-Lease stores included.

[1] A more complicated system of deflating consumption expenditure gives this same result (see Nathan, op. cit. pp. 161, 649).

It may be seen from Table 13 that the reduction in the volume of most imports was severe, whether foodstuffs such as rice, materials such as wood, or manufactures such as iron bars, cotton piecegoods and machinery are considered. The largest general reduction was in manufactured articles, for even the value of manufactures fell from £9·3 million in 1939 to £5·9 million in 1943, while the volume index fell from 100 to 20 over the same period. Furthermore, the total figures of this table conceal changes in source. Wheat and barley, for instance, now came from Syria and Iraq rather than Canada and Australia, and this meant that the quality was not as good and prices were higher. The importance of this latter phenomenon will be seen in § 3.

Briefly, then, total civilian consumption in Palestine was cut by some 20%[1] owing to the reduction of imported supplies and the diversion of home production to war. But this is after all only a rough guide, for the 20% reduction can hardly be compared with the 20% fall in consumption in Great Britain which took place over the same period.[2]

In the first place, the general standard of living in Palestine was lower in 1939 than in Great Britain (national income per head of the population came to £20 in Palestine and £108 in Great Britain in that year). It was therefore inevitable that any substantial cut in consumption would have to come out of basic necessities as well as luxuries and semi-luxuries. It is significant that bread and other basic foodstuffs were rationed in Palestine,[3] whilst bread and potatoes were unrationed in Britain. It is also probable that this reduction in consumption of necessities was extended further because of somewhat indiscriminate purchases by the military authorities, and because of the lack of any really effective import policy during the early war years.

In the second place, it is possible that the reductions in consumption were more unevenly distributed between the different income classes than in Great Britain. Although, as we shall see in § 2, there is no evidence that real earnings of workers were reduced (except in the early war years), and although the poorest sections of the working classes gained considerably, it is undoubtedly true that the

[1] Consumption per capita was cut to a greater extent owing to the increase in population.

[2] See *Impact of War on Civil Consumption*, H.M.S.O. 1945, pp. 23–4.

[3] Average consumption of flour was reduced from 1980 g. per head per week in 1937–9 (av.) to 1715 g. in June 1943. Sugar was reduced from 350 to 185 g. (League of Nations, *Food Rationing and Supply*, 1943–4, p. 64).

merchant classes made the most of the increases in activity and prices. Considerable losses were inflicted on minor Government officials and small salaried men whose incomes failed to rise at the same rate as prices. But the most important reason why the reduction in consumption was unevenly spread is not connected with changes in real income but with the physical distribution of consumers' goods, for efficient rationing only really applied to the towns, and a very large proportion of the restricted supplies available found its way into the towns. As the poorest sections of the community were to be found in the villages, the wartime hardships imposed on the country as a whole by the reductions in consumption were inevitably increased.

Finally, it should be remembered that the Palestine fall in consumption was accompanied by a piling up of sterling balances (see Table 21), which will to some extent compensate for the wartime impositions when it is possible to use them.

§ 2. Financial Changes

In § 1 we have dealt with the wartime changes in man-power usage and allocation, the expansion of the real national output, the share that was devoted directly or indirectly to war production, and the accompanying reductions in civilian consumption. It is now time to look at the financial changes which accompanied these real changes. We must now look at the changes in the quantity of money and currency, in the price levels, and in the size and composition of overseas assets. When we have done this it will be possible to form a fairly complete picture of the modifications wrought by war to the Palestine economy. We shall then be in a position to inquire why wide changes in prices and incomes took place.

Supply of Money

The increase in the supply of money may be seen from Table 14, which shows the vast expansion of the currency and notes in circulation and the deposit liabilities of the commercial banks.

Prices

Wholesale and retail price indices are reproduced in Table 15. The retail price index is that devised by the Wages Committee in 1942; it has been extrapolated to include the earlier war years.

TABLE 14. *Supply of money*

Date	Currency and notes in circulation		Bank deposits (demand)	Bank deposits (time)	Bank deposits (total)	Index bank deposits	Index currency and notes and bank deposits
	£m.	Index	£m.	£m.	£m.		
Aug. 1939	10·0	100	12·8	4·5	17·3	100	100
Dec. 1939	8·5	85	12·8	3·4	16·2	93	91
June 1940	11·7	117	11·9	2·8	14·7	85	96
Dec. 1940	10·6	106	13·0	2·7	15·7	91	96
June 1941	13·6	136	13·8	2·5	16·3	94	109
Dec. 1941	13·4	134	19·2	2·5	21·7	126	129
June 1942	18·0	180	21·5	2·5	24·0	139	154
Dec. 1942	24·0	240	28·9	2·7	31·6	183	204
June 1943	29·1	291	37·9	3·3	41·2	238	259
Dec. 1943	36·0	360	49·1	4·5	53·6	309	328
June 1944	38·2	382	57·7	6·2	63·9	370	375
Dec. 1944	41·5	415	64·2	7·0	71·2	414	414
June 1945	45·7	457	69·7	7·6	77·3	448	451

Source. General Monthly Bulletin of Statistics.

Notes. (1) Deposits of Co-operative and Savings Banks are excluded.

(2) There was a change in accounting practice in June 1944 which eliminated £3·2 million of duplication in bank deposits. The true rise in bank deposits is therefore greater than the published figures suggest. On the other hand, some of the additional currency and notes were in circulation in Transjordan and not Palestine.

TABLE 15. *Price movements*

Date	Prices (wholesale)	Prices (cost of living index)
Aug. 1939	100	100
Dec. 1939	123	111
June 1940	128	116
Dec. 1940	155	131
June 1941	179	138
Dec. 1941	226	166
June 1942	246	185
Dec. 1942	302	211
June 1943	336	248
Dec. 1943	341	230
June 1944	333	238
Dec. 1944	365	252
June 1945	330	257

Sources. General Monthly Bulletin of Statistics; Abstract of Statistics.

Increases in prices of individual commodities, even when controlled, diverged to an enormous extent. On the whole food prices rose less than those of manufactured goods. Potato and onion prices, for instance, rose by 227 and 300% respectively between June 1939 and June 1945, whereas shoe prices rose by 380%, men's jackets by 420% and metal goods most of all (aluminium cooking pots rose by 1158%). The explanation of these discrepancies is to be found mainly in the huge reduction in the supply of manufactured imports, but also in the inefficient methods and unscrupulous character of many entrepreneurs[1] producing substitutes for imports.

Before we make any comparisons between the currency and price movements, it should be pointed out that, as usual, in Middle East countries, the black market was a thriving institution, and for many people black-market prices are much more representative than the controlled prices on which the indices are based. The enormous discrepancy between black-market and ordinary wholesale prices is borne out by Table 16.

TABLE 16. *Free and controlled prices (December* 1943)

Commodity	Controlled price	Free price	Ratio
Wheat (long ton)	£19·125	£90	4·7
Sugar (long ton)	£45	£250	5·6

Source. Special information.

Furthermore, the deterioration in the quality of imported wheat and barley, and the inferior nature of those goods manufactured at home to replace those normally imported from abroad, are not taken into account in the indices.

In so far as a comparison of official price indices and the money supply index is worth while, it may be seen that until 1942 prices increased faster than the quantity of money. This was partly due to the devaluation of the sterling area in 1939 and the initial rises in import prices, and partly to the various crises in the early war years which shook the public confidence and in fact caused a serious run on the banks.[2] The imposition of controls began to make itself felt in 1942 and although currency continued to expand, the relative rise in prices was much less after that date. The expansion in time deposits in the later war years is an indication of the general increased willingness to hold money.

[1] It is interesting to note that, despite the general tendency for prices to rise higher and controls to be more loose in Egypt than in Palestine, the contract prices for 4-gallon petrol containers in Palestine were the equivalent of 17·4 piastres each as against Egyptian prices of 11·4 piastres (100 piastres = £1E.).

[2] Cf. *The Economist*, 30 January 1943.

Incomes

Little information is available on changes in profits, rents and salaries, and therefore our description will be mainly confined to changes in wage rates and earnings.

The general movements of wage rates may be seen from Table 17.

TABLE 17. *Index of wage rates*

Year (June)	Jewish labour		Arab labour (male)	Cost of living index
	Male	Female		
1939	100	100	100	100
1941	108	114	140	138
1942	140	159	118	185
1943	202	271	194	248
1944	251	338	272	238

Sources. *Survey of Palestine*, vol. II, ch. XVIII, 1946; *Abstract of Statistics*.
Note. Statistics are based on unweighted geometric average of selected occupations.

From information collected in the wartime wage censuses it is possible to compare the movements in average earnings over a wide range of industry.

TABLE 18. *Average earnings (mils per man-day)*

Item	Arabs			Jews		
	July 1939	June 1945	Index (July 1939 = 100)	July 1939	June 1945	Index (July 1939 = 100)
All industry	150	450	300	330	1183	358
Food	143	437	306	326	1027	315
Paper	74	245	331	198	887	448
Printing	162	434	268	336	957	285
Metals	208	600	288	302	1070	354
Minerals	120	342	285	400	1253	313

Source. Special information.
Note. 1000 mils = £1 (P.).

The traditional doctrine that wage rates tend to lag behind prices in the early stages of an inflationary situation does appear to be borne out, particularly when it is remembered that the cost of living index probably underestimates the true price rise; but by 1943–4 the gap had disappeared. If changes in earnings are compared with the increased cost of living (the index stood at 257 in June 1945), it is clear that both Jews and Arabs had improved their position relatively to 1939. Even in the early war years the longer hours and more regular work available did much to compensate for the lag in wage rates. A weighted average of wage rates and earnings in ten industrial groups showed that while real wage rates had declined by some 20%, real earnings had only declined by 13% by June 1941.[1]

Of course these general averages of figures hide many varied changes in different communities, industries and occupations. It may be seen from a comparison of the figures in Tables 17 and 18 that while the movement of wage rates favoured Arabs rather than Jews, the movement of earnings favoured Jews more than Arabs. These relative movements of wage rates are explained by the differential nature of cost of living allowances which favoured low-paid workers, and also by the much heavier gains of Arabs in trades involving hard manual work, as will be evident in a moment. The relative movements of earnings in industry are explained by the fact that the largest increases in hours were those of key men or highly specialized workers who were mainly Jews, and by the fact that pre-war Arab hours of work were normally longer than those of the Jews, and there was therefore less scope for increases.

Wage increases in different industries differed to an enormous extent. On the whole the constructional trades showed larger increases than agriculture, and agriculture larger increases than industry. Wage rates of unskilled Arab building labour rose from an average of 109 mils per day in 1939 to 550 mils per day in 1945 (405%), whereas those of citrus general labourers rose by some 300%, which was much larger than the increases of carpenters (190%) or fitters (178%). Although the discrepancies were not so marked in the case of Jews, unskilled building labour wage rates rose from 315 to 1350 mils per day (329%), while citrus general labourers' increases were 295%, fitters 210% and carpenters 173%. The great change of wage rates in constructional work was, of course, due to Army demands, as building work for domestic purposes was reduced to a very low level during the war. Although official Army rates were not normally above local rates, workers did, in fact, receive substantial increases through being upgraded far more than in proportion to skill and experience. In so far as they were partly paid in kind through the provision of meals the differences are still greater. The influence of military demand is obvious in the variations in agricultural wage rates in different districts. In 1943 daily harvesting rates for Arab labour

[1] *General Monthly Bulletin of Statistics*, July 1941.

ranged from 500 to 1000 mils per day, whereas an average pre-war figure would have been 100 mils per day. This increase was particularly evident in districts where there was a good deal of military activity, such as Haifa (1000 mils), Acre (750) and Lydda (750).

There were many variations in different occupations. Broadly, the pattern was that the lowest paid workers gained most, as can be seen in the case of constructional trades from Table 19.

TABLE 19. *Wage rates in constructional trades (mils per day)*

Trade	Arabs			Jews		
	1939	1945	Index (1939=100)	1939	1945	Index (1939=100)
Stonemason	392	1500	383	470	1650	351
Bricklayer	350	1500	429	450	1650	367
Plasterer	300	1500	500	476	1800	378
Unskilled	109	550	505	315	1350	429

Source. Survey of Palestine, vol. II, ch. XVII.

Similarly in citriculture, Jewish personnel on pruning had increases from 200 to 800 mils per day (300%) over the same period, whilst packers only had increases of 114% from their pre-war rates of 700 mils per day. In industry, too, the same tendencies are apparent.

Finally, as an example of the way in which these changes were experienced by a single firm the changes in wage rates paid to daily employed labour by the Palestine branches of an Oil Company may be quoted.

TABLE 20. *Wage rates of Oil Company*

Period	£ per month	Index
Before 30. xii. 40	6	100
1. i. 41–30. xi. 41	7	117
1. xii. 41–30. ix. 42	7·2	120
1. x. 42–31. xii. 42	9·1	152
1. i. 43–30. vi. 43	11·9	199
1. vii. 43–30. ix. 43	14·9	248
1. x. 43–31. i. 44	14·5	241
1. ii. 44...	13·8	230

Source. Oil Company figures.

To summarize, we may say that although wage rates did lag behind the cost of living until the later war years, the opportunities for earning more did much to compensate for this lag. Those receiving the lowest wage rates gained the largest percentage increases. Therefore the traditional doctrine that an all-round rise in money values *necessarily* means a long period of reduced real *income* (as distinct from consumption) for workers must be regarded with some scepticism, even in countries where labour is not solidly organized in strong Trade Unions. Moreover, such evidence as there is suggests that those classes not entirely dependent on money wages did not incur great falls in real income either. The large number of Arab fellaheen who paid rent in kind continued to contribute their traditional two-fifths of output; and Jews living and working in the Collective Farms or *Kvutza* did not lose much by the changes in money values. Further, the enormous reduction in the burden of debt must be considered. Nathan[1] estimates that in 1939 average indebtedness of the fellaheen was £25–30 per head, and rates of interest paid were normally about 30%. Not only was a considerable amount of these debts repaid but the real burden of the remainder is no longer so completely and utterly crushing as it was.

External assets

The changes in external assets are closely bound up with the changes in the quantity of money. These changes are comparatively simple in the case of Palestine, as there was practically no redemption of sterling (or other foreign) debt,[2] and therefore the change in assets is represented by the change in sterling balances which is shown in Table 21.

TABLE 21. *Sterling balances (estimated)*

Year (Dec.)	Value (£m.)	Annual increase (£m.)
1939	20	—
1942	50	30 (3 years)
1943	75	25
1944	100	25
1945	130	30

Sources. Economist; *Palestine Economist*; *Survey of Palestine*, vol. II, ch. XIV.

To realize the magnitude of the increase in sterling assets they must be compared with the national income (£90 million at factor cost in 1943). As in the case of Egypt (see p. 144), the gains are proportionately greater than those of India.

[1] Op. cit. p. 197.

[2] The Shemen Oil Company was sold in 1944 by British interests to a group of Palestine investors. There was also a very small debt repayment in 1942.

Summary

The figures in this section tell their own story without need of much comment. The supply of money and the general price level did not increase as much as in some other Middle East countries, but there was, nevertheless, a considerable degree of inflation. We may now ask how the war contribution described in § 1 links up with these phenomena.

§ 3. Inflation and Controls

In this section we shall discuss, first, the relationship between the events of §§1 and 2, i.e. how the war effort led to such a degree of inflation, and, secondly, we shall see how the position was aggravated by other factors not directly connected with the war effort.

We have seen that the main physical feature of the war effort was an increased pressure of demand on a precarious supply of goods. This demand took several forms; the vast increase in military expenditure, the more gradual but still appreciable increase in Government expenditure and the steady contribution of exports. The whole of Government expenditure and the total value of exports cannot be described as part of the war contribution, but as it is impossible to divide these items into war and non-war contribution with any degree of accuracy, it will be found most convenient to treat the separate elements together. As we shall see, much the most important item, both in size and results, was military expenditure, and we shall therefore concentrate mainly on this aspect of increased demand and only return to the others and discuss them briefly at a later stage. On the supply side the position was complicated, as there were present two opposite influences of reduced imports and expanded home production. How did these various conflicting aspects of the economy fit together and why was inflation of prices and incomes the result?

The first and most obvious line of approach is to look at the methods of financing military expenditure. This was largely financed by credit creation, for as we shall see other sources of obtaining currency, such as a Palestine import surplus or budget surplus, proceeds of gold sales or voluntary supplies of savings, were not nearly sufficient to meet the requirements of the Allies. Palestine currency was therefore usually made available to the military authorities in return for the crediting of sterling assets.

The relationship of military expenditure to the increase in the supply of money may be seen in Table 22 (the significance of the other columns will be apparent later).

TABLE 22. *Military expenditure, imports and supply of money (£m.)*

Year	Annual increase in currency and bank deposits	Annual increase in sterling balances	Military expenditure	Import surplus
1940	1·6	—	8·5	8·3
1941	8·8	—	20·7	8·5
1942	20·5	30	25·4	12·1
1943	34·0	25	31·5	15·9
1944	23·1	25	25·0	21·7
Total	88·0	80	111·1	66·5

Source. Tables 4, 14, 21 and 27.

Notes. (1) Import surplus includes official gold sales in imports.
(2) 1942 figure for sterling balances includes 1940 and 1941.

However, war expenditure in all countries resulted in an increased supply of money; in no country was it covered *in toto* by 'genuine' savings or by taxation, and yet large price increases did not always result. Why did it cause such a high degree of inflation in Palestine?

In the first place, the military authorities were free to spend their currency in different districts or industries, as they required, more particularly in the early war years. This was inevitable when a large part was spent on securing the services of local bricklayers, carpenters, fitters, etc.; another large part on locally grown foodstuffs and another large part by individual foreign soldiers. Local scarcity and shortages of goods, and therefore higher prices, were bound to arise. But even apart from that little attempt was made in the early war years to ensure that military contracts would be made with those factories which could supply them most easily, although there was some planning of supplies by the War Supply Board in the later war years.[1] Not only were restrictions lacking on the districts and goods in which the extra purchasing power was spent, but also there was little effective control over the prices paid for goods and services. As we have seen, there were methods of overcoming War Office regulations on wage rates that might be paid for local labour.

Thus receipts of manufacturers and farmers were bound to increase haphazardly as a result of military expenditure, and there was little attempt to limit incomes by direct measures in the early war years.

[1] See p. 116.

In April 1942, an anti-profiteering order was introduced which prohibited excess profits of contractors, manufacturers and dealers. This was the first law of its kind in the Middle East, but it is doubtful whether it had much effect until 1944. Measures of a rather different type were taken to deal with importers' profits as we shall see when we discuss price control.[1] The principal measure introduced to limit farmers' incomes was the requisitioning of crops surplus to needs at controlled prices, but this was not really successful either, as so many were able to sell their crops in the black market, or smuggle them over the borders to Syria or Transjordan where prices were higher.

What attempts were made to limit wages? We have already seen how wages of both Jews and Arabs increased. In the early war years these advances were haphazard and uneven, and it was found by the Wages Committee that employers were not opposing demands for higher wages. But after the agreement between the Manufacturers' Association and the Federation of Jewish Labour in February 1942, the registration of Approved Manufacturers in October 1942, and the Wages Committee Report of 1943, wages were tied rigidly to the cost of living index by a complex bonus system. A family allowance system was also introduced. The Government certainly paid attention to the principle of equity of wage rates, but in doing so it laid itself open to the charge that it accelerated the vicious spiral of rising wages and prices.[2]

Thus in sharp contrast to the Sudan there was no effective mechanism for direct control of incomes. How far did taxation perform this function? That there were considerable increases may be seen from Table 23.

TABLE 23. *Tax receipts (£m.)*

Year	Taxation paid	% Government expenditure	% Government expenditure and military expenditure
1939–40	4·6	76	53
1940–41	5·2	70	32
1941–42	6·2	82	22
1942–43	8·4	82	23
1943–44	11·5	78	25
1944–45	15·1	83	35

Source. Budget accounts.

Notes. (1) Year is March–March.

(2) Tax figures include railway and miscellaneous receipts, but exclude grants from His Majesty's Government.

[1] See p. 113. [2] The subsidy policy was, of course, an exception to this (see p. 113).

It will be seen from this table that despite the increases in taxation the percentage of Government expenditure financed by other means remained substantially the same. In the peak war years of 1941–3 taxation did not absorb more than about 25% of the expenditure of the military authorities and Government together, and so there was not much of an offset to the large volume of public expenditure. The totals of taxation hide considerable changes in the relative yields of various forms of tax. The most important innovation was income tax, which was introduced in 1941. This was a very light burden at first, in fact, incomes of less than £400 per annum were totally exempt, and the receipts in 1941–2 were only £197,000. But owing to increased rates of tax (including the imposition of a surtax in 1943), and, of course, increases in incomes, the yield was £2·5 million in 1944–5. All indirect taxes were increased at various stages, and the total yield rose from £856,000 in 1939–40 to £7,602,000 in 1944–5.[1] No E.P.T. was ever introduced, and business firms were only subject to a Company Tax which was really part of the income tax. On the whole taxation did little to prevent increased expenditure out of the higher incomes due to military activity, for the Government could not even cover its own expenditure, as that had increased so immensely with the high cost of living allowances and the extensive subsidy policy.

The fact that people are receiving higher incomes, even after taxation has been paid, is not serious if they can be induced to increase their level of saving voluntarily, but the difficulty of persuading poor peasants and labourers not to spend their increased earnings is well known and may be seen time after time in this survey. Some attempts were made in Palestine to encourage small savings, but it was not until April 1942 that a Post Office Savings Bank was inaugurated; regulations concerning the issue of Defence Bonds and Savings Certificates were only published in June 1942, and it was October 1943 before a savings campaign of any force was really in being. All in all these efforts to attract small savings by the methods used in Western countries met with little success.[2] The most successful method was the introduction of Premium Bonds in 1944. 100,000 bonds of £10 each were sold bearing interest at 1% and due to be redeemed after 20 years. 159 prizes were offered, ranging from

[1] Including Customs and Excise duties, matches, salt, tobacco, liquor licence and stamp duties.

[2] The cumulative total of 'small' savings was estimated at only £690,000 in March 1944.

£1000 to £20, at the quarterly drawings. These Premium Bonds proved highly popular and were easily subscribed, as in most other Eastern countries where they had been sold. However, it is apparent from this brief résumé of savings that in the early war years, when a large amount of voluntary savings would have helped to damp the fire under the boiler, there was little response. Savings were inevitably brought about by increased investment; but only by the mechanism of rising prices.[1]

Gold sales were introduced as an anti-inflationary measure. Between August 1943 and April 1944 some £3 million of official gold coin and bullion were sold through the banks at prices varying from 96*s.* to 103*s.* per gold sovereign. It is doubtful how important this weapon was as a counter to inflation, as the proceeds from gold sales never covered more than a small part of military expenditure, even though they did come at a critical time. There is no evidence of any correlation between falls in gold prices and reductions in the general price index.

In this country rationing of a wide range of commodities undoubtedly played a large part in holding down price increases as well as in securing equitable distribution of goods. How far was rationing used as an anti-inflationary measure in Palestine?

In the early war years little was done. Some attempts were made to control a number of foodstuffs, chemicals and other essential articles; for these licences had to be held by traders, and permits by purchasers. But these controls were not really effective, and nothing approximating to a general control of distribution and allocation was developed at this stage. The first consumers' rationing to start was actually in April 1941. This was a simple quantitative restriction of sales of sugar, wholesale and retail, to 50% of what they had been in the 'base' period. In February 1942 coupon rationing was introduced for sugar and its extension to flour was considered, but it was not successful, largely because of differences in Arab and Jewish standards. In November 1942 a complicated points rationing scheme was introduced. This applied to about ten commodities at first[2] but was later extended to twenty more, and there was an ingenious scheme of adjusting points value to keep supply and demand in step. The scope of this scheme was different from rationing in Britain in

[1] Fairly effective measures to prevent exports of capital or new issues of domestic capital did direct such savings as were made available into the right channels.

[2] Flour, sugar, macaroni, margarine, edible oil, jam, tea, coffee, cocoa and meat.

that the very basic necessities, e.g. bread, were rationed, but milk and fresh fruit were not. For each adult 168 points were allowed weekly, and these had to cover meals in restaurants, which cost 7 points each, as well as normal food purchases.[1] The predominance of bread and flour in the scheme can be seen from the fact that purchases of these normally accounted for 50% of points expenditure (1 kg. of bread cost 32 points). Any alteration in points value for them meant changes in demand for all other commodities. This coupon scheme, however, only applied to urban areas, which covered some 650,000 people, although there were allocations of bulk supplies and restrictions of sales of commodities in country districts.

The Government intervened much more actively in the later war years, and for many imported commodities it became the sole importer and controlled distribution through all stages to the consumer. The work of the Controller of Light Industries was typical for home-produced goods. Utility textile goods, metal goods, and footwear were introduced; textile manufacturers were compelled to assign two-thirds of their output to utility and military goods; the use of paper for many commodities was completely banned. But it is on the whole true to say that rationing in Palestine was much more an attempt to secure some degree of social justice in the light of a shortage of commodities than a planned attempt to limit consumption expenditure.

Another powerful anti-inflationary method is price control. How far was it used in Palestine? Maximum prices were fixed for some commodities at the beginning of the war, but owing to the general fall in prices in the summer of 1940 they fell into disuse. Sporadic attempts were made to improve controls in 1941, e.g. a controlled price was fixed for locally milled flour based on a controlled price of imported soft wheat with an addition for local milling costs. But many circumstances rendered these and similar controls ineffective: the scarcity of foodstuffs after the poor harvest of 1941 rendered more acute by the hoarding of peasants and the unchecked activities of the speculators; the lack of knowledge of stocks of many commodities and the lack of machinery to requisition them; the great increase in the price of imported goods, particularly from other Middle East countries; and the inability to enforce the prices laid down. Consequently prices rose steadily throughout 1942. It was not until really comprehensive measures were introduced for controlling the

[1] *Crown Colonist*, October 1942.

supply and distribution of imported goods and foodstuffs that any success was achieved in price control. In the case of imported goods this took several forms, either prices were fixed (usually when the Government had a monopoly of imports), or a fixed percentage or absolute amount was allowed to be added on to landed costs. A system of tender and monopoly licence was started in 1943 for imports.

The most outstanding innovation in methods of price control in the later war years was the subsidy policy. This first started with the subsidization of flour prices in 1942; meat followed soon afterwards, and by April 1944 a number of essential foodstuffs, as well as cotton yarn, were being subsidized. Whereas Syrian export prices for wheat rose to £50 a ton, the wholesale price of flour in Palestine was kept at £23 a ton; between September 1943 and February 1944 some £525,000 was spent on subsidizing beef, and it was estimated that this commodity was kept at half its 'natural' price. Total expenditure on subsidies may be seen from Table 24.

TABLE 24. *Subsidy expenditure*

Year	Subsidy (£000's)	Budget deficit (−) or surplus (+) (£000's)
1941–2	93	+ 861
1942–3	1140	−1402
1943–4	3353	−3300
1944–5	4703	− 700

Source. Budget accounts.

The subsidy programme helped to keep down prices and wages by keeping the cost of living index at a lower figure than it would have reached without assistance, but it is significant that budget deficits were incurred by the Palestine Government in the later war years, and these can be attributed largely to the subsidy policy, which accounted for the main increase in expenditure.

In comparison with the Allied military expenditure these deficits were a relatively minor item, and, of course, they played no part in the initial price rises in the first years of the war. It has, in fact, been argued that as the subsidies, to which the budget deficits were largely due, were mainly used to stabilize prices of imported goods, the effective result of the policy was to enrich foreign exporters—or, in other words, the increased budget deficit was offset by an increased import surplus.[1] This argument slides over the question of what the

[1] *Report of Committee on Subsidies and Surcharges.*

import surplus would have been in the absence of a subsidy policy. It would only be valid if subsidies enabled the Palestine Government to purchase a larger value of imports than they would have done otherwise, and there is little evidence to show that this was so. Therefore the argument that subsidies largely wasted themselves in higher import prices is incorrect and under-emphasizes the effect of subsidies as an inflationary factor. The real argument against putting any emphasis on the inflationary aspect of subsidies is the simple comparison with the other phenomena involved.

Despite these various attempts at price regulation it is open to doubt how far official prices were not merely shadow prices, in the sense that black-market prices of the type listed in § 2 were the significant prices for the majority of the population, at any rate in the early war years. It is true that the coupon rationing system evolved for the towns did work fairly well in the later years, and goods were normally available at controlled prices, but the limited nature of the scheme—in duration and in areas covered—should be borne in mind. In so far as the statistics quoted in Table 16 may be taken as representative, it should be pointed out that they indicate a higher ratio of black-market to controlled prices than anywhere else in the Middle East, though this, of course, may be an indication of the weakness of controls elsewhere in the Middle East rather than a sign of evasion in Palestine. Finally many home-produced goods were sold at extremely high prices, as manufacturers were able to claim and exact very high rates of yield and depreciation on plant and equipment.

We have now explored some of the reasons why the excess money demand was not diverted or held in check. It is therefore time to consider the methods by which, and the extent to which, supplies were made available to meet these demands.

Imports were very restricted in volume, owing to the lack of shipping and supplies, and therefore shortages were inevitable. The tremendous cut shown in Table 25 goes far to explain why it was impossible to prevent the great expansion in money demand from pushing up prices considerably above pre-war levels.

The importance of this reduction cannot be overestimated, but it should be noticed that in the early war years there was no vigorous scrutiny of the type of goods imported despite the existence of a licensing scheme, and it was reported in November 1941[1] that inessential goods were still being imported to the detriment of raw

[1] *The Economist*, 22 November 1941.

materials. The joint Government and Middle East Supply Centre[1] control of imports in the later war years ensured that supplies of bare essentials were secured, the import of 200 articles being completely forbidden. The expansion of imports in 1944 was a powerful drag on inflationary forces.

TABLE 25. *Index of volume of imports of merchandise (excluding military and N.A.A.F.I. stores)*

1939	100
1941	50
1942	60
1943	41
1944	52

Source. General Monthly Bulletin of Statistics.
Note. Diamonds excluded.

Not much attempt was made to organize man-power. A Directorate of Man-power was set up in 1942 to organize the supply of labour for essential work, but few effective controls on labour supply and recruitment were imposed, although some attempt was made to freeze labour in its current employment.[2]

In agriculture the main preoccupation in the early war period was to keep the citrus industry alive; Government advances and guarantees to the local banks were issued for that purpose, although gradually the policy was whittled down to one of keeping only selected groves alive. Government encouragement of other sections of agriculture was limited to loans and propaganda at first, little being done to ensure that the most vital crops would be grown or to secure them from the scattered smallholdings once they had been grown. However, the supply position became acute by 1942, and this led to direct Government intervention in production, trading, and requisitioning which broadly followed the pattern described in other chapters on Middle East countries, with such measures as the issue of seeds, seedlings and fertilizers at subsidized prices. As we have seen, the vegetable position improved enormously, with the result that Palestine was not only able to meet the needs of its own civilians and military, but also to export seeds to Egypt and the Lebanon.

[1] The official decree of 30 April 1942 listed a number of commodities which could only be imported in the future on Government account, and a further long list of commodities which could only come from Middle East countries and even then only in extreme circumstances.

[2] *Foreign Commerce Weekly*, 10 October 1942.

In industry some plans were made in 1940 to coordinate and encourage industrial production, e.g. the Central War Supply Board was started in February 1941 to coordinate Palestine industry and bring it within the orbit of the Eastern Group Supply Council; later it worked with the M.E.S.C. Government allocation of raw materials to essential firms and Government advances of capital also started (this may be seen from the statistics of advances and discounts made by the principal banks and Co-operative Societies which fell from £13·8 million in July 1939 to £11 million in July 1942, despite the great increases in production).[1] In general, however, it is fair to say that industrial production was left very much to private enterprise in the early years of the war. Later more active steps were taken to coordinate the industrial output to the war effort. The reorganization of the commodity supply and control organization which was carried out in 1942[2] brought all commodities in short supply under official control. The Anti-Inflation Committee which functioned in 1943 made recommendations which led to the setting up of the War Economic Advisory Council which had general coordinating duties and subsequently performed useful work in securing the enforcement of controls which had previously been nominal. The Controller of Heavy Industries (who was also Director of War Production) now ensured that industries under his control were harnessed to the war effort. After January 1943 Army contracts were, with the exception of a few N.A.A.F.I. orders, placed through the Government and not direct with the manufacturers.

We can now return to the points we mentioned at the beginning of this section but did not explore: the increase in Government expenditure and the increase in the value of exports. The importance of these factors in aggravating the situation we have described will now be examined.

The increase in Government expenditure did not expand incomes further in so far as it was met by increased taxation. Our real interest is in the budget deficit, when taxation and miscellaneous receipts but not grants from the United Kingdom are counted towards revenue. As may be seen from Table 26 this was never large in comparison with military expenditure.

The increase in the value of exports may be seen from Table 27, and this was of some importance in contributing to higher producers'

[1] *The Economist*, 30 January 1943.
[2] *Foreign Commerce Weekly*, 13 February 1943.

incomes. On the other hand, it was more than offset by the increase in the value of imports, which drained off much purchasing power. On balance, imports and exports of merchandise were an inflation-reducing element, even though the annual import surpluses did not nearly match the annual military expenditure until 1944, when, it is significant to note, the pace of inflation lessened considerably.

TABLE 26. *Government revenue and expenditure (£000's)*

Year	Revenue	Expenditure	True deficit (−)
1939–40	4,635	6,005	−1370
1940–41	5,179	7,450	−2271
1941–42	6,226	7,464	−1238
1942–43	8,431	10,253	−1822
1943–44	11,439	14,819	−3380
1944–45	15,107	18,196	−3089

Source. Budget accounts.

Notes. (1) Revenue figures exclude grants from U.K.
(2) In view of the smallness of the sums involved, deductions have not been made from expenditure in respect of sinking fund contributions, or interest on loans and pensions paid to foreigners.

TABLE 27. *Imports and exports of merchandise (£m.)*

Year	Imports	Exports and re-exports	Import surplus
1939	14·6	5·4	9·2
1940	12·5	4·2	8·3
1941	13·3	4·8	8·5
1942	21·3	9·2	12·1
1943	27·2	13·2	14·0
1944	36·2	15·6	20·6

Source. General Monthly Bulletin of Statistics.

Notes. (1) These figures are not strictly comparable as they do not include Transjordan before mid-1941, but the error introduced is very small.
(2) Figures include credit Lend-Lease of civilian goods, but exclude all military and N.A.A.F.I. stores.
(3) See Table 11, Note 3.

In view of the statistics of Tables 26 and 27 it seems difficult to ascribe a great deal of importance to the Government deficit or to the rise in exporters' incomes. We must now examine two more phenomena which featured in the inflationary movement: high import prices and private capital imports or invisible items on current account.

It has been claimed[1] that high import prices were a major factor in the Palestine inflation. The main grounds for this argument rest on the evidence shown in Table 28.

TABLE 28. *Value of Palestine imports (excluding military and N.A.A.F.I. stores)*

Item	1939	1942	1943
Total value of imports (£m.)	14·6	21·3	27·2
Index of volume	100	60	41
Total value 1939 prices	14·6	8·8	6·0
Average value of imports	100	242	453
Wholesale price index	100	246	336

It can be seen that a volume of imports which would have cost £6 million in 1939 actually cost £27·2 million in 1943 (and thus average import prices rose from 100 to 453 over this period), whereas the index of wholesale prices only rose from 100 to 336. Furthermore, not only did import prices in general rise, but those which rose most were the essentials of life, such as cereals, meat and textiles.

The two main explanations of this rise are the reorientation of Palestine's sources of imports during the war (in 1943 55% of the total value of imports was coming from the Middle East compared with 16% in 1939),[2] and the vastly increased freight and insurance rates on those goods which did come from overseas sources of supply.[3]

The mechanism by which these high import prices raised general prices and wages was simple. The system of price control was such that wholesale and retail prices largely depended on import prices, and after 1942 cost of living bonus sliding scale arrangements made wages move more or less automatically with the cost of living index. As Palestine is dependent on overseas producers for a large proportion of the basic items, such as cereals and meat, which enter into the cost of living index, the link was all the stronger. Thus high import prices

[1] E.g. Nathan, op. cit. p. 596: 'The greater part of the inflation of Palestine's price level may be attributed to the direct and indirect consequences of the high prices she has had to pay for her imports.'

[2] See *Review of Commercial Conditions* (Palestine). This change of course is greater than the percentage change in volume simply because prices of goods from M.E. countries showed a larger percentage increase than prices of goods from other countries, even when allowance is made for the increase in c.i.f.

[3] In November 1944 machine tools procured through Lend-Lease channels cost 300% more than similar British products in 1939.

of wheat and wheat flour led the Government to increase retail prices of bread by 22% in July 1942, and the cost of living index rose by 10 points in August 1942. Furthermore, high prices in neighbouring countries of wheat and barley helped to make the supply position worse inside the country. Because prices were known to be higher elsewhere, and, *a fortiori*, when prices were thought to be still rising elsewhere, peasants hoarded their grain in the hope of higher prices, or were tempted to smuggle it over the frontiers.

These then were the principal ways in which high import prices helped to push up prices and wages in the country. How important were they compared with the pressure of Government and military expenditure? Here it seems necessary to draw a distinction between the earlier years of the war up to 1942, and the years after that date. When prices in neighbouring countries were rising rapidly and the Palestine system of price control was in its rudimentary stages, these high prices did play some part in pushing up prices and wages, although, of course, the mere fact that at the same time the import surplus was high was an anti-inflationary force. In the later war years it is doubtful whether rising import prices really did produce much reaction in retail prices and wages, because of the extensive subsidy programme which, as we have seen, was adopted with the specific intention of isolating this phenomenon. It is noteworthy that although prices of wheat in Syria and barley in Iraq continued to rise after 1942, the controlled price in Palestine was kept fairly stable. On the other hand, the indirect effect of the subsidy programme in leading to an increased budget deficit must not be forgotten. In so far as subsidized commodities were smuggled out to neighbouring countries the Government was effectively taxing the country to swell the incomes of the smugglers. But it should be remembered that, particularly in the early war years, black-market, and not controlled, prices were usually more relevant, and as we saw in Table 16 black-market prices of wheat and sugar in Palestine were considerably above controlled prices which in turn were largely based on import prices. Therefore we must be cautious about any argument relying solely on a comparison of import and controlled prices.

Another factor which was of some considerable importance and peculiar to Palestine among the Middle East countries was the receipt of substantial remittances both by Government and private institutions or individuals. These remittances were the normal peacetime method of paying for the import surplus and balancing the budget.

Their importance may be gleaned from Table 22, where the relative magnitudes of increases in currency and bank deposits, of sterling balances, of annual levels of military expenditure and import surpluses are set forth. In view of the fairly close correspondence between the total figures of estimated increased sterling balances and the additions to the supply of money, it is reasonable to compare the total of military expenditure and overseas remittances with the total of the import surpluses and the increased supply of money. Military expenditure was £111·1 million from 1940 to 1944, the increase in currency and bank deposits was £88·0 million, and the import surplus was £66·5 million. The sum of net capital imports and net invisible exports must clearly have been of the order of £40–50 million.

The main constituents of these items were grants-in-aid from His Majesty's Government to the Palestine Government, funds from institutions abroad (such as Zionist Societies in the U.S.A.) and imports of capital by private individuals. Grants-in-aid from His Majesty's Government were £10·4 million from 1939 to 1944. It was estimated that from 1940 to 1944 all Jewish receipts of funds amounted[1] to about £38 million, and although the exact division between private and institutional receipts is not known, it may be roughly estimated, on the basis of what happened in the earlier war years, that private receipts were about £8 million and institutional receipts about £30 million.

What was the importance of these items in contributing to the inflationary process? We have already excluded the grants-in-aid from Government receipts,[2] and it would therefore be double counting if we reckoned it as an export receipt as well. How important the other receipts were in contributing to an expansion of outlay it is impossible to determine. Clearly, however, they cannot have been anything like as important as military expenditure, not only because of their smaller size but also because all money created on military account was spent and thus went into the active circulation, whereas it is probable that some portion of these overseas receipts were treated as capital assets and not spent. It is a reasonable assumption that the velocity of circulation of 'military' money was greater than that of 'overseas remittances' money.

[1] *Survey of Palestine*, vol. 1, p. 464. [2] See Table 26.

§4. Critique of War Organization

In this section the question of whether it might have been possible to avoid such a high degree of inflation as actually took place will be examined.

There were several influences which made some measure of inflation inevitable. First, the size of the war effort and the expansion of the national output entailed could never have been achieved by the methods of orthodox finance. Credit creation was the only way in which the necessary purchases of the military authorities could be financed. It is never completely possible to prevent a large injection of new money which goes straight into the expenditure stream from having some effect on prices and incomes, even under normal supply conditions, but when the usual sources of imports were disrupted the effect was bound to be greater. Secondly, the nature of the war effort made an expansion of prices and incomes extremely likely. The major problem was to divert a large slice of the country's resources to satisfy Allied military requirements, and as we saw in Chapter I this made the employment of normal fiscal methods difficult, even though there was closer liaison between the Government and the military authorities than in some countries. Thirdly, even though it was found possible in Palestine to enlarge industrial output with more success than in other primary economies, there were special features of the country which were responsible for many of the snags that arose. The most important of these was the political state of the country, for even though there was a reduction in the number of actual clashes between Jews and Arabs during the war the truce was at best an armed one. Typical of the difficulties raised by this situation was the vehement opposition of the Arabs to the imposition of estate duty, ostensibly on religious grounds but more fundamentally because of the fear of enforced sales of Arab lands and their subsequent acquisition by the Jews.[1] It has, in fact, been said, with possibly more truth than cynicism, that the only matter on which the Jews and Arabs were ever in unanimous agreement was opposition to further increases in taxes. Furthermore, the very existence of two very different races inside one State introduced considerable administrative difficulties. Rationing, for instance, was made much more difficult by the completely different character of Jewish and Arab consumption. The standard difficulties encountered in primary economies in

[1] Budget estimates 1943–4.

increasing production and reducing consumption were present in varying degrees. It is true that it was relatively easy to increase the output of manufactured goods and of modern agriculture, but in many cases the manufacturers exacted a high rate of profit for their efforts which helped in the price-inflation process. All the normal difficulties in expanding the output of primitive agriculture were incurred, and the position was rendered especially difficult by the severe curtailment of imports which might have helped to increase production, either directly by supplying necessary implements[1] or indirectly by supplying more consumption goods. The persistence of higher prices in neighbouring territories made it hard to ensure that grain or other products would ever reach the markets where they were most needed. On the other hand, there is no evidence to show that Palestine suffered as acutely as some colonies from a shortage of administrative staff.

Fourthly, as we have already seen, inflation in Palestine is partly explained by the extraneous factors of high import prices and overseas remittances. Here again it might well be claimed that it was impossible to isolate these factors completely from the economy.

Finally, a number of remedies which might seem theoretically valid were for various reasons impracticable. Exchange appreciation would have reduced import prices (in view of wartime restrictions any possible adverse repercussions due to elastic demand combined with inelastic supply may be neglected), and this would have mitigated the effect of the great wartime rise. It is difficult to believe, however, that the British Treasury would have viewed such a manipulation with pleasure, both because of the adverse effects it would certainly have had on sterling balances and the effects it might have had in reducing the useful dollar income from Palestine exports of polished diamonds. And even apart from these considerations the inflationary effect of the reduced import surplus (the volume of imports was limited by purely physical considerations) might have offset the anti-inflationary effect of lower import prices. Nor is it possible to argue that higher interest rates would have induced people to save more or to lend their savings to the Government. In the first place the Moslem tradition against usury was strong as in other Middle East countries.[2] Secondly, there was no tradition of lending to the Palestine Government, and, as in

[1] See *Crown Colonist*, November 1943, where it was reported that the lack of tractors was holding up the food production campaign, as 50% of the pre-war ones were worn out and very few new ones arrived in 1942 and 1943.

[2] See Hansard (Lords), 15 November 1944.

other colonies, an adequate framework for a money market was non-existent. Finally, any system of deferred savings was impracticable, for this would have incurred the worst of both worlds—it would have aroused all the opposition to higher taxation as well as the normal prejudices against loans.

Inflation in Palestine can be explained on the lines of these five general sets of arguments, but it is doubtful whether its scale can be excused. There does seem to be a *prima facie* case for believing that it should have been possible to accomplish the increase in industrial production and allocation of resources for war purposes without such expansion of incomes and prices as actually took place. In the first place, the war contribution of Palestine, significant as it was, does not seem to have absorbed such a large proportion of the country's resources as it did in the principal belligerent countries.[1] It is difficult to measure war contribution, but as a rough and ready guide we may compare the calculations of Table 11 which show the ratio of the value of Allied expenditure plus Government defence expenditure plus exports to the value of net national output plus imports with similar figures for the United Kingdom and the U.S.A. The peak ratio was 54% in the United Kingdom and 46% in the U.S.A., whereas in Palestine the peak ratio was 38%.[2] Furthermore, the war contribution of the United Kingdom was maintained at or about this high level for a longer period of time than was that of Palestine. The difference in ratios can, of course, be explained very largely by the much higher initial standard of living in the U.S.A. and the United Kingdom, but the comparison is still useful for putting the war demands on Palestine in their true perspective.

In the second place, there was a considerable reserve of labour and capacity in 1939 in Palestine. The immigration of Jews during the previous decade had brought in a large number of skilled craftsmen for whom there was not sufficient employment in the 1939 economy, and there was a large reserve of unskilled labour to be found in the mass of under-employed workers who attempted to scratch a poor and

[1] No comparison of relative *sacrifices* is intended here.

[2] The figures for U.K. and U.S.A. are from *Impact of War on Civilian Consumption*, Appendix XII. This comparison is not strictly valid, however, for two main reasons, even apart from any slight difference in national income concept. First, the Palestine ratio is at market prices and that of the U.K. and U.S.A. is taken at factor costs. Secondly, a more accurate measure would be to take gross national output, but as no gross figure is available for Palestine the net figure has had to be used in all three cases. Therefore, in so far as the ratio of net to gross income differs in each country, the comparison may not be fair.

wretched living from the soil. Furthermore, the dislocation of the citrus export trade in 1940 should have made a still larger labour force available. Capital equipment had been imported steadily for some years before the war, and 1939 found Palestine with a larger value of capital equipment per head of the population than any other Middle East country.

If, in view of these facts, the influence of the size and nature of the war effort, the special features of the country and the extraneous factors listed above are insufficient to justify the degree of inflation in Palestine, it must be asked whether the methods of securing the war contribution were as adequate as they might have been.

The wartime controls introduced in Palestine are a formidable and imposing array at first sight, for, as we have seen, most aspects of the economy were covered. Some controls found necessary in other countries are more conspicuous by their absence, however. There was never any real control of labour despite the attempts made by the Directorate of Man-power to freeze workers in essential occupations, and although this was no loss in respect of unskilled labour, it is probable that some local bottlenecks of skilled and semi-skilled labour could have been avoided by more effective labour control. Nor was there ever an adequate system of controlling primary producers' incomes despite the attempts to fix the prices of requisitioned crops.

Many controls which were adopted later on were either not introduced in the early years of the war at all or at least not in an effective form. Import licensing was not at all strict until 1942;[1] the anti-profiteering ordinance and the subsidy programme were only drafted in that year, and the machinery for the control of prices and distribution only creaked along up to that time. And even though income tax receipts were £2·5 million by 1944–5, the exemption limit for a married couple was still £300 per annum.

It was, in fact, possible for an observer to report in September 1942: 'There are surprisingly few of those severe restrictions which have been experienced in England...there is no clothing rationing in Palestine, nor does one see any queues outside shops' (*Crown Colonist*, October 1942).

The explanation of the lack of queues might be that there was so much to buy that there was no need to queue, or that prices were so high as to be prohibitive for most people, or that there was nothing to buy at all. On the whole, the second explanation is the most likely.

[1] See p. 114.

Furthermore, controls in Palestine sometimes suffered from their very complexity. The points rationing scheme, for instance, was admirably logical on paper and on the whole worked well, but it did present the administration with many headaches in, for instance, reconciling total demand and supply of points. The system of changing weights embodied in the Wages Committee cost of living index was also too complicated for easy handling.

Perhaps the key to the whole structure of controls may be found in the following quotation:

'Changes were forced by circumstances rather than planned in advance, the present (i.e. 1943) provisions being adopted only after it had been demonstrated that the early provisions were inadequate' (*Foreign Commerce Weekly*, 13 February 1943).

It can reasonably be claimed that the size and nature of the war effort and the characteristics of the country explain to some extent why the early provisions were inadequate and why the necessary measures were not planned in advance. We have already seen that these points account very largely for the difficulties in raising taxes. At the same time it does seem that with rather more prescience it should have been possible to accomplish the war contribution without such a high degree of inflation. It is doubtful, for instance, whether the hard task involved in trying to increase production and supply in face of reduced imports of machinery and raw materials was fully realized and whether adequate allowance was made for it. The comfortable feeling that there was a large margin of resources in reserve was fostered still further by the closing of the Mediterranean sea route and the collapse of the citrus trade in 1940. Finally, the Colonial Government tradition of *laissez-faire* in economic matters had to be overcome. This was bound to take time, but it cannot be denied that the lack of clear directions from His Majesty's Government in the early part of the war about the probable war contribution that would be needed lengthened the process. Such points as these largely explain the Government's failure to impose adequate controls in the beginning of the war years, when they might very well have restrained the growth of inflation.

CHAPTER IV

EGYPT[1]

§ 1. PHYSICAL CHANGES

Man-power

The main wartime demand on Egyptian man-power resources was the direct employment by the Allied Armies of general labourers for airfield construction, road building, railway extensions, and dock and harbour work. A large number of skilled labourers were also employed as fitters, turners, welders and carpenters on these works and in the many War Department repair shops and depots. Others were employed as black-coated workers, drivers, mess orderlies, cooks and the like. All in all the peak figure for direct employment of these categories was about 200,000 in 1943, although it had declined to 150,000 by 1945.[2] In addition to these direct demands a large number of workers were employed by private entrepreneurs either producing commodities for the requirements of the military in Egypt or elsewhere, or performing services of various kinds. The largest categories of this sort were in general manufacturing work and in public construction. Although the numbers of workers so employed are not known exactly, the peak figure in 1943 was probably about 80,000. Finally, the Egyptian Army itself was not large but increased from 22,000 in 1937–8 to 40,000 in 1945.[3] Thus an overall estimate of the peak wartime drain on man-power reserves would be about 300,000.[4] Of course, the number of individual people employed on war work of these various sorts was much larger than this, as the turn-over of many categories of labour—and more particularly of unskilled labourers who came off the land—was extremely high. For this reason the post-war problem of reabsorption of this labour may be much more difficult than even the figures above suggest.

To what extent did these commitments make a serious inroad on Egypt's man-power reserves? In the first place, the population of Egypt is large, and in common with other Middle East countries is increasing at a rapid rate. The 1907 census revealed a total of 11·2 millions, whereas in 1927 it was 14·2 millions and in 1937 15·9

[1] Unless otherwise stated financial statistics are in £E.
[2] *The Times*, 31 May 1946.
[3] *The Economist*, 17 August 1946.
[4] Cf. *Économiste Égyptienne*, 7 November 1943.

millions. It was estimated that the population was 17·0 millions in 1941,[1] and assuming the same rate of growth over the later war years, it may be put at about 18·0 millions in 1944–5. Secondly, the fundamental Egyptian economic problem is rather like that of India—how to find sufficient work for a population which cannot possibly be supported on the land at present and for which there appears to be no adequate outlet. It is perhaps not generally realized that density of population per square kilometre of inhabited area was as much as 500 in 1941; or to put it in another way, some 18 million people are living in an area no larger than Yorkshire and Lincolnshire together. Quite apart from this perennial problem of under-employed rural labour there was a large reserve of unemployed labour in the towns in 1940. The contraction of some staple exports, the decline in private building activity and the suspension of Government public works all helped in this process.[2] In view of these factors of expanding population for which there is insufficient work and of a reserve of unemployed town labour, it is difficult to believe that the war demands for man-power seriously reduced the supply available for normal civilian production. But in common with other countries there were many shortages of particular categories. The 1937 census showed that there were only about 478,000 occupied in manufacturing industry and handicrafts, and of this number a very large proportion were concentrated in a few industries, such as clothing manufacture (108,000), woodworking (77,000), textiles (76,000), food processing (54,000) and fuel and power (40,000). Between them, these five industrial groups absorbed 355,000, or 74% of the total. All the many varied metal and machinery trades had only about 60,000 workers altogether. In addition to this total of 478,000 workers in manufacturing industry there were some 120,000 workers occupied in building and various kinds of constructional work. It is important to realize that manufacturing industry and building were practically the only sources from which skilled or semi-skilled labour could be drawn for military requirements; and these were heavy for many types of skill, covering both the traditional Egyptian kinds, such as carpenters and masons and the more modern electrical and engineering crafts. About 60,000, or one-third of those employed direct by the military authorities in 1944, were classed as skilled men, and although this figure is misleading to the extent that men of little skill and

[1] *Statistical Handbook of the Middle East.*
[2] *The Economist*, 16 November 1940.

experience were sometimes upgraded so that higher wages might be paid, there is little doubt that when the expansion of employment in private industry working for the Army is taken into account, the reserves of skilled or semi-skilled labour in Egypt in 1942–3 must have been very small.

Production

The best index of the wartime increase of demand for goods and services is to be found in the vast expansion of military expenditure shown in Table 1.

TABLE 1. *Annual military expenditure (estimated)*

Year	Expenditure (£m.)	Cost of living index (base June/Aug. 1939 = 100)
1939	5·0	100
1940	15·2	109
1941	47·7	134
1942	75·2	178
1943	76·8	241
1944	56·7	273

Source. Special estimate.

Notes. (1) All expenditure by Allied military authorities and troops in Egypt is included, except that deductions are made for such items as N.A.A.F.I. receipts (less expenditure on local goods), value of sales in officers' shops and home remittances via Army channels.

(2) Cost of living index refers to June of each year.

(3) £ are sterling.

It is not easy to appreciate the significance of this expenditure in a country where national income statistics are almost entirely lacking. It is normally reckoned that in 1939 the national income per head of the population was of the order of £12 or slightly more,[1] and peak military expenditure was at 1939 prices about £2·4 per head. This is a very crude estimate, but it does give some idea of the order of magnitude of military expenditure in relation to the pre-war economy. Military expenditure took many forms. In the first place, there was a considerable demand for light manufactured commodities and many processed foods such as canned fruits, chocolate and sweets, dehydrated products, beer,[2] textiles, ropes and twine, leather goods and metal containers and tins were produced. Secondly, staple food-

[1] Cf. *Foreign Commerce Weekly*, 14 March 1942. Somewhat lower figures are given in *The Economist* (7 September 1946), where an estimate of £8·5 per head is made for 1937. The 1944 figure is put at £23 per head.

[2] Egypt was producing 1 million bottles per week by September 1943.

stuffs were purchased locally for the Allied Armies, but it is doubtful whether this was a large imposition on Egyptian resources. It was reported, for instance, in 1942[1] that the 1941 annual rate of wheat and wheat-flour consumption was only 25,000 tons or 2% of the total crop, of maize and maize flour 7800 tons or 0·5% of the total crop, and that all the vegetables purchased could be grown on about 600 acres. Purchase of sugar, too, was confined to surpluses above civilian requirements. In later years Army purchases may have been larger in some cases, but they were only made after agreement with Egyptian authorities. Thirdly, as we have seen, there was a large demand for labour on constructional work, either working directly for the Army or for contractors, and in terms of man-power this undoubtedly accounted for a very large part of the drain on Egyptian resources. Finally, there was a large demand for personal services by the Forces both in their collective and individual capacities.

For the sake of completeness Egyptian defence expenditure must be considered. This was unimportant as it did not increase substantially above the pre-war level of £5–6 million per annum (excluding high cost of living bonuses). There was virtually no reverse Lease-Lend expenditure, as airfields, etc., provided for the U.S. Forces were normally paid for out of the proceeds from the sale of Lend-Lease supplies and therefore are already listed in Table 1, which includes all Allied expenditure.

The other main way in which most countries contributed to the Allied war effort was by their exports. Some of the principal items of Egyptian exports are detailed in Table 2.

It will be clear from this table that the volume of exports fell considerably by 1942–3. No indices of volume or export prices are available, but the index of retail prices rose from 100 to 241 between June 1939 and June 1943, and if, as a crude measure, we deflate the average of the value of exports in 1942 and 1943 by this index it would appear that, very roughly, the volume had declined to about a third of pre-war levels. The figures of raw cotton and cotton seed which are such a large proportion of Egyptian export trade show a decline from 683,000 tons in 1938–9 (av.) to 170,000 tons in 1942–3 (av.), which seems to indicate an even greater decline in overall volume than the crude price comparison shows. In fact, the only important commodities to show any sustained increase at all were raw flax and fuel oil.

[1] Hansard (Commons), 19 February 1942; *The Economist*, 7 February 1942.

Thus although military expenditure did increase enormously in Egypt and absorbed a substantial amount of real resources, it is fairly clear that there was at the same time a very great fall in exports. But to see the impact of these demands on the Egyptian economy in their true light we obviously need estimates of the changes in volume of the national output. In the absence of these the most that we can do is to see whether there was any tendency for the volume of output to rise or fall in the principal industries.

TABLE 2. *Principal exports*

Commodity	Quantity		Value f.o.b. (£000's)	
	1938–9 (av.)	1942–3 (av.)	1938–9 (av.)	1942–3 (av.)
Raw cotton (000's tons)	383	152	22,760	16,250
Cotton seed (000's tons)	300	18	1,455	98
Cotton-seed cake (000's tons)	228	0·3	809	0·9
Refined sugar (000's tons)	71	12	720	308
Rice (000's tons)	91	83	903	1,788
Onions (000's tons)	164	5·2	922	22
Raw flax (000's tons)	1·45	6·4	90	1,240
Fuel oil (000's tons)	81	171	240	900
Total value (including re-exports)	—	—	33,700	24,700

Source. Egyptian Customs Returns.

Notes. (1) Figures include exports to Sudan.
(2) Military and N.A.A.F.I. stores excluded.
(3) Figures of rice are for bleached and unhusked together.
(4) Wheat exports have not been included as they vary so much from year to year with the harvests. In 1940, for instance, 42,000 tons were exported (£402,000) and in 1942, 7 tons (£202).
(5) Tons are metric.

From the earliest days of recorded history agriculture has played a supreme part in the Egyptian economy. The 1937 census showed that out of the total occupied population of 6·1 millions some 4·3 millions (or 71 %) were engaged primarily in agriculture, although, of course, many did other seasonal or temporary jobs, such as unskilled building work in the off seasons. The changes in output in the main cash and food crops over the war years may be seen from Table 3.

It is apparent from Table 3 that apart from cotton and cotton seed, where there was a substantial decrease, and millet, where there was some increase, there were no obvious trends in the output of the main crops during the war years. The policy of reducing cotton output was specifically devised to increase the acreage available for growing food crops to feed the civil populations of the Middle East. The mere fact that agricultural output as a whole did not increase[1] appreciably should not lead us to suppose that it was military absorption of labour or of land which was the principal bottleneck. The total cultivated area was in fact greater, as the increase of acreage under food crops was greater than the reduction of the cotton area (see Table 4).

TABLE 3. *Agricultural output* (000's *metric tons*)

Crop	1936–9 (av.)	1942	1943	1944
Cotton	417	190	164	199
Cotton seed	777	336	270	327
Wheat	1266	1263	1291	946
Barley	234	277	314	227
Millet	455	964	776	765
Maize	1585	1499	1407	1543
Rice (paddy)	678	930	676	811
Beans	296	277	284	326
Cane sugar	2296	2690	2104	2300

Source. Statistical Handbook of the Middle East.

TABLE 4. *Area under crops* (000's *feddans*)

Crop	1936–38 (av.)	1943
Cotton	1776	713
Maize	1526	1994
Wheat	1398	1917
Millet	347	731
Rice	404	642
Beans	389	381
Barley	286	419
Sugar-cane	67	87

Source. Statistical Handbook of the Middle East.

Note. 1 feddan = 4210 sq. metres = 1·04 acres.

From Tables 3 and 4 it may be seen that average yield of maize per acre was reduced by some 32% between 1936–9 and 1943, wheat by 24% and millet by 30%. The outstanding reason for these changes was the decline in imports of fertilizers.[2]

[1] Vegetables did increase quite considerably. Output of onions was 235,999 tons in 1936–8 and 741,999 in 1941, although it is true that output was reduced later. Potatoes also were grown in some quantity. The output of flax increased from 3999 tons in 1940 to 12,000 in 1943.

[2] See p. 154.

The increased supply of Egyptian manufactured goods to the military authorities did not mean that the supply of these available for the civilian population was seriously reduced, as the overall increases in production were sufficient to compensate for military purchases. Many pre-war industries, such as cotton textiles, petroleum refining, soap making, sugar refining, superphosphates production, paper and cement, were developed and many completely new ones, such as food canning or processing, dehydrated products, starch making, refractory brick production, were started. Statistics of production are scanty, but some evidence of increases in output or capacity is available in Table 5.

TABLE 5. *Industrial production*

Commodity	1938–39 (av.)	1943–44 (av.)
Cotton piecegoods (m. sq.yd.)	83	210
Cotton yarn (000's tons)	23	32
Crude oil (000's tons)	591	1,290
Petroleum (000's barrels)	4,100	10,000
Manganese ore (000's tons)	137	7
Phosphate rock (000's tons)	503	315
Cement (000's tons)	284	700
Refined sugar (000's tons)	160	190
Refractory bricks (000's tons)	4	20
*Paper and cardboard (000's tons)	12	30
*Glassware (000's tons)	2	12
*Preserved foods and jams (tons)	400	20,000
*Starch (tons)	Nil	3,000
*Dehydrated products (tons)	Nil	2,500
*Soap (000's tons)	45	60
*Superphosphates (000's tons)	4	16
*Sulphuric acid (000's tons)	5·5	11

Sources. *Statistical Handbook of the Middle East, Review of Commercial Conditions* (Egypt); *Annuaire Générale de l'Industrie Égyptienne*; *Petroleum Press Service*, November 1945.

Note. For commodities marked with an asterisk the figures indicate capacity only, as actual production figures are not available.

In addition to these industries there were many other increases—particularly in engineering and metal trades—and other innovations, such as the production of vastly increased amounts of paper or jute manufactures, of which statistics are not available.

To summarize this subsection we may say that military demands for Egyptian resources, and particularly man-power, were considerable, but on the other hand the volume of exports of domestic goods declined sharply. Although agricultural output did not increase appreciably there was a substantial expansion of industrial output and capacity in many lines of production.

Consumption

Little is known about pre-war stocks of commodities and the size of the labour force engaged in capital goods industries in Egypt in 1939. However, although domestic building activity was reduced to a bare minimum, it is improbable that many resources could have been made available for war or civilian consumption by means of this sort.

The main point we have to determine here is whether there is much evidence of a great reduction in the supply of consumers' goods during the war years. The most important factors are clearly the increase in home production, and the diversions to military demand, which we have dealt with, and the reduction in imports which we must consider now.

The main changes may be seen from Table 6.

TABLE 6. *Principal imports*

Commodity	Quantity			Value c.i.f. (£000's)		
	1938	1941	1943	1938	1941	1943
Sugar (000's tons)	109	14·6	2·2	653	212	55
Tea (000's tons)	7·9	6·6	2·9	831	1,240	959
Coffee (000's tons)	9·0	7·8	10·3	300	400	1,100
Beer (000's litres)	3,521	8,735	5,847	82	575	315
Tobacco leaves (000's tons)	5·9	6·4	9·0	604	863	3,490
Soap (000's tons)	3·8	2·2	0·3	111	85	28
Kerosene (000's tons)	309	173	246	1,130	1,200	1,640
Cotton yarn (tons)	772	1,080	144	112	263	76
Cotton piecegoods (000's tons)	16·9	7·5	1·7	2,780	2,670	1,470
Paper, printing (000's tons)	15·5	10·9	2·5	250	574	227
Fertilizers (000's tons)	514	5	159	2,950	119	3,410
Coal (000's tons)	1,548	400	240	2,010	2,070	1,440
Iron bars and pipes (000's tons)	108·5	12·0	5·5	1,200	320	150
Wood (for building) (000's tons)	230	10·0	10·7	1,220	151	222
Machines and looms for weaving (tons)	3,522	553	291	184	67	45
Pumps, steam and i.c. (tons)	1,095	148	105	88	23	29
Engines, stationary, i.c. (number)	958	327	81	217	66	45
Tractors (number)	305	74	29	72	27	7
Total value	—	—	—	37,700	34,500	38,900

Source. Egyptian Customs Returns.

Notes. (1) Stores imported on military and N.A.A.F.I. account are, broadly speaking, excluded from these figures. N.A.A.F.I. stores clearly should be excluded, as the figures in Table 1 are net of N.A.A.F.I. receipts. It is suspected that some stores of staple foods which were intended for military use only are included in the Customs Returns but the error introduced thereby is very small.

(2) Imports from Sudan and civilian Lend-Lease goods included.

(3) Tons are metric.

It is clear from Table 6 that the chief increases were in such items as beer and tobacco intended for sale to the Forces,[1] and the chief reductions were in raw materials and manufactured goods such as fertilizers, coal, wood, cotton piecegoods, iron bars and pipes and machinery. Of these reductions the most vital of all was in fertilizers, for this was the principal limitation on expansion of agricultural output. Egypt is normally dependent on coal imports, and their decline made it necessary to convert many locomotives to oil burning. Imports of cotton piecegoods formed about two-thirds of the annual consumption requirements before the war. Egypt is so nearly self-sufficient in most foodstuffs that pre-war imports were not important. Tea imports were reduced from 7580 tons in 1939 to 2970 tons in 1943, but this was the only important reduction, as the change in sugar imports was largely offset by a reduction in exports.[2]

The order of magnitude of the main changes in consumption is difficult to determine in Egypt in view of the paucity and inaccuracy of the statistical material available. The sustained production of food grains, the small military demands, the relatively small exports and the insignificant level of pre-war imports, make it extremely doubtful whether the overall supply of cereals was ever very much below pre-war requirements. On the other hand, it must be remembered that the output of maize, the principal grain eaten by the fellaheen, was somewhat lower than in the immediate pre-war years, and there was a substantial increase in population over the war years. There is not much evidence of great reductions in total consumption of other foodstuffs. Increases in production of vegetables were probably sufficient to compensate for Army demands, and although the supply of raw materials for edible oil was curtailed by the reduction in cotton output, imports from the Sudan went some way towards alleviating the shortage. Meat supplies for the civilian population were cut by the imposition of three meatless days a week in 1942, but as many hardly ever saw meat before the war it is doubtful whether this was ever a severe hardship. Perhaps the cut in tea imports was felt most keenly.

The fall in the supply of textiles is more apparent. Before the war home production of cotton textiles amounted to about one-third of

[1] These figures, of course, do not represent all imports of these items but only those made through normal commercial channels.

[2] Sugar consumption of the civil population was estimated to be 132,000 tons in 1939–40 and 145,000 tons in 1943–4 (*Report of Annual Meeting of the Egyptian Sugar Company*, 1944).

annual consumption, but output of cotton piecegoods was more than doubled between 1938–9 and 1943–4, as it was increased from 83 to 210 million sq.yd., and it was estimated that by 1944 this output would have supplied about 70% of total consumption at the pre-war rate.[1] However, some of this output was taken up for military purposes,[2] although the imports allowed by M.E.S.C. partly compensated for these demands. It must also be remembered that the population was increasing, and this was a further aggravating factor. Moreover, imports of wool fabrics which were 1600 tons in 1938 were reduced to 300 tons in 1943, and this situation was further aggravated by military consumption of home-produced supplies.

Although there was a large expansion of manufactured goods in general during the war, they clearly cannot have compensated entirely for the reductions in imports. Metal goods are probably the best example. We have seen in Table 6 how the total imports of iron and steel bars and pipes declined. Even by 1941 annual imports of nails, bolts, nuts, screws, hinges, etc., had been reduced to nearly one-quarter of 1938 tonnage. Kerosene was one of the two universally rationed commodities in Egypt,[3] and although rations were at first fixed at the same level per family as pre-war consumption rates, they were reduced by 37½% by September 1942. Furthermore, it was estimated that by December 1943 monthly consumption of coal had been cut to one-third of pre-war rates.

From this picture it is apparent that there were reductions in general consumption of some essential commodities, even if not of basic foodstuffs. But the hardships imposed were probably greater than any simple statement such as this conveys, for some of the poorer classes in Egypt suffered unduly during the war years. In the first place the changes in real income were uneven; in the second place schemes for rationing and distribution favoured the rich at the expense of the poor, and the towns at the expense of the country.

It is well recognized that the large landowners, industrialists and traders were very prosperous during the war years.[4] It is also well recognized that the lower branches of the salariat, such as minor Government officials, suffered acutely, as their cost of living bonuses were nothing like sufficiently large to compensate for the increases in food prices and the raising of rents in the towns. This latter point

[1] *Économiste Égyptienne*, 15 July 1945.

[2] This was known to be at the rate of 3000 tons (or about 27 m. sq.yd.) per annum in 1944.

[3] The other was sugar.

[4] See p. 141.

was of some importance, for not only was domestic building activity reduced to a standstill owing to such factors as military demands for local building labour and raw materials and cuts in imported materials (e.g. wood, see Table 6), but also the demand for accommodation in the towns, particularly Cairo, increased tremendously with the influx of both Allied military personnel and Egyptian rural population. As there was no effective control over rents at all in Egypt until the very end of the war, they inevitably increased an enormous amount in some urban districts.[1] Lastly, increases in textile prices were another severe blow at this class.

Whether the fellaheen suffered falls in real income it is difficult to tell. The predominant characteristics of land tenure in Egypt are the concentration of large estates into a few hands and a large number of very small holdings. Some cultivators earn sufficient on their own land, but the great majority eke out a living by working as general labourers or farmers on the large estates, and in the latter case métayage systems are common. Money rents of land in rural areas increased during the war, but it is doubtful whether these were more than doubled on the whole, in contrast with grain prices which were often trebled. Where rents and wages were paid in kind there is no evidence that landlords absorbed a greater proportion of the crop than before. It is true that labourers did not have the protection of compulsory higher cost of living allowances as did those in the towns, but those employed on military work can hardly be said to have suffered on that account. Moreover, such evidence as there is points to a substantial reduction in indebtedness during the war, and even those who did not repay their debts were left with a much lighter real burden when interest payments were fixed in terms of money. Although, as we shall see, consumption of some commodities was reduced, consumption of foodstuffs such as grain and vegetables appears to have increased. It was, in fact, difficult for the real income of the fellaheen to fall simply because his normal requirements are so limited[2] and because he is so often largely self-supporting.[3]

The rationing and distribution systems undoubtedly favoured the towns rather than the country and the richer classes rather than the

[1] See p. 141.

[2] Even textiles are almost a luxury: 'The fellah requires cotton for his clothing, fertilizers for his fields, and is either directly or indirectly a consumer of various petroleum products, but beyond these his requirements are small' (Turner, *Economic Conditions in Egypt*).

[3] This, of course, is no refutation of the long-term tendency for the standard of living to fall through the Malthus-like pressure of expanding population on the land.

poorer. Kerosene was rationed on the basis of the purchasing power of the inhabitants and the amount normally used; sugar was rationed, in Cairo at any rate, on the same principle; the so-called 'popular textiles' were allocated to governorates and districts on the basis of the 'number of inhabitants, purchasing power and moral standing', which turned out to mean a ration in the cities which was twice as large as in the smaller towns and three times as large as in the villages. Consequently, there were very frequently great shortages of sugar and cloth (and also tea) in the rural areas, which were quite out of proportion to the changes in supplies available. It is not improbable that the shortage of cloth in Upper Egypt was an important cause of the malaria epidemic of 1944.

In summary, then, we may say that despite the stability of most food supplies and the emergence of increased supplies of local manufactured products to compensate for reduced imports and increased military demands, there were reductions in consumption of basic necessities among some of the poorest elements of the population.

§2. Financial Changes

Money

The increases in the supply of money are set out in Table 7.

Table 7. *Supply of money (£m.)*

Date	National Bank of Egypt notes in circulation	Currency and subsidiary notes in circulation	Index all notes and currency	Bank deposits: Demand	Bank deposits: Time	Bank deposits: Total	Bank deposits: Index of total	Index all money
Aug. 1939	22·0	5·0	100	29·8	8·2	38·0	100	100
Dec. 1939	26·4	5·1	116	36·3	8·5	44·8	118	117
June 1940	32·6	—	—	—	—	—	—	—
Dec. 1940	37·3	6·3	162	48·9	8·7	57·6	152	155
June 1941	41·6	—	—	—	—	—	—	—
Dec. 1941	50·6	8·6	218	77·4	9·4	86·8	228	224
June 1942	64·8	—	—	—	—	—	—	—
Dec. 1942	75·3	9·4	313	108·7	7·9	116·6	308	309
June 1943	82·4	—	—	—	—	—	—	—
Dec. 1943	95·6	9·3	388	175·5	5·9	181·4	479	440
June 1944	99·0	—	—	—	—	—	—	—
Dec. 1944	116·7	9·1	464	227·8	9·0	236·8	625	560
June 1945	123·9	—	—	—	—	—	—	—

Sources. National Bank of Egypt Reports; League of Nations, *Monthly Bulletin of Statistics.*

Notes. (1) Small quantities of National Bank of Egypt notes are in circulation in the Sudan and Cyrenaica, and therefore the totals above are subject to a small systematic error.

(2) Bank deposit figures exclude Sudan.

The main comment on this table will be made after the wartime price movements have been shown, but it is interesting to note in passing that £50 and £100 notes formed some 17% of all currency and notes in circulation in December 1939, but 29% by December 1943. This is partly due to the fact that the proportion of National Bank Notes (including £50 and £100 notes) to the supply of all currency and notes had risen over these years from 84 to 91%, and partly to the general increases in prices and activity, but it is indicative of the growth of hoarding and illicit trading, as people engaged in such traffic were the chief hoarders and users of large notes.[1]

Prices

The relative movements of wholesale and retail prices over the war years are set out in Table 8.

TABLE 8. *Wholesale and retail price movements*

Date	Wholesale price index	Cost of living index
June–Aug. 1939	100	100
Dec. 1939	121	108
June 1940	130	109
Dec. 1940	143	122
June 1941	161	134
Dec. 1941	182	156
June 1942	209	178
Dec. 1942	251	215
June 1943	269	241
Dec. 1943	293	257
June 1944	313	273
Dec. 1944	330	288
June 1945	325	288

Source. League of Nations, *Monthly Bulletin of Statistics.*

Before any deductions are drawn from the statistics of Tables 7 and 8 it may be noted that, as might be expected, the general indices of wholesale and retail prices conceal wide differences in price rises of individual commodities and commodity groups. Wholesale prices of cereals, for instance, only rose from 100 to 231 between June–August 1939 and December 1943, whilst prices of edible oil rose from 100 to 329, and of paper from 100 to 1704 over the same period. One explanation of such divergences was the reduced supply and higher landed costs of imports, but the degree of control exercised inside the country was probably much more important.

[1] Cf. *National Bank of Egypt Reports*, President's address, 1944.

Variations in retail prices of some of the main items of expenditure may be seen from Table 9.

TABLE 9. *Retail prices of selected commodities*

Commodity	Aug. 1939		June 1943		June 1945	
	Price (piastres)	Index	Price (piastres)	Index	Price (piastres)	Index
Onions (oke)	0·5	100	2·5	500	5·0	1000
*Tea (lb.)	12	100	—	—	31·2	260
Meat (oke)	14	100	—	—	50·9	364
*Rice (oke)	1·7	100	3·3	194	4·0	236
*Edible oil (oke)	3·0	100	10·6	352	12·6	420
*Beans, white (oke)	2·0	100	15·0	750	20·0	1000
*Sugar, gran. (oke)	3·2	100	5·9	185	7·0	219
Spirit lamp (each)	10	100	45	450	60	600
Shoes (pair)	200	100	—	—	600	300
Woollen cloth (metre)	50	100	—	—	400	800
All food	—	100	—	180	—	241
Clothing	—	100	—	210	—	445
Fuel	—	100	—	170	—	186

Source. Oil Company statistics.

Notes. (1) 1 oke = 2¾ lb.; 97·5 piastres = £1 sterling and 100 piastres = £1 (E.).
(2) Controlled prices are used for 1943 and 1945 where they existed. These items are marked with an asterisk.

It is difficult to draw any sweeping conclusions from these figures, as the divergences of individual commodities within the food group make any simple comparisons between the rise in all food and all clothing prices rather misleading. As with wholesale price variations the main explanation probably lies in the degree of control of distribution. The supply of beans, for instance, was not reduced appreciably by reductions of imports or military demands, nor is there any evidence that internal civilian demands for normal purposes expanded in such a way as to drive prices up tenfold. The reasons why the general index rose further than the food index may be partly found in high import prices, for imported goods play a larger part in the index as a whole than in the food section, but the main point is probably the simple one that home-manufactured goods made by high-cost methods had to be substituted for imports in many cases. This certainly applied in the case of clothing.

In common with other Middle East countries, wholesale prices tended to rise further than retail prices. The explanation is to be found in the different weightings employed in the two indices, and the more consistent attempts to control some of the main items of retail sales rather than in any subsidy policy. It may be noted on this point that between August 1939 and June 1945 an Oil Company cost of living index shows a rise from 100 to 279 for their lowest paid employees, which confirms the official Government figures fairly closely.

Before we can make any comparisons between prices and money movements it is necessary to observe the spread of free prices from controlled prices. By the nature of the subject this is difficult, but commonly quoted figures for December 1943 are shown in Table 10.

TABLE 10. *Free and controlled prices, December* 1943

Commodity	Controlled	Free	Ratio
	£ *s.* *d.*	£ *s.* *d.*	
Wheat (long ton)	21 15 0	29 0 0	1·38
Sugar (long ton)	63 6 0	92 0 0	1·46

Source. Special information.

These figures do not show such a large divergence as might have been expected, but in some cases the true ratio of free to controlled prices was higher than these figures indicate, as extortionate charges were frequently made for such facilities as packing sugar in bags, and the degree of extortion was usually greater in the free markets.

Finally, to come to the comparisons between money changes and price changes, it is clear that, generally speaking, the increase in the supply of money was greater than the increases in wholesale or retail prices. The main exception to this was the period at the very beginning of the war when wholesale prices shot up rapidly on account of sterling bloc devaluations (which increased the cost of non-sterling area imports) and because of increased freight charges. Although the threat of invasion in the summer of 1942 led to a heavy demand for cash and some rush on the banks there was never in any sense a flight from the £E. There was, in fact, a rush to hold £E. by Syrians after 1943 when the £S. was made convertible, and in the free market in Syria the £E. was quoted at a substantial premium.[1]

Incomes

It is well recognized that some classes benefited in no small degree from the war, for the big landlords, contractors and merchant classes undoubtedly made large profits, but it is quite impossible to assess

[1] See p. 230.

their gain in any quantitative manner. It is true that published figures of company profits are full of statistical pitfalls for the unwary, and that one cannot generalize about the whole economy from the experiences of a few firms. Nevertheless, with these points in mind, the experience of such firms as the Industrie Meunière d'Alexandrie, which was unable to pay anything to its shareholders at all in 1939 but paid dividends of 20% in 1942 and 60% in 1943, in addition to issuing in the latter year four bonus shares for every five held in 1942, may not be without interest or significance.[1] It has already been mentioned that landlords were able to push up rents both in urban and rural areas. It is impossible to generalize safely about the extent to which rents rose, but they were commonly quoted in 1942–3 as being four times as high as pre-war levels in Cairo.[2] Inadequate as this evidence is, the conclusion can be safely drawn that many of the classes normally thought of as fixed-income receivers in Western countries were not left behind the inflationary band-wagon in Egypt.

In the absence of any adequate statistics on Egyptian wages, even in pre-war days, it is not possible to give as full a picture of changes in the war years as we could in the case of Palestine or even India. In general, urban workers obtained some increases, as Egyptian Government rates of cost of living bonus were enforceable by decree on all commercial and industrial enterprises as well as applicable to their own employees. For the lowest paid workers increments were some 60–70% of pre-war rates by June 1944. The experience of an Oil Company is shown in Table 11.

TABLE 11. *Wage rates of daily paid general labourers*

Period	Wage rates per day (in piastres)	Index	Cost of living index (Jan.–June 1939 = 100)
1. ix. 39–31. iii. 41	10	100	122 (Dec. 1940)
1. iv. 41–31. xii. 41	11	110	134 (June 1941)
1. i. 42–30. ix. 42	13	130	178 (June 1942)
1. x. 42–30. xi. 43	15	150	241 (June 1943)
1. xii. 43–June 1944	17	170	273 (June 1944)

Source. Oil Company information.

Note. Rates are for a day of normal length.

The fall in real income was not as great as a simple comparison of the above figures would suggest, as in common with many other

[1] *Egyptian Stock Exchange Yearbook*, 1944.

[2] *Foreign Commerce Weekly*, 18 September 1943.

Middle East countries hours were longer and work was more regular than before the war. Wages of labour employed by the Forces were, in general, higher than in private industry, both because rates for equivalent work were higher and because workers were more easily graded as skilled or semi-skilled. Average earnings for unskilled work in 1942 were about 12 piastres a day, and in 1945 25–30 a day, whereas in pre-war years 9 piastres was an average figure in the towns, which indicates a rise of approximately threefold by 1945. Skilled artisans frequently received up to 80–100 piastres a day in 1945 compared with 15–20 before the war.[1] Thus those industrial workers on war work received wage increases sufficient, or more than sufficient, to compensate for the increases in the cost of living, for quite apart from these wage increases, free meals and similar facilities unknown before the war were frequently provided. On the relative position of urban workers as a whole it is difficult to generalize, not only because of the lack of statistics, but because of the wide discrepancies shown in different occupations and areas by such statistics as there are.[2] Despite the greater regularity of work it is possible that there were falls in real income in the earlier war years even if this was not the case after 1942–3. There is no doubt whatever that many black-coated and similar workers were not able to increase earnings relatively to wage rates, and therefore they did suffer heavily.[3]

We have already seen that there is good reason to doubt whether the war brought any fall in real income to the fellaheen. Grain prices rose by 200%, and while prices of textiles tended to rise more it must be stressed that for many of the poorest cultivators these are not a major item of their budgets. Money rents, as we have seen, were probably not more than doubled. Little evidence is available on wages, but whereas these were often quoted at 2–3 piastres a day before the war[4] they were more frequently about 10 piastres a day by 1944. And, of course, those on Government work were often able to earn 25–30 piastres a day. Perhaps the best indication of the change in the fellaheen's position is the reduction in indebtedness.

[1] *Manchester Guardian*, 17 June 1946.

[2] *Statistical Handbook of the Middle East* shows that average weekly wages in July 1943 varied from 67 piastres (clothing manufacture) to 174 (road construction) and from 47 in Upper Egypt to 176 in the Suez area.

[3] A vivid picture of the squalor, ignorance and heavy indebtedness of Egyptian policemen is given in *Annual Report of Cairo City Police* for 1941, where it is claimed that 'this (cost of living) allowance has by no means compensated the policemen for the great rise in prices of all commodities'.

[4] Bonné, *Economic Development of the Middle East*, p. 29.

According to the Crédit Foncier Egyptien,[1] outstanding mortgages amounted to £17·66 million in 1939; by 1943 these had fallen to £9·6 million and by 1944 to £8·4 million. Similarly, arrears of payment had been reduced from £1·3 million to £583,000 and to £429,000 over the same years. Thus, even though the rural population did suffer shortages of staple consumption goods, such as textiles, tea and sugar, there is little evidence of much fall in real income. The poorer fellaheen ate more grain and vegetables; the richer ate more meat and by-products, such as chickens and eggs, which they had to sell before the war to make ends meet.

Foreign balances

The main change in the Egyptian capital position was, of course, the accumulation of sterling assets. In addition to this there was some repatriation of external debt. Estimates of these figures are set out in Table 12.

TABLE 12. *Estimated changes in sterling assets (£m.)*

Date	National Bank of Egypt holdings	Other holdings	Total holdings	Net annual increase	Debt repatriation	Gross annual increase
31. viii. 39	17	2	19	—	—	—
31. xii. 40	34	16	50	31	—	31
31. xii. 41	52	38	90	40	—	40
31. xii. 42	82	60	142	52	—	52
31. xii. 43	111	84	195	53	11	64
31. xii. 44	135	125	260	65	—	65

Source. *Bank of International Settlements Report*, 1943–4 (and evidence of Egyptian delegation at Bretton Woods Conference).

Notes. (1) 'Other holdings' of sterling are all holdings of commercial banks and other institutions and private persons.

(2) Figure of £11 million for debt repatriation is a net figure, as although £16 million of external debt was repatriated in 1943, some £5 million was contributed from external sources to the new loan floated that year.

These figures clearly do not reveal the exact change in Egypt's position on capital account, as the estimates from which they are compiled are subject to some degree of error. Nevertheless, they do show the magnitudes of the overall and annual changes reasonably well, and they are certainly sufficient to indicate the extraordinary

[1] *Annual Report* for year ending 31 October 1944. The Crédit Agricole d'Égypte also had a similar history, for it had outstanding loans of £6·0 million in 1939 and by 1943 these had fallen to £4·1 million, although they showed some tendency to rise in the following year (13*th Annual Report*, 1945).

degree to which Egypt improved her capital position as a result of the war. In fact, by the end of 1945, when balances are estimated to have stood at some level over £325 million, the equivalent of 9–10 months national income, at 1944–5 prices, had been reached. Even the improvement of India's capital position pales beside these figures, for in that country the reduction of sterling debt and increase of sterling balances amounted to some £1350 million between March 1939 and March 1945 (see Table 19, Chapter 2). This only represents about half the estimated national income for 1942–3 (see p. 32), and therefore would be a smaller fraction still of the 1945 national income, even if allowance is made for the further increase in sterling assets during the later months of 1945.

§ 3. INFLATION AND CONTROLS

Our first task is to assess the importance of the various forms of income-generating expenditure in Egypt during the war period. We have already seen the magnitude of annual military expenditure in Table 1, but before we go on to discuss the way in which this reacted on the economy we must put it in perspective with the other main factors.

First, deficit financing was practically non-existent in Egypt. In fact, there was a surplus over the whole of the war period after 1939–40, and this acted as an offset to the expenditure of the military authorities. Details are shown in Table 13.

TABLE 13. *Revenue and expenditure (£000's)*

Year	Revenue	Expenditure	Surplus (+) Deficit (−)
1939–40	39,408	41,174	− 1,766
1940–41	43,677	42,559	+ 1,118
1941–42	56,336	46,062	+10,274
1942–43	67,059	56,553	+10,506
1943–44	77,190	68,940	+ 8,250
1944–45	87,731	84,959	+ 2,772

Source. Journal Officiel, various issues.

Note. As from 1940–1, the budget of the State Railways, Telephones and Telegraphs was incorporated in the general budget.

These budget figures do not cover all transactions, however, as purchases of the cotton crop were made in 1941–2 out of loan funds, and some repayment of debt was affected in 1943–4 in conjunction with the Conversion operations. But the cotton purchases only involved expenditure of £17½ million, and this was in turn recouped when the crops were disposed of to other purchasers; and the repayment of debt to internal holders only amounted to some £5 million.[1] Whether any appreciable fraction of this sum was spent is open to doubt. Therefore all in all the extra-budgetary expenditure cannot be said to impair the general impression of a substantial annual surplus.[2]

Secondly, in all years except 1939 there was an import surplus, and from 1942 to 1944 it was really substantial. Table 14 shows the details.

TABLE 14. *Imports and Exports of Merchandise (£m.)*

Year	Imports (c.i.f.)	Exports (f.o.b.) and re-exports	Balance: export surplus (+) import surplus (−)
1939	34·7	36·0	+ 1·3
1940	32·2	30·0	− 2·2
1941	34·5	24·7	− 9·8
1942	57·5	21·8	−35·7
1943	39·9	27·6	−12·3
1944	53·6	30·0	−23·6

Source. Customs Returns.

Notes. (1) Figures include trade with Sudan.
(2) Estimated gold imports are included.
(3) Military and N.A.A.F.I. stores mainly excluded (but see p. 133).

It is possible to form a rough estimate of net invisible exports and private capital imports by comparing the figures of military expenditure and import surplus with the growth of sterling assets, as shown in Table 15.

It is clear from Table 15 that although other external items were of some importance in 1940 and 1944, the main influence in the years when the inflationary process in Egypt was at its height was military expenditure. We shall therefore consider the problems arising from military expenditure and then briefly glance at other factors, such as external trade, just as we did in the case of India and Palestine.

[1] Some £21 million was repaid by April 1944 (*The Economist*, 22 April 1944), but of this £16 million was to external holders (Table 12). The balance of the unconverted debt (about £12 million) was held by persons living in enemy-occupied territory.

[2] It is significant that Egyptian Government deposits with the National Bank expanded from £2·9 million in December 1938 to £24·0 million by December 1943, and to £64·0 million by December 1944 (*Annual Balance Sheets, National Bank of Egypt*).

As in other countries in the sterling area military expenditure was financed by credit creation against sterling assets, in so far as imports of merchandise or gold or repayment of sterling loans did not provide sufficient £E. The enormous amount of money created for this purpose went straight into the active circulation, and although this is true of other countries it had peculiarly vicious results in Egypt. In the first place, the Egyptian authorities probably had little power to control the effects. It is doubtful whether they knew the exact amount of total current military expenditure, although, of course, the

TABLE 15. *Sterling assets, military expenditure and import surplus (£m.)*

(1) Year	(2) Net increase of sterling assets	(3) Military expenditure	(4) Import surplus	(5) Other external items (derived by subtracting the algebraic sum of cols. 3 and 4 from col. 2)
1940	(31)	15	−3	(+19)
1941	40	48	−11	+3
1942	52	75	−36	+13
1943	64	77	−12	−1
1944	65	57	−25	+33

Source. Previous tables.

Notes. (1) The figure of £19 million for 1939–40 is definitely too high, as £31 million represents the net increase in assets from August 1939 to December 1940, whereas military expenditure and the import surplus figures only refer to the calendar year 1940. It will be remembered that military expenditure was £5 million in 1939, and that there was an export surplus of £1·3 million in that year. A more accurate figure would be of the order of £14 million.

(2) The slightly different import surplus figures are due to the exclusion of trade with the Sudan, which does not involve receipts or payments in foreign currency.

(3) It is probable that in some years figures of military expenditure are too high, as French remittances to Egypt to cover costs of locally stationed troops, etc., appear to have been larger than was really necessary and to have contained some capital exports from Syria. No figures are available.

increases in notes and currency issued were a partial guide. It is certain that they did not know either current levels in different areas and industries, or future levels as a whole. The general policy of the military authorities was to make purchases, or at best short-term contracts, and thus it was never known whether any particular demand was likely to be purely temporary or not. The Army itself ran very few factories, and apart from the Government petroleum refinery at Suez and a few similar enterprises, private enterprise was responsible for all production. There was no proper system of placing purchases or contracts through any centralized machinery, and thus no overall attempt to adjust demand for economic resources to the available supplies. This was particularly true of demands for foodstuffs which local commanders were encouraged to purchase in their own areas, and although the overall demand for Egyptian foodstuffs was not large,[1] a situation such as this was bound to produce local shortages. Similarly, heavy demands for unskilled labour in specific areas could only be satisfied by offering high wages. In the second place, quite apart from these limitations, it is doubtful whether the Egyptian authorities were particularly willing to attempt to soften the impact of war expenditure on incomes. It is true that attempts were made to limit margins in distribution, but these were never successful. Crops were also requisitioned at fixed prices in the later war years, but there was no policy to keep the increases in the incomes of cultivators below the increase in the cost of living as there was in the Sudan. Thus prices paid to the cultivator for cane sugar were raised successively from 37 milliemes[2] per cantar in pre-war days to 71 by 1943 and 95 by 1944. Wheat prices to cultivators were advanced from £3 per ardeb in 1943 to £4 in 1944, largely on the insistence of the landlord interests in the Egyptian Parliament. There were no real attempts to limit manufacturers' or merchants' incomes by any blanket anti-profiteering ordinance. Wages, too, were allowed to move in any fashion in the early war years, even though a system of fixing minimum cost of living bonuses which became operative later did introduce some orderliness into the scene.

To anticipate later discussion, there appear to have been three main reasons for this failure to attempt to control incomes. First, it is possible that the crucial importance of controlling incomes rather than prices was not recognized. Suggestions of increases in indirect taxation by the M.E.S.C. authorities were, for instance, rebutted on the grounds that these would raise prices and therefore increase the degree of inflation. Secondly, even if income control was recognized as essential to check the inflationary process it is doubtful whether the oligarchy of industrialists and landlords behind the Government were particularly anxious to check it. Thirdly, the Government itself probably felt that it could not administer the necessary controls with the requisite degree of ability.

We must now ask what attempts were made to check consumption expenditure out of higher incomes by taxation or savings. The

[1] See p. 129.

[2] 1000 milliemes = £1 (E.); 1 cantar = 44·9 kg.; 1 ardeb = 150 kg. (for wheat).

relation of tax receipts to Government and military expenditure is shown in Table 16.

TABLE 16. *Tax receipts and expenditure (£m.)*

Year	Tax receipts	Total receipts	% tax receipts/ Govt. exp.	% tax receipts/ Govt. exp. and mil. exp.	% total receipts/Govt. exp. and mil. exp.
1939–40	29·6	39·4	71	64	85
1940–41	28·3	43·7	66	49	76
1941–42	35·6	56·3	77	37	60
1942–43	45·0	67·1	80	34	51
1943–44	50·9	77·2	73	35	53
1944–45	58·7	87·7	69	41	62

Source. Journal Officiel.

Notes. (1) Tax receipts include all receipts except those from Government trading, railways, telephones and telegraph and ports.

(2) Military expenditure for 1939 is added to expenditure for 1939–40, 1940 to 1940–1, etc.

From this table it can be seen that the ratio of both tax receipts and total receipts to the sum of Government expenditure and military expenditure showed an abrupt decline to 1942–3 and then a slight rise afterwards. The main changes in public finance were the introduction of taxes on income. Before 1939 direct taxation of incomes was unknown, but in that year three new taxes were introduced on earned income, unearned income, and company profits and in 1941 an excess profits tax was also started. By means of these taxes, which were successively increased, direct taxation under these headings was raised from £2·7 million in 1939–40 to £15·4 million in 1943–4. Furthermore, an additional tax, which was simply a percentage addition to other taxes, was introduced in 1940 at the rate of 1%. By 1944 it had been increased to 10%, and it yielded £2·5 million during the first nine months of 1944–5. Despite the decline in imports, receipts from customs duties, excise and tobacco increased from £18·5 million in 1939–40 to £24·1 million in 1943–4. Land-tax receipts fell slightly, but trading profits of railways and other State concerns, as might be expected, rose considerably. Railway receipts, for instance, were £13·6 million in 1943–4 against £7 million in 1940–1, and railway rates were by mid-1943 100% above the pre-war level.

The heavy budget surpluses in the crucial years of the war are proof that quite substantial efforts were made to offset Allied expenditure. Even in 1943, when the ratio of taxation to Government expenditure plus military expenditure was lowest, it was still higher than in any other country in the Middle East. But it is doubtful whether this tax burden was distributed fairly, or whether it was as great as it could have been even when the fact that Egypt was not at war is taken into account.[1] In 1943, for instance, income-tax returns were such that anybody earning £700 per annum or more, whether married or single, paid 12% of his income[2] in tax, but this ratio did not increase *at all* on higher incomes. The standard for E.P.T. was 12% of capital invested, and although rates were graduated the maximum was 50% for the greater part of the war. There also appear to have been many cases of people who escaped assessment altogether or were under-assessed, although it is only fair to add that this was partly the fault of the military authorities, who were not prepared to co-operate with the Egyptian tax officials by disclosing adequate details of Service contracts. Nor did income taxes or E.P.T. apply to earnings from land, which was perhaps the greatest omission of all, as land tax rates were unchanged and so the large landowners were able to reap their war profits unhindered. Finally, as we have already seen, misconceived objections to increasing indirect taxes were raised and these prevented any substantial advances in that direction.

Voluntary savings in Egypt did not make any contribution towards checking the inflationary spiral. No public loans were raised except for the purposes of financing cotton purchases in 1941 and 1942 and converting old internal debt and repatriating external debt in 1943. For the latter operations a net sum of about £33 million was received from internal sources.[3] It must be emphasized that these were the only attempts to drain off purchasing power by public loans, and throughout the war period there were no real efforts to encourage voluntary savings as a general anti-inflationary weapon.[4]

Gold was sold from November 1943 to April 1944 by the leading clearing banks on both British and American account, but the amount

[1] 'Egypt still remains one of the least taxed countries in the world' (Address by President of National Bank, 1945).

[2] If earned in business.

[3] *The Economist*, 22 April 1944. Actually some £46 million was received through conversion of old loans and some £38 m. which represented new subscriptions. But about £5 million of this came from overseas sources.

[4] There was a campaign run by the British Embassy which was mainly intended for British residents.

was not large enough to influence the course of events appreciably. It is estimated that some £1 million was sold in 1943 and some £3 million in 1944 at prices which ranged from about 90*s*. to 95*s*. for a gold sovereign. But Allied expenditure was running at the rate of £5–6 million a month at that time, and even if the purchasing power mopped up by these sales did not come out of hoards, the contribution of the whole process as a counterblast to rising incomes and prices cannot have been very great, as there is no trace of any connexion between gold prices and the general price level such as would indicate indirect psychological effects.

We have already seen that consumers' rationing did not ensure a very equitable distribution of goods in Egypt. Kerosene and sugar were the only commodities rationed by coupon, and in both cases the towns were favoured rather than the country and the rich rather than the poor. Similarly, tea and popular textiles were allocated on the basis of previous consumption levels. It cannot be claimed that rationing in Egypt was ever a means of cutting down consumption expenditure appreciably. In the first place, the number of commodities rationed was small. In addition to kerosene, sugar, tea and popular textiles, the only other restrictions of importance were the imposition in 1942 of three meatless days a week (in which purchase and sale of meat were forbidden), various restrictions on the number of courses served and prices charged for meals served in restaurants, and a percentage allocation system of rationing edible oil. Wheat consumption was also cut down by adulterating flour with millet or rice after July 1942. Secondly, the ration of these individual commodities was liberal, in the early war years at any rate. Kerosene and sugar supplies were maintained at pre-war consumption levels until September 1942 (sugar, for instance, for class 1 families in Cairo was 800 dirhems[1] per head per month). The restrictions on hotels and restaurants were not introduced until 1943, and the percentage allocation rationing of edible oil only started in September 1943. Thirdly, the very people who had surplus purchasing power as a result of the war were given most opportunities to spend it. It was precisely the consumption expenditure of the merchant and business classes which any rationing system should have cut down, but in actual fact the system of differential rationing allowed them to purchase much the same quantities as before. Fourthly, quite apart from these deficiencies there were many defects in administration of the various

[1] 800 dirhems = 2 okes = $5\frac{1}{2}$ lb.

schemes. Typical of these were the inconsistencies such as occurred in sugar and kerosene rationing in 1944. On 30 July the Minister of Supplies announced a cut in kerosene and sugar rations; on 31 July it was announced that this would not apply to all rations but only to those 'not fixed in conformity with the regulations'. In actual fact when people went to purchase their rations in August they found that the reduction was a general one. On 14 August the Minister reversed the decision and said that the cut in supplies would be restored, but neither in August nor September was there any sign of the goods.[1] Of course, the fact that supplies of rationed goods were frequently not available (and sugar was a conspicuous example of this)[2] was a means of restricting consumption expenditure, but in so far as it drove people to purchase their supplies on the black market where there was never any shortage it increased expenditure.

Finally, quite apart from the inequality of the rationing schemes and the failure to restrict consumption expenditure, there was no attempt to use rationing as a lever to force grain holdings on to the market. This criticism is not so important in Egypt as in other countries, for there was little hoarding by cultivators.[3] But it may well be that the combined effect of high prices and shortages of essential consumer goods in rural areas was to make cultivators consume more of their grain or sell more of it to dealers only too anxious to add to their speculative hoards.

Nor can it be claimed that direct methods of price control were a great success in Egypt. A Central Price Regulation Committee fixed maximum prices for consumer goods from as early as 1939, and by 1944 this list covered some fifty foods and other essentials.[4] Various methods were also adopted to ensure the proper distribution of supplies whether from foreign or home sources. Pools were formed of some essential imports, and in 1943 an order was introduced regulating maximum profits of dealers in imports; Lend-Lease supplies all went through Government channels; a number of general restrictions clamping down on speculative traders by a system of registration, limiting traders' stocks of goods to four months' demand, and ordering retailers to display prices in shop windows were introduced at various times. The supply of grain to the right channels was ensured by requisitioning from producers at fixed prices, and in 1943,

[1] See *Egyptian Gazette*, 5 September 1944 and 12 September 1944.
[2] See *Économiste Égyptienne*, 24 October 1943 and 9 January 1944.
[3] See p. 160.
[4] *Egyptian Gazette*, 23 July 1944.

for instance, some 1·1 million metric tons of wheat, barley, millet and rice were secured by this means out of a total production of about 3 million tons. The supply of cloth was regulated by forcing manufacturers to produce a certain percentage of popular textiles, and a general control over wholesalers and retailers was enforced. Similar regulations were introduced for other manufactures such as hosiery. The price of flour and bread to consumers was kept stable from December 1941 to April 1944 by a Government subsidy, which was used to bear costs of grain transport or storage,[1] but after that date there was a rise in costs and prices owing to a fall in grain yield per acre. There was also some subsidization of sugar and kerosene prices in the later stages.

Many of these schemes, however, were far better on paper than in practice. It is broadly true to say that those goods which were rationed or allocated—sugar, tea, kerosene, meat, edible oil, popular textiles and bread—were more frequently available at controlled prices than unrationed goods, but there were many deficiencies in the system. Even if rations were available at controlled prices (and that was far from always being the case with sugar at any rate) extra supplies could always be bought anywhere at prices above the controlled level. Moreover, these controls meant very little in rural areas where, after all, the great mass of the population lives. Imported goods, such as fertilizers, iron and steel bars, crockery, were sometimes available to purchasers at reasonable margins such as 20–30% above c.i.f. prices, but for many commodities control of supply and distribution was so perfunctory that all the parasitic classes of speculators were able to reap their harvests and prices went extremely high. Chemicals, dyes, paints and paper[2] are all examples of this. And quite apart from failures to enforce established controls there were deliberate reversals of policy such as in early 1942, when controls were temporarily thrown overboard and grain prices increased by 50% in the hope of persuading hoarders to part with supplies.[3]

Therefore, military expenditure generated great increases in incomes, and the attempts to prevent these incomes increasing or, at

[1] This, of course, made the Government budget surplus less than it otherwise would have been, which was, *pro tanto*, undesirable from a counter-inflationary point of view.

[2] Wholesale paper prices rose by 1604% between August 1939 and December 1943.

[3] *The Economist*, 8 August 1942.

least, to restrain consumption expenditure, were not very successful. It is now time to survey the attempts to tackle the situation from the supply side.

In Table 6 we saw that even by 1941 there was a substantial reduction in the imports of many different commodities such as fertilizers, coal, wood, cotton piecegoods, iron and steel products, and machinery. The normal dependence on imports of raw materials and manufactures of this sort was bound to make the supply position difficult, however good the administration, but it is also probable that official policy made it more difficult than it need have been. Until September 1941 there were no official restrictions on imports into Egypt, and even then only a few goods such as fruit, biscuits, soap, cement and hardware were completely prohibited, and a relatively small number of others subjected to a licensing and quota system. It was not until 1942, on the insistence of M.E.S.C., that any severe import restrictions were imposed, and these really did not come into effective operation until 1943. The result of this was that at the period of the war when shipping rather than availability of supplies was the limitation on overall tonnage imported, semi-luxuries were imported at the expense of essentials. For instance, in 1941 some 8·7 million litres of beer were imported by private traders (for subsequent sale to the Allied Armies), and this may be estimated to have taken up about 15,000 net tonnage of shipping. 1938 imports of beer were 3·5 million litres. On the other hand, imports of cotton textiles, which were 16·9 million tons in 1938, were reduced to 7·5 million tons in 1941. It must be emphasized that this was a real and not merely a theoretical choice, for external supplies of textiles were available at the time and a considerable amount of beer could have been produced from internal resources. It is a clear example of where hardship may be inflicted on the community at large through the weakness of a Government and the eagerness of private traders to exploit the most profitable opportunities without any regard for the public interest. Even in the later war years, when regulations were so much stricter, a perpetual battle had to be fought by the M.E.S.C. authorities to scotch conspiracies of Egyptian and American traders to secure non-basic imports by illicit means.

There were several reasons why it was not found possible to expand agricultural output except in such lines as vegetable production. The most important was the shortage of fertilizers on which Egyptian agriculture is so completely dependent. In pre-war years, approximately 500,000 tons were imported annually, but in the war years imports were as follows:[1]

	000's *metric tons*		
1939	471	1942	149
1940	357	1943	159
1941	5	1944	272

The tremendous reduction in 1941 was partly due to factors outside Egyptian control. Some 70% of the volume of pre-war imports had come from Norway, Germany and Chile. Supplies could no longer be obtained from the first two, and the difficulties of securing shipping for the long haul from Chile explain the reduction in supplies from that country. On the other hand, it was reported that the U.S.S.R. offered fertilizers to the Egyptian Government in 1941, but it lost its opportunity by taking so long to consider the offer.[2]

The second main reason why it was impossible to expand output is that there is hardly any more land which can be brought under cultivation in Egypt except by extensive land reclamation and irrigation projects, and in wartime these were extremely difficult to carry out. The work on the Esna barrage was held up through lack of materials; the labour normally employed on reclamation work by the Government was diverted to military works; the machinery of some of the big land companies was also used by the Armies. Furthermore, the unceasing battle for adequate water supplies was rendered more difficult by the reduction of imports of new irrigation machinery such as pumps,[3] and the impossibility of obtaining spare parts during the war for machines which were of Continental manufacture. Other import reductions, too, played some part in restricting agricultural output. Seed potatoes, for instance, were no longer available from previous sources, and although some did come from the U.K., shipments were not frequent. Agricultural machinery imports practically ceased altogether,[4] but it is doubtful whether this was so very im-

[1] In assessing the importance of the reduction in fertilizer supplies it must be remembered that the proportion of total acreage devoted to cotton was much less in the war years, and although the evidence is not conclusive it is not improbable that more fertilizers are needed per acre of cotton than of grain.

[2] *Économiste Égyptienne*, 19 September 1944.

[3] See Table 6. In 1938, 1095 tons of pumps (steam and i.c.) were imported, but in 1943 only 105; similarly, imports of stationary engines (i.c.) were reduced from 958 to 81 over the same period.

[4] See Table 6. 305 tractors were imported in 1939, only 29 in 1943.

portant in view of the system of land tenure and the normally primitive methods of cultivation.

Thirdly, although the conversion of cotton-growing land to food crops did secure a large increase in acreage under food crops,[1] the scheme was not without its drawbacks. Normal crop rotations were upset by the continued growing of grain without the interspersion of cotton crops, and this was a contributory factor in reducing yield per acre. Further, it should be remembered that it was not until 1941 that any really energetic measures were taken to reduce cotton acreage; the driving force in that year was the British Purchasing Commission, which refused to take more than half the crop or to pay more than the previous year's prices.

Finally, the structure of Egyptian agriculture must be taken into account. In 1940, out of some 2·5 million proprietors some 1·76 millions owned less than 1 feddan each (with a total of 724,000 feddans) and some 12,000 owned over 50 feddans each (with a total of 2,168,000 feddans). This extreme subdivision of holdings inevitably makes it difficult to appeal to the great majority of cultivators by normal propaganda methods and makes it impossible to secure any sudden changes in technique. Nor is there any evidence that the larger estates are normally well run and anxious to develop new methods, for very many landlords are absentees taking little interest in their lands. Such measures as the establishment of rural centres in March 1944 with the idea of improving agricultural efficiency[2] could hardly make much impression in these circumstances.

There were several reasons why industrial output could not expand beyond fairly narrow limits. In the first place there was no control over man-power at all.[3] In the absence of any statistical information it cannot be stated with any certainty but only with a fair degree of confidence that the attractive conditions of military employment robbed civilian industry of many key skilled workers. Undoubtedly, the turn-over of unskilled labour in industry was very greatly increased as a result of military demands, for a frequent occurrence in the textile industry, for instance, was for unskilled rural workers to start work there and then migrate to military work after a few weeks. Secondly, the lack of capital equipment was important, for before the war the average size of firms was very small (only 3% of establishments

[1] See Table 4. [2] *Anglo-Egyptian Chamber of Commerce Journal*, June 1944.

[3] Except a military order (no. 147 of 16 June 1941) giving the Government authority to requisition the services of skilled workmen.

enumerated in the 1937 census of industry employed more than nine persons), and as an indication of the amount of capital equipment, only 6659 establishments out of 92,000 used any motive power at all. When it is remembered that machinery imports during the war years fell to a very low level (e.g. tonnage of machines and looms for weaving fell from 3522 in 1938 to 291 in 1943), the inherent limitations of Egyptian industry become apparent.[1] Thirdly, although attempts were made to allocate key materials, such as tin, coke, jute sacks, tyres and cement, some industries suffered from raw-material shortages. Productive capacity was available to turn out more edible oils but materials were lacking; in 1944 leather factories had to reduce output because of a shortage of tanning materials and reduced imports of hides from the Sudan;[2] some 20,000 hands were reported to be out of work in hand-loom weaving in 1943 owing to lack of yarn.[3] Finally, as in other countries, there were many transport difficulties due to the reduction of imports of road and rail transportation equipment, the immense Army demands for transport facilities and the small supply of coal, which made it necessary to convert many locomotives to oil firing, with some consequent reductions in efficiency. Even when production was increased it was often by very uneconomic methods as firms were so very small. In the glass industry, for instance, total output was only about 9000–12,000 tons per year in 1943, but there were twenty firms sharing this output. The fact that the manufacturers, no less than the merchants and the landlords, were willing to seize every opportunity to exploit both the Egyptian consumer and the British taxpayer pushed prices up still further.

We must now look very briefly at other items which were considered at the beginning of the section: Egyptian Government finance, imports and exports of merchandise, and the net balance of invisible items and movements of private capital.

On the subject of Egyptian Government finance it is not necessary to make any further comments, as the extra-budgetary transactions had negligible effects on the recorded annual surpluses of receipts over expenditure.

Nor was there ever any problem of increased incomes due to

[1] It may be noted that one of the main textile mills was able to increase output by 19% after the arrival of spare parts in 1944.

[2] *Report of Chamber of Egyptian Leather Industries*, July 1944.

[3] *Report of Egyptian Federation of Industry*, 1943.

annual export surpluses as in India. The very substantial import surplus every year from 1940 to 1944 was a powerful counterweight to inflationary forces. It is not easy to see any secondary effects of external trade in merchandise, for there is no evidence to show that Egypt exported commodities which could ill be spared (there was a tight control over exports of food surpluses, for instance), nor is it apparent that exporters' incomes were increased unduly by exporting to higher priced countries. No index of average import prices is available to compare with an index of internal wholesale or retail prices, but, excepting a few commodities in the early war years, it is doubtful whether Egypt had the same difficulties as Palestine on account of import prices. The main reason for this is that the bulk of her imports were manufactured goods and raw materials, and these, coming mainly from the Western hemisphere or India, did not show great price rises such as wheat from Syria or barley from Iraq, despite the increases in c.i.f. due to war risks and the long hauls round the Cape. It is probably true that average import prices increased faster than average home prices in the first years of the war, but as there was no close relationship between the cost of living index and the wage level, as in Palestine, the result was not serious.

Finally, we have to take 'other external items' into account, and the estimates in Table 15 show that on balance these were an income-generating item in all years except 1943. External payments decreased owing to the cessation of interest payments to European holders of Egyptian securities, the reduction in expenditure by Egyptian nationals or foreign residents on overseas travel, and the smaller use of foreign shipping services. The two main reasons for increased receipts were the purchase of Egyptian balances by Syrian nationals after 1943,[1] and the fact that the purchases of cotton by the M.O.S. were often completed before the crop was shipped. As the holdings of cotton stocks in Egypt were higher in 1944 than in 1939, there was an apparent balance in Egypt's favour on this account. The exact division of these external items between current and capital accounts is unknown, but clearly the total influence cannot have been very great in comparison with the overriding factor of military expenditure.

[1] See p. 230.

§4. CRITIQUE OF WAR ORGANIZATION

It is clear that there were many reasons why large rises in prices and incomes were inevitable in Egypt during the war. The importance of Egypt, both as a base for active operations and as a vital link in the system of communications, meant that additional military demands on her resources were likely to be large which, *prima facie*, meant injection of new money into the active circulation and rising prices and incomes. The facts that these military demands were never exactly known to the Egyptian authorities, and that they mainly took the form of employing unskilled labour or making individual purchases rather than long-term contracts, made it difficult to devise any adequate and continuous anti-inflationary policy. In the nature of the case it was difficult to secure popular assent to further increases in taxation when a large annual budget surplus was being achieved in the country, and when the country was not at war. The population could hardly be expected to see that measures to restrain the growth in the volume of money demand were very necessary when the bill for the defence of Egypt was being footed by other countries. The wartime reductions in imports of key materials and goods, such as coal, wood, paper, textiles, and above all fertilizers, both impeded production and enforced cuts in consumption. Moreover, there was a surfeit of troubles in 1941–2 (not unlike the Indian experiences of 1942). In the first place fertilizer imports went down to 5000 tons. Secondly, the normal routine of the country's economic activity was upset by the very real fear of invasion. This gave rise to persistent rumours and was a golden opportunity for the hordes of rapacious speculators waiting to seize any opportunity of profit for themselves. Thirdly, there was a rain failure, and as a consequence there was a crisis of grain supplies in May 1942, disaster only being averted by the early collection of the new spring crop.

Quite apart from purely wartime considerations, the normal features of Egyptian economic organization in themselves presented many difficulties. Most of the usual characteristics of primary producing countries were to be found. The administration was small and there was no possibility of recruiting many additional workers of the right type. This was a particularly severe handicap in income-tax assessment and collection. Furthermore, the corruption and inefficiency of the administration were marked in pre-war days, even when judged by Middle East standards, and the inevitable result of scarcity and high prices without adequate compensation of higher wages to public servants was to make matters worse. There was no pre-war tradition whatever of interference with economic affairs, as they were considered to be a matter for private enterprise only. Perhaps the best indication of this is the scarcity and defective nature of the statistical material available. Nor were the merchant and manufacturing classes and landlords distinguished by their concern for the poorer classes of the population, or by their regard for established laws if these interfered with their own potential profits.[1] The war was for them the opportunity of a lifetime to increase their wealth. The poorer classes themselves were apathetic and uninterested, and this was not surprising in view of the fact that the country was not at war until 1945. The absence of an organized money market or of any classes traditionally willing to save[2] did not make it easy to float loans, although there is reason to believe that this difficulty was exaggerated.[3] The pre-war structure of industry where establishments were very small, and agriculture where all available land was cultivated and holdings were minute, imposed severe bottlenecks on output, especially where imports of industrial machinery and agricultural fertilizers were reduced so much. Finally, as in the case of India, any appreciation of the currency would not have helped materially to check inflation. Allied demands for Egyptian resources were completely inelastic; there were no difficulties with high import prices as in Palestine, and there is no evidence that the speculative activities of the commercial classes were due to any lack of confidence in the £E., or that they would have been mitigated by raising the parity with sterling.

But these reasons do not adequately account for the extent of the rises in prices and incomes which did occur over the war years. In many ways Egypt had far less burdens imposed on her in wartime than other countries and was much better equipped to meet them. First, peak military expenditure at 1939 prices was only about £2·4 per head in Egypt compared with, for instance, £9·4 per head in Palestine. National income per head in Palestine in 1939 was about £20, whereas in Egypt it was estimated to be about £12,[4] but the general deduction is that the war demands on Egypt were less than on Palestine.[5]

[1] In 1942, for instance, the King sold all his grain to the Government at a low fixed price, but no other great landlords were observed to follow his example.

[2] The richer classes often prefer to live luxuriously. [3] See p. 161. [4] See p. 128.

[5] This conclusion is reinforced if the relative increases of internal defence expenditure and falls in volumes of imports and exports are taken into account.

If we deflate annual military expenditure by the cost of living index in each country in order to reduce the expenditure for each war year to 1939 prices and then sum the adjusted annual expenditures, we obtain a total of £150 million in Egypt and £62 million in Palestine for the years 1939–44 (inclusive). This indicates an average annual military expenditure per head of £1. 9*s*. in Egypt and £6. 8*s*. in Palestine, and therefore there is little justification for claiming that the burden borne by Egypt was intensified because it was more prolonged.

Secondly, the types of demands made on Egypt were not exacting. The main demand was for unskilled labour, which did not impose nearly as heavy a burden as if she had been called on to supply a vast amount of foodstuffs for consumption by the Armies or for exports. It is precisely this labour which is normally most plentiful in Egypt and which can be spared without any real imposition on productive capacity or civilian consumption. Even though Egypt was called on to produce manufactured goods for the Armies and the other civilian populations of the Middle East, there is little ground to suppose that war demands fell on those resources which could ill be spared as in India.

Thirdly, Egypt is normally self-sufficing for many of her needs and is far more fortunately situated in this respect than most of the other countries dealt with in this survey. There was a great deficiency of fertilizers, but other falls in imports were not so catastrophic as in other countries. Oil supplies, for instance, were amply sufficient to fill the place of coal. Furthermore, Egypt was not troubled appreciably by a phenomenon which is normally attributed to all primary countries. The cultivators as a whole did not hoard their produce with an eye on future consumption or future rises in prices. For this there were two simple reasons; the soil of Egypt is normally damp for storage underground and few small cultivators possess any storage accommodation above ground.[1]

Finally, there is another cogent reason why it should not have been difficult to impose controls fairly effectively in Egypt, even given the deficiencies of the administrative machinery and the apathy of the population. Egypt, unlike India or the Sudan, is a small country—or at least the cultivated portions are. This should have made it relatively easy to requisition supplies from cultivators, control movements and distribution and avoid local shortages.

[1] It is significant that a large amount had to be spent on constructing extra silos in 1943 for wheat storage. The following passage may also not be without interest: 'And he (Joseph) gathered up all the food of the seven years which were in the land of Egypt, and laid up the food in the *cities*: the food of the field, which was round about every city, laid he up in the same' (my brackets and italics) (Genesis xli. 48).

It is abundantly clear that the inflationary process in Egypt assumed large dimensions because of the absence of adequate controls. We have, indeed, already seen that there were no controls over skilled labour, no effective restrictions of imports till 1942, no proper premium bonds or voluntary savings campaigns, and that such controls as rationing and price fixing were not effective in practice. The main reason for this was simple. The real rulers in Egypt were the great merchants, manufacturers and landowners who were making fortunes out of the increased activity and prices. It was to their interest for this movement to continue, for the further it went the more did they gain. There can be little doubt that this was the real reason for the passivity of the Egyptian Government. This attitude only really showed signs of weakening when it was feared the sterling balances might be nearing such a high figure that the prospect of repayment would be dimmed. This seems to be the true explanation why more loans were not floated; the normal excuses of Moslem antipathy to usury and the absence of money-market machinery seem a little thin when the outstanding success of the 1943 Conversion operations is recalled. On this point it may be noted that the Koran also condemns hoarding, but it can hardly be said that there was great eagerness to follow this injunction.

There was no excessive keenness to take effective counter-inflationary measures, but there seem to have been cases of false reasoning about some of those which were taken. The crucial importance of controlling incomes rather than prices in a country where the cost of living index is not closely related to any wages mechanism does not seem to have been grasped. As we have seen, it was considered that indirect taxation could not be taken any further because it would push up prices. Furthermore, rationing of consumers' goods was designed to favour the towns rather than the country. Quite apart from questions of economic welfare involved in the lower standard of life in rural areas, this meant that it was precisely those people whose production was necessary—the grain cultivators—who were starved of the necessary inducements.

Finally, it is possible that loans could have been floated by the British authorities, even if the Egyptian Government was unwilling or unprepared. This would have involved paying higher rates of interest than on sterling balances, but if the price rise had thereby been reduced the aggregate value of the loans might clearly have been much smaller than the massive proportions which sterling balances eventually assumed.

CHAPTER V

SUDAN[1]

§ 1. PHYSICAL CHANGES

Man-power

Wartime demands for man-power in the Sudan were not heavy even in comparison with other Middle East countries. The main change was the growth of the Sudan Defence Force, which had a strength of 4500 in 1939 but grew to 26,000 by 1944. A number of additional workers were employed by the British War Department, the Sudan Government Departments and the Defence Force, but the peak number of all these never exceeded 10,000.[2] Therefore the total direct man-power drain was only about 30,000 out of a population of about 6·5 millions. It is true that the main demands were concentrated on the northern regions, and that there was, as elsewhere, a heavy demand for skilled labour. Furthermore, there was indirect absorption of labour on war activities by the larger commercial firms, but although no accurate estimate is available the number cannot have been nearly as large as that of auxiliary workers employed by public departments. It certainly does not impair the general impression of a relatively light demand for labour.

Production

The main impact of war upon the Sudan's resources may be seen from the statistics of military expenditure presented in Table 1.

TABLE 1. *Estimated military expenditure*

Year	Expenditure (£000's)	Price index (cost of living) (1938 = 100)
1939	297	100
1940	1052	110
1941	4583	130
1942	3418	151
1943	3167	177
1944	1018	160

Source. Special estimate.

Notes. (1) Figures refer to all Allied military expenditure, including pay of troops (net of any expenditure on N.A.A.F.I. goods).
(2) £ are sterling.
(3) Prices are for December of each year.

[1] Unless otherwise stated, financial statistics are in £E. [2] Special information.

No figures of national income are available at all for the Sudan, but if we deflate the peak figure (1941) by the price index, it may be seen that average expenditure per head at 1939 prices was only about £0·60. This is low in comparison with Egypt (£2·4) and lower still in comparison with Palestine (£9·4), and it is very doubtful whether national income per head is so very much less than in Egypt. On the other hand, it should be made clear that the bulk of this expenditure was in the northern areas, as the south was hardly touched at all by the war, and therefore the impact of war expenditure may have been more serious than the figures suggest.

This expenditure took many forms.[1] The British Government contributed to the upkeep of the Sudan Defence Force and its auxiliaries; labour was employed direct by the War Department on airfield and road construction; a number of manufactured goods, such as camp equipment, leather goods, stationery and tentage, were produced; some agricultural products were exported on Army account (e.g. cotton seed, timber), and a good deal of servicing and conversion work on lorries, guns and railway trucks was performed by the Sudan Government Stores, Railways and Public Works departments; finally, there was the personal expenditure of British troops, although this was a small item.

In addition to British military expenditure, the Sudan Government paid all the cost of the maintenance and expansion of the Sudan Defence Force for a year after war broke out; after that it paid a fixed annual contribution based on 1939 expenditure.[2] Furthermore, three free gifts of £100,000 each were made—two to His Majesty's Government and one to the Indian Government.[3]

The changes in the volume of exports can be seen from Table 2. As a result of the 25% cut in cotton acreage adopted to free land for food crops, cotton exports, which are by far the most important item, were reduced to lower levels. The most important other point to note is the increased exports of cattle and sheep which were mainly sent to Egypt to feed the Allied Armies. Sudan exports of sesame and cotton seed also supplied an appreciable share of the oil requirements of the Allied Armies and civilians in the Middle East countries.

Other changes in output during the war years were not substantial.

[1] See Henderson, *Survey of Anglo-Egyptian Sudan*.

[2] For 1941 and subsequent years this was £599,000.

[3] These, of course, did not involve any contribution in real terms over and above the combined value of military expenditure and exports.

The output of the main food crops does not appear to have been greatly affected by war conditions. The durra crop was 544,000 tons in 1943 compared with 713,000 for the average of the years 1936–9, but this reflects the vagaries of the climate and the impact of the locust swarm rather than the direct effect of war. The wheat crop was 8000 tons in 1936–9 (av.) but 24,000 in 1943, which more than compensated for a reduction in wheat-flour imports. The very fact that industrial output—apart possibly from some primitive spinning and weaving of textiles—was negligible in pre-war days means that the utilization of resources for war purposes cannot have made much difference to that side of the economy.

TABLE 2. *Principal exports*

Commodity	Quantity			Value f.o.b. (£000's)		
	1938–9 (av.)	1942	1943	1938–9 (av.)	1942	1943
Raw cotton (000's tons)	62·0	49·3	38·5	3412	4204	3079
Gum (000's tons)	23·8	13·7	14·8	687	491	597
Cotton seed (000's tons)	95·6	29·6	52·7	239	106	255
Sesame (000's tons)	18·4	10·7	15·7	208	239	294
Sheep (000's)	9·7	152	93	8·6	264	185
Cattle (000's)	8·3	50	40	36	403	348
Value of exports	—	—	—	5490	7151	6016
Value of re-exports	—	—	—	393	351	590
Value of all exports	—	—	—	5883	7502	6606

Source. Sudan Trade Returns.

Note. Military and N.A.A.F.I. stores excluded, as payment for these is already counted in Table 1. In 1943 they amounted to £396,000, the main constituent being 60,000 tons of cotton seed, valued at £262,000 (for use in manufacturing edible oil, etc.).

Consumption

It is impossible to make any precise estimates about the reductions in consumption which were forced on the Sudan during the war, but the best rough guide is the reduction in imports, of which details are given in Table 3.

It can be seen from Table 3 that there were many reductions in imports of consumption goods in general demand, such as cotton piecegoods, tea, sugar, soap and kerosene. In the case of kerosene and textiles respectively it was estimated that consumption had been reduced 30 and 50% below pre-war standards by 1943. On the other hand, despite the reductions in wheat-flour imports the grain supply for the population does seem to have been maintained reasonably well. Paper and timber are typical of the reductions in materials.

There is no evidence that cuts in consumption were distributed unjustly as in Egypt. In the first place, efficient measures were taken to prevent the cultivators and exporters (with the possible exception of the livestock owners) who stood to gain from war demands and high prices from making large profits. In the second place, although individual rationing did not apply to the rural areas there were many

TABLE 3. *Principal imports*

Commodity	Quantity			Value c.i.f. (£000's)		
	1938–9 (av.)	1942	1943	1938–9 (av.)	1942	1943
Wheat flour (000's tons)	20·5	17	5·5	158	378	151
Rice (tons)	3416	428	1503	30·5	7	41
Coffee (000's tons)	7·7	8·8	7·9	188	357	398
Tea (000's tons)	2·6	2·4	1·3	260	415	204
Tobacco (tons)	176	234	270	178	474	499
Sugar (000's tons)	33	24	18	650	848	485
Soap (tons)	1819	2001	895	35	67	38
Cotton piecegoods (000's tons)	9·1	7·0	4·4	1074	2353	2772
Kerosene (000's tons)	6·9	5·0	4·1	25	35	29
Paper	—	—	—	36	7	1·5
Timber	—	—	—	142	30	15
Machinery	—	—	—	374	146	177
Total imports (value)	—	—	—	5938	8878	9220
Total imports (volume)	100	74	55	—	—	—

Source. Sudan Trade Returns.

Notes. (1) All imports of private traders and Government included except military and N.A.A.F.I. stores.
(2) Base of volume index is 1934–8.

schemes of allocation and 'percentage distribution' to rural areas of such commodities as grain, matches, textiles, sugar, tea, etc., and these did work fairly well in practice. Finally, in the case of Omdurman, where there was a fully fledged individual rationing scheme,[1] the results were that the consumption of the rich was reduced but the poor actually purchased more of rationed goods than in pre-war days.

§ 2. FINANCIAL CHANGES

Money

Some statistics are available in respect of the supply of money. They are reproduced in Table 4. Further comment will be made on these figures after the course of prices has been surveyed.

[1] See p. 172.

TABLE 4. *Money supply*

Date	Currency and notes issued (£m.)	Index	Bank deposits (demand and time) (£m.)	Index
Aug. 1939	2·7	100	N.A.	—
Dec. 1939	2·7	101	1·2	100
Dec. 1940	2·8	105	1·3	108
Dec. 1941	4·1	153	2·5	207
Dec. 1942	4·6	172	3·3	275
June 1943	5·6	209	3·5	291
Dec. 1943	5·1	192	4·3	357
June 1944	5·0	187	4·8	400
Dec. 1944	4·2	156	4·8	400
June 1945	4·8	178	5·1	425

Source. Sudan Government Returns.

Note. No exact figures of currency and notes *in circulation* are available.

Prices

The movements of wholesale and retail prices are reproduced in Table 5. Several points are at once obvious from Tables 4 and 5. First, the rise in wholesale prices relatively to retail reflects the importance of higher costs of imported goods which were isolated from retail prices by a subsidy system. While import prices rose from

TABLE 5. *Wholesale and retail prices*

	Wholesale prices (1938 = 100)	Labourers' cost of living index (1938 = 100)
Dec. 1939	113	100
Dec. 1940	139	110
Dec. 1941	168	130
Dec. 1942	206	151
June 1943	220	175
Dec. 1943	220	177
June 1944	217	167
Dec. 1944	228	160
June 1945	217	166

100 in 1934–8 (av.) to 305 in 1943,[1] prices of home-produced staple goods rose by about 50%, e.g. durra rose 58% and sesame 49%, although cattle prices rose by as much as 107%. Secondly, the peak rate of increase of currency and prices was reached earlier than in the other Middle East countries. Currency and notes, for instance,

[1] See p. 173.

rose by 48% between December 1940 and December 1941, which was a faster rate of increase than in the later years. Wholesale prices hardly moved in 1943, whilst in other Middle East countries they were mounting rapidly upwards. The obvious explanation is that the war was closest to the Sudan in 1941–2 in terms of actual fighting as well as financially. Finally, a comparison of price and money movements shows that there was never any tendency for prices to move upwards more rapidly than currency, except in the first year of the war when the impact of the rise in import prices for the sterling area was felt. This conclusion is reinforced by the fact that these price indices only reflect town prices and not rural prices which were on the whole lower, particularly in the southern regions.

Incomes

Little quantitative evidence is available on cultivators' incomes but, as we shall see in § 3, the overriding principle was to keep them below the increase in the cost of living index. Rents were officially controlled throughout the war, and this prevented exploitation such as occurred in Egypt, but, nevertheless, there were many of the usual dodges such as demanding heavy sums for key money. Some information is available on the wage rates of daily paid labour and small-salaried monthly paid labour employed by a number of commercial firms. Perusal of these figures shows that in 1945 cost of living allowances payable to men earning a basic wage of £8 a month varied between extremes of £2 and £7 a month. The Sudan Government itself was paying £2. 5*s*. a month. The disparity is not really so great, however, as in many cases low cost of living allowances were supplemented by free meals or issues of textiles,[1] and in other cases by cash bonuses. Very roughly, it may be said that earnings (including special allowances) of these workers rose by some 50% on the average, in contrast with the 60–70% rise in the cost of living index.

§ 3. Inflation and Controls

In this section we shall deal first of all with the causes tending to generate higher incomes in the Sudan and the direct methods used to limit these incomes. Then we shall consider the various other means used to prevent substantial price increases.

[1] See *Report of Special Committee on Cost of Living in Sudan*, December 1943.

We have already seen the size of military expenditure in the Sudan in Table 1. The inflationary effect of this expenditure was not aggravated by a local budget deficit as Table 6 makes clear. At first sight it seems as if the balance of import and export payments was also a case of a moderate counter-inflationary factor. Table 7 shows that with the exception of 1941 there was no surplus of receipts from exports over payments for imports.

TABLE 6. *Budget receipts and expenditure (£m.)*

Year	Receipts	Expenditure	Surplus
1939	5·1	4·9	+0·16
1940	4·6	4·5	+0·88
1941	5·4	5·0	+0·33
1942	5·8	5·3	+0·47
1943	5·8	5·5	+0·28
1944	6·58	6·53	+0·05

Source. Sudan Government Publications.

Notes. (1) Local Government budgets excluded.
(2) It has not been possible to exclude external receipts and payments from these figures but the *difference* between the two is thought to be small.

TABLE 7. *Value of exports and imports (£m.)*

Year	Imports (c.i.f.)	Exports + re-exports (f.o.b.)	Import surplus (−) Export surplus (+)
1938	6·1	6·0	−0·1
1939	5·7	5·7	Nil
1940	5·6	5·5	−0·1
1941	8·3	9·0	+0·7
1942	8·9	7·5	−1·4
1943	9·2	6·6	−2·6
1944	10·0	9·4	−0·6

Source. Sudan Trade Returns.

Notes. (1) Military and N.A.A.F.I. stores excluded.
(2) Lend-Lease civilian stores included.

In fact, however, the incomes received by producers were much less than the figures of export values show (even after allowing for merchants' margins, duties, etc.), and therefore the counter-inflationary effect was, *pro tanto*, greater than these figures indicate. For the Government did not allow the benefit of high prices in the other Middle East countries to be reaped by producers, but appropriated the difference between the prices at which goods were sold externally and internal prices. This was the famous policy of the Price Stabilization Reserve and, as it was the keystone of Sudan war controls, we must examine the ways in which it worked in more detail.

The fundamental aim of this policy was to control cultivators' incomes, and, in this respect, the policy was instrumental in mitigating inflationary effects from military expenditure as well as from higher volumes and prices of exports. The prices paid to producers of most agricultural products were kept throughout the later war years below those ruling in the second half of 1941—which meant that cultivators' incomes increased less than did the cost of living index. By this means the difficulties which arise when high or rising prices are received by primitive producers were avoided. If prices had been high they would have made cash gains which would have been available for spending on the reduced supplies of consumption goods. If consumption goods were not available the probable results would have been reduction of output, or grain hoarding, as voluntary saving in cash or bonds is almost unknown. In any of these eventualities, the pressure of money demand on supply would have been more acute and prices would almost inevitably have risen greatly.

The mechanism by which this policy worked in the case of exports was in three parts. First, it was agreed in 1941 that exports of a number of staple products, such as sesame, hides, haricot beans, chick peas, cereals and groundnuts, should be centralized through the United Kingdom Commercial Corporation. These crops were obtained from producers at fixed prices,[1] and any surplus of selling price abroad over requisitioning price at home was, after allowance for intermediate charges, paid into a Reserve Fund which was available for subsidizing high-cost imports, if the necessity arose.[2] Although the scheme was originally only applicable to the six commodities listed above, it was later found necessary to extend it to a number of other cash crops which had become more lucrative for producers in the absence of any such controls. Secondly, special arrangements were made for the purchase of the whole of the cotton crop at fixed prices by the British Ministry of Supply. Any profits such as were made by reselling to India where prices were higher were placed at the disposal of the Sudan Government, and these were partly used to swell the cotton

[1] See p. 172.

[2] This, of course, mitigated the counter-inflationary effects of the policy to some extent. See p. 173.

reserve funds which had been built up in pre-war days, as an insurance scheme for cultivators.[1] Despite the fact that the scheme of centralized exports covered many products, the concentrated nature of Sudan exports is apparent when it is realised that the second scheme covered 57% of total exports (by value) in 1943 as against the 10% covered by the first. The third scheme to restrict export producers' incomes was in connexion with cattle, sheep and gum. Limited panels of exporters were allowed to trade and charge prices which, although higher than internal prices, were much lower than prices in other Middle East countries. There was no scheme for Government appropriation of any part of these proceeds, which accounted for 18% of the value of all exports in 1943. The remaining 15% of exports was undertaken by private traders, when suitably licensed.

Apart from these far-reaching attempts to control incomes of producers by direct methods, the Sudan Government was slow to increase its employees' incomes by cost of living allowances. The recommendations of the 1943 Committee Report on the cost of living[2] show that they were anxious not to push up incomes unduly, and proposed a policy of issuing cloth to Government servants as well as bonuses. And in 1945, as we have seen, Government bonuses were below the levels paid by many commercial firms to workers earning the same basic rates.

We shall now consider the other main weapons employed by the Sudan Government in its battle against rising prices. The effectiveness of its taxation policy can be seen from Table 8.

TABLE 8. *Receipts and total expenditure*

Year	Receipts (£m.)	Total expenditure (£m.) (Sudan Government plus military)	% receipts/total expenditure
1939	5·1	5·2	98
1940	4·6	5·5	84
1941	5·4	9·6	56
1942	5·8	8·7	67
1943	5·8	8·7	67
1944	5·97	7·5	79

Note. Local budgets excluded.

[1] A description of the Gash Delta scheme is given in Keen, *Agricultural Development of the Middle East*, pp. 22 ff.

[2] Op. cit.

The minimum percentage ratio of receipts to total expenditure in the Sudan was 56%, which contrasts with 51% in Egypt and 22% in Palestine, although, of course, it must be remembered that the Sudan task was very much easier as military expenditure was never very high. The main changes in taxation were the increase of the rate of tax on business profits from 10 to 30%, the 50% increase in charges for traders' licences and the higher taxation on animals and crops. Mainly as a result of these increases the yield from direct and other taxation[1] was approximately doubled between 1938 and 1944, although even then it was still a low percentage of total receipts in comparison with other Middle East countries, and this was mainly due to the absence of a general income tax. Changes in indirect taxation (i.e. customs, excise and sugar profits) were highly selective, as the Government tried to avoid increases in the cost of living index through this factor.[2] Whether this was really necessary in a country where there is little direct relationship between incomes and the cost of living index is open to doubt. To carry the policy to the length of allowing the yield of indirect taxes to fall by some 10% between 1938 and 1944, certainly seems unnecessary.

Attempts were made to increase savings by several means. First, a compulsory savings scheme was welded on to the business profits tax in 1943. For profits not exceeding £2500 per annum, the rate was 3%. Secondly, a voluntary scheme was started whereby employers could deduct pay and deposit it in the Post Office Savings Bank, with the consent of the employee. Thirdly, a campaign was waged to increase private deposits in the Post Office Savings Bank and War Savings Certificates.[3] Many free gifts were made to Allied funds by private persons and institutions,[4] as well as by the Government.[5] Finally, some gold was absorbed through official sales—about £60,000 in all.

We have already mentioned consumers' rationing schemes in our discussion of consumption changes. As in other Middle East countries these were, generally speaking, attempts to secure equitable distribution of commodities in short supply rather than methods of restriction,

[1] Including land tax, animal tax, date tax, house tax, as well as business taxes and traders' licences.

[2] This was also the reason given for keeping the rates of house tax constant (a tax roughly corresponding to our local rates).

[3] Post Office Savings Bank deposits reached £700,000 in December 1943.

[4] Henderson (op. cit.) gives a total figure of about £200,000.

[5] See p. 163.

of individual consumption outlay. There was no individual rationing except in towns such as Omdurman, the principal method in the rural areas being allocations to districts of scarce commodities, on the basis of previous consumption. The Omdurman scheme provided for monthly rationing of sugar (2 lb. per person), paraffin (½ gallon for a medium-size household), durra (28 lb. per person), cotton piecegoods (10 sq.yd. for an adult male per year). Coffee beans and wheat flour were also in the scheme. It is interesting to note that in order to make the scheme work effectively, many of the normal retailers had to be cut out completely, as they were found to be far too dishonest. Paraffin and coffee beans, for instance, were distributed by selected retailers; cotton piecegoods by three shops run by the town council; sugar by Government shops (the experience of running a Government monopoly of sugar supply and distribution since 1919 was an invaluable source of experience). Finally, petrol and tyres were strictly rationed, as in other Middle East countries.

The methods of controlling prices by direct measures were essentially tied up with procurement and distribution controls. In dealing with home-produced crops it is roughly true to say that in the early war years up to 1943, there was little attempt to do anything except declare maximum ceiling prices. Wholesale and retail prices for durra, sesame and groundnuts were fixed in 1941, but without any attempt to control supplies. The usual results followed: hoarding by cultivators—this was, in contrast with Egypt, a particularly widespread habit—and speculative purchases by dealers. In 1942 attempts were made to fix prices at such levels that cultivators would not be tempted to hoard supplies on the one hand or receive much higher incomes on the other, but success was only really achieved with the imposition of requisitioning and physical controls over distribution. In 1943, for instance, a Durra Purchasing Commission was established to inspect producers' supplies, purchase all surpluses[1] and ensure fair allocations to different districts. This Commission worked with authorized dealers only, but the real factor which secured its success was strict Government control over transport facilities. In the case of wheat, all producers' surpluses were purchased by a pool of dealers operating on behalf of the Government and strictly controlled on all

[1] 80,000 tons were purchased by the Government between October 1943 and March 1944 at a price of £5 per ton. Other Middle East Government prices for millet in 1943 were £17·8 in Egypt and £26 in Transjordan. The expenses of running the Purchasing Commission were defrayed from the Price Stabilization Reserve Fund.

matters of price, storage and distribution. In 1943, 18,000 tons of wheat were purchased in this way. Finally, small-scale systems of exchanging consumers' goods for grains were established at various times. Wide publicity to convictions also proved a good deterrent to potential offenders.

The main methods of keeping down prices of imported goods were to centralize a number of goods through Government channels only (e.g. flour, sugar, iron and steel, cement) and to impose a strict licensing system of other imports. Private traders were only allowed to deal in imported goods if they declared themselves willing to abide by the Controller-General of War Supply's regulations on such matters as maximum selling prices and percentage of cheap goods allowed for re-export purposes. Allocations were made to regions by issuing directives to private stock-holders. Wholesalers were linked up with groups of retailers, and in some towns (e.g. Omdurman) traders were 'concentrated' on British lines. Finally, not only were supplies of imported goods effectively controlled in this way but prices were kept down by means of subsidies from Government export profits. Grain,[1] meat, tea and cotton piecegoods prices were in this way restricted. Of course, this meant that less purchasing power was absorbed by imports than the total value of imports for each year suggests, and therefore more was available for expenditure on other goods and services. It is also doubtful whether the increase in wage rates in response to higher import prices and a higher cost of living index would have been sufficiently large or sufficiently widespread to affect the general level of incomes very much. But at any rate the complications, which arose in Palestine due to the reluctance of cultivators to sell their crops through official channels when import prices were high, were avoided. The success of the policy in isolating import prices from the cost of living index may be seen from Table 9.

TABLE 9. *Import prices and cost of living index*

Year	Retained import price index (1934–8 = 100)	Cost of living index (1938 = 100)
1940	170	110 (Dec.)
1941	223	130 ,,
1942	279	151 ,,
1943	305	177 ,,

[1] Home produced as well as imported.

It is perfectly true that the major item in the cost of living index is home-produced grain, but many imported foods (tea, sugar, coffee) and manufactured goods (textiles, hardware) also enter into it.

In these various ways—income limitation and price fixing, taxes, savings and rationing—the Sudan Government attempted to soften the impact of war on the economic life of the country. Various other measures were taken to keep production up to the highest possible levels. Import controls were gradually tightened and luxury imports cut down to very low levels. There were never any strict man-power controls, but in 1943 regulations were issued freezing labour in some eighty-one occupations (mainly clerical or technical) in certain areas.[1] A Resources Board was set up in 1939 to mobilize the country's economic resources, and in 1941 this was changed into a War Resources Board, and a Controller-General of War Supply was appointed with wide powers over production and trade. The usual measures to maintain or increase agricultural output were adopted—propaganda, issue of fertilizers, loans, etc. Wheat production, as we have seen, was very much increased, the production of soya beans was started, and the cotton acreage restricted by 25% to divert land and labour to food crops. The Sudan Government had obtained several years of valuable experience before the war in co-operating with cultivators in the Gezira irrigation scheme, and this proved extremely useful in wartime. Although industrial production for civil purposes was not important in the Sudan, a considerable amount of work, such as servicing and repairs, was done for the military authorities in the appropriate departments of the Sudan Government. Finally, a number of attempts were also made to restrict usage of scarce commodities such as fuel, cotton seed and dom nuts being used instead.

§ 4. Critique of War Organization

To appreciate the problems of war economics in the Sudan, it is essential to realize the nature of the country and the people. The first point is the huge size of the country—1,000,000 sq. miles. It is relatively easy to survey and assess agricultural output where it is concentrated in a narrow strip of land as in Egypt, but not nearly so easy when cultivation is scattered among such diverse terrains as river valleys, irrigated areas and mountainous regions. The ease with which

[1] *Foreign Commerce Weekly*, 29 May 1943.

crops can be hidden is only equalled by the difficulty of transporting them in a country where railways have always been few and roads unmade. It might reasonably be expected that breakdowns would occur in the distribution of imported manufactures as well as cereals under such conditions. Secondly, the extraordinary mixture of Arabs, Nubians, Berberines and sundry miscellaneous races, all with their different styles of living, created many difficulties in planning allocations of consumption goods and rationing of scarce commodities. Thirdly, there was no real administration of the country at all before 1898, when the joint Anglo-Egyptian Condominium was proclaimed, and even now some of the more remote areas have hardly progressed beyond savagery. Fourthly, the soil will not grow a large variety of crops as in Egypt, and therefore the possibilities of extensive conversion in accordance with wartime necessities were limited. The very primitive agriculture and shifting cultivation general in the south were further obstacles. Finally, although Allied military expenditure was never very heavy in the Sudan, on the other hand, imports were heavily curtailed and, in the case of manufactured goods, there was no possibility of replacing these by home-produced commodities. Textiles are perhaps the best example of this.

It is in the light of these factors that the Sudan achievement in restricting retail prices to 70% above pre-war levels must be judged. It is possible to draw several conclusions from these experiences. The first is the vital importance of a good administration, working with and not against the population. The Sudan was perhaps the only one of the Middle East countries fortunate enough to have both a Civil Service which was experienced and efficient and a public which was, on the whole, not unwilling to co-operate with it. In Palestine the administration was adequate, but Jews and Arabs were far more anxious to fight one another than to co-operate with it. Egypt was distinguished neither by her administrative efficiency nor by public willingness to make sacrifices for the Allied war effort. The second point is the very much easier problems raised by expenditure which had more of a peacetime than a wartime character about it. The main problems the Sudan had to face in 1942 and 1943 (when pre-war stocks were beginning to vanish and imports became really tight) were not a vast amount of expenditure by authorities willing to pay high wages for labour or by troops accustomed to much higher standards of living than the local population, but problems of high-cost imports and exporters earning or trying to earn large incomes. These problems were not of the same nature, magnitude or complexity as those due to large-scale military expenditure. Nevertheless, the achievement of the Sudan Government should not be underrated. It undoubtedly made mistakes—it could be argued that a more effective price-control policy could have been started in the early war years, and that some types of indirect taxation could have been pushed further—but it did recognize the necessity of making income control the keystone of an anti-inflationary policy in a primary producing country. This more than anything else explains its success.

CHAPTER VI

CYPRUS

§ 1. Physical Changes

Man-power

Increased demands for labour in Cyprus came from several sources during the war years. The Cyprus Armed Forces were negligible in 1939, but by 1945 had grown to 10,000, with 8500 in the Cyprus Regiment and 1500 in the Cyprus Volunteer Force. Direct employment of labour by the Allied Armed Forces varied enormously, as may be seen from Table 1. The bulk of these demands was for unskilled labour for road work and similar building operations.

Table 1. *Employment of labour by Armed Forces*

Date	Number
July 1941	6,000
Sept. 1941	10,000
Nov. 1941	25,000
June 1942	17,000
Oct. 1943	8,000
Oct. 1944	6,000
Mar. 1945	3,500

Sources. Commission on Wages and Employment 1944; *Report of Acting Commissioner of Labour*, 1945; *Report of British Goodwill Trade Mission to Iraq, Syria, the Lebanon and Cyprus* (Board of Trade, London, 1946), p. 48.

Note. R.A.F. employment is included.

Apart from these main drafts on labour supplies, there were two other subsidiary demands. The number employed by local contractors on military work was estimated to be 2500 in 1944. Furthermore, there was an increase in numbers employed by the Government. This was subject to continuous variation in wartime, as a large proportion of workers were casual labourers, and, in fact, fluctuated between lower and upper limits of 6000 and 11,000, compared with a normal pre-war demand of about 5000. Employment in August 1945, for instance, was 9500 (7800 casual workers and 1700 regular).

It has not been possible to obtain continuous statistics showing the variation in numbers employed in these different capacities for all the war years, and therefore it is not possible to be exact about the peak man-power drain. Roughly, however, the peak was about 30,000 in the winter of 1941–2, but by mid-1944 the total number had shrunk to 22,000; at the latter date the Armed Forces accounted for 10,000, military employment 7500, contractors 2500 and additional Government employment about 2000. The main point is that the peak absorption by the Armed Forces (1944) did not coincide with the peak employment by the military authorities (1941–2).

To put this wartime demand for labour in perspective the total population of Cyprus was about 397,000 in 1939 and as it was growing at the rate of about 5000 a year it may be put roughly at 430,000 in 1945.[1] The peak war demand for labour thus absorbed about 7·4% of the total population compared with 6·1% (Palestine) or 1·7% (Egypt), although it should be remembered that the peak was sustained for longer periods in the latter two countries.

There were several sources from which these additional demands were met. The most important was unemployed labour, as a considerable reserve of labour appeared in wartime, owing to the decline of mining operations consequent on the loss of the European market and the suspension of private building activity. The unemployment position was in fact so bad in March 1941 that a considerable amount had to be spent in providing relief work for some 4200 men who were otherwise without means of subsistence.[2] Figures are not available for the reduction in numbers employed in domestic building, but the labour force in the mines was reduced from 10,000 in 1938 to 1500 in 1944.[3] This figure of 8500 accounts by itself for more than one-third of the supply of labour needed to meet wartime demands in 1944. Another source was agricultural labour, particularly from the citrus groves, which was often attracted to military work in rural areas. Finally, the total population increased, as we have seen, and consequently the total man-power available for work was greater.

On the whole there do not seem to have been disproportionate drafts on skilled labour, as the main military demands were for unskilled and building workers. Nevertheless, even these were sufficiently heavy to cause such acute shortages of labour at times that men had to be temporarily released to perform urgent work in the towns.[4]

[1] *Statistical Handbook of the Middle East.* This implies about 125,000–130,000 males of working age.

[2] Ashiotis, *Labour Conditions in Cyprus*, 1939–45.

[3] 1944, *Commission on Wages and Employment.*

[4] *Report of Acting Commissioner of Labour*, 1945.

Production

As in the other countries of the Middle East, the principal additional demand on productive resources was due to military expenditure. Allied military expenditure (of all types) increased from negligible proportions before the war to £2·25 million in 1941, £4·25 million in 1942, £3·7 million in 1943, and £4·1 million in 1944.[1] If we deflate the 1942 expenditure by the cost of living index this gives us an expenditure of about £1·93 million in terms of 1939 prices—or about £4·7 per head of the population, which is quite high compared with Egypt and the Sudan, where the peak figures were respectively £2·4 and £0·60 per head. The usual limitations of such analysis must be borne in mind, however.

The main outlet for this expenditure was the employment of labour on military projects. There was, of course, some demand for local foods, both processed, such as jam and macaroni, and unprocessed, such as vegetables. Wines and spirits were also in very heavy demand. Other items were the purchases of large supplies of timber[2] and a few manufactured goods such as buttons. Finally, there were the outgoings of individual Allied soldiers.

In comparison with military expenditure the Cyprus Government Defence expenditure was not large as Table 2 shows.

TABLE 2. *Local defence expenditure (£000's)*

Year	Amount
1939	31
1940	47
1941	236
1942	295
1943	302
1944	346

Source. Financial Reports.

Note. This expenditure includes the annual contribution of about £10,000 to His Majesty's Government.

[1] *Economic Report on Cyprus.* As in the case of other Middle East countries these figures are net of such items as N.A.A.F.I. receipts and remittances of troops to Britain via Army channels.

[2] From 1939 to 1943, some 580,000 cu.ft. were exported for war purposes, some 575,000 used by the military forces on the island and some 183,000 supplied for A.R.P. purposes. The combined demand was thus extremely heavy, for pre-war exports were negligible.

The trend of exports from Cyprus during the war years may be seen from Table 3.

TABLE 3. *Principal exports*

Commodity	Quantity			Value f.o.b. (£000's)		
	1938–9 (av.)	1941	1944	1938–9 (av.)	1941	1944
Carobs (000's tons)	50	13	40	261	85	304
Raisins (000's cwt.)	39	61	70	22	30	184
Potatoes (000's cwt.)	303	143	189	87	88	222
Citrus fruit (m.)	54	1·8	18·3	81	2	81
Copper concentrates (000's tons)	130	Nil	8·9	756	Nil	67
Buttons	—	—	—	21	91	301
Timber (000's cu.ft.)	Nil	138	21	Nil	22	6
Wines (000's gall.)	1607	1468	697	81	68	89
Spirits (000's gall.)	11	116	410	3	38	266
Total value (incl. re-exports)	—	—	—	2450	1072	2450
Vol. index	100	54	82	—	—	—

Source. Statistics of Imports and Exports.

Notes. (1) Military and N.A.A.F.I. stores excluded.
(2) Volume index is calculated on basis of main items only.
(3) Individual items do not include re-exports, but these were unimportant for the items listed except in the case of timber. Quantities of timber re-exports were nil in 1939, 34,000 cu.ft. in 1941, 154,000 cu.ft. in 1944.
(4) Tons are long.

The main reason for the decline in volume and value of total exports between 1939 and 1941 was the reduction in mining activity. Despite the revival of the raw silk industry in Cyprus, exports of raw materials and semi-manufactures fell from £1,589,000 in 1939 to £388,000 in 1941, £228,000 in 1942 and only rose to £413,000 in 1944. Exports of foodstuffs, drink and tobacco declined from £639,000 in 1939 to £472,000 in 1941, but increased to £1,480,000 in 1944, mainly owing to the increased exports of wines and spirits to the Middle East Armies, cereals to Palestine and potatoes to Egypt. The share of Palestine, in fact, in Cyprus export trade increased from 2% of total value in 1939 to 19% in 1944, whilst that of Egypt increased from 6 to 36% over the same period. Finally, exports of manufactured goods rose continually over the whole period from £73,000 in 1939 to £122,000 in 1941, and £366,000 in 1944, the main cause being the increased exports of buttons to the United Kingdom.

The character of the wartime absorption of resources in Cyprus is now clear. There was a considerable volume of military expenditure in the early war years, and although exports were at a low ebb at that time, they recovered in such a way that by 1944 total volume was some 82% of 1939 volume.

Against this picture of war demands we now have to see how output changed in the main lines of production. In agriculture the principal task was to grow sufficient food to feed the local population. Output changes of the main crops may be seen from Table 4.

TABLE 4. *Agricultural output* (000's *metric tons*)

Crop	1936–9 (av.)	1940	1941	1942	1943
Wheat	56	48	24	62	55
Barley	44	32	22	50	30
Potatoes	31	29	15	22	18
Carobs	46	40	25	36	47·5
Olives	5	13	2	9	6
Oranges	27	25	23	11	N.A.
Vetches (000's bushels)	238	329	80	135	368

Source. Statistical Handbook of the Middle East.

The explanation of the very low output of wheat and barley in 1941 and the high output in 1942 is to be found in differences in weather and harvest conditions. Cyprus is normally fairly self-sufficient in foodstuffs, and therefore the main aim was to maintain pre-war rates of production rather than to secure any large increase. The reduction in output of oranges was parallel with that of Palestine.

The main changes in industrial output may be seen from Table 5.

TABLE 5. *Industrial output*

Item	1939	1943
Minerals (tons)	538,000	52,660
Cupreous concentrates (tons)	103,000	30,000
Asbestos (000's tons)	1,262	146
Buttons (m.)	113	185
Crushed carobs (tons)	29,540	28,513
Soap (000's okes)	988	1,136
Tobacco (000's okes)	229	246
Macaroni (000's okes)	362	736
Tanning products (000's okes)	142	171
Jam (okes)	234	137,000
Silk (kg.)	Nil	420
Hemp (okes)	Nil	30,000

Source. Cyprus Blue Book, 1943.

Notes. (1) Figures exclude cottage production.
(2) 1 oke = 2·75 lb.

The character of the changes is fairly easy to see. The decline in mining output was due to the loss of the European markets. The main increases were to meet additional export demands (buttons and silk), or military demands (jam, macaroni) or local consumption needs (soap, hemp). Although the total output of carobs and tobacco did not show great increases, these, together with wines and spirits, were by far the most important outputs from the point of view of total value, as gross values of output were £198,000, £580,000 and £1·1 million respectively in 1943.[1]

Consumption

Before we can assess the main changes in consumption forced on Cyprus during the war, the reductions in imports must be surveyed.

From Table 6 it can be seen that in general the reduction in imports was fairly heavy. We must now relate the individual changes to home production and consumption changes.

On the whole, the supply of foodgrains was kept up to pre-war levels of 65,000 tons for food consumption and 55,000 tons for animal and seed requirements. Imports were adjusted by the Middle East Supply Centre to compensate for changes in home production (thus the bad harvest of 1941 was followed by much higher imports of barley, wheat and wheat flour in 1941–2) and military demands on local foodgrains were negligible. Finally, some barley was exported in pre-war years, but this was very much curtailed in wartime. On the other hand, it should be remembered that there was an 8% increase in population during the war years. Vegetable production was also maintained fairly well, and the Middle East Supply Centre kept imports sufficiently high to maintain consumption near pre-war levels. Imports of cotton-seed oil were reduced, but more olive oil was available for consumption; this, however, was more expensive, and it was not a substitute as far as the poorer sections of the population were concerned. The only really clear example of a reduction in staple foods was in sugar, where consumption was reduced to a rate of 1800 tons a year in 1943–4 compared with 2000 tons a year before the war. A system of three meatless days a week was imposed as in Egypt, but this is no proof that there was an overall deficiency in supplies, for although military demands expanded, the numbers of cattle in the

[1] The figure of £1·1 million for wines and spirits may be compared with that for 1939—£160,000. Corresponding carob and tobacco values in 1939 were £153,000 and £255,000.

TABLE 6. *Principal imports*

Commodity	Quantity		
	1938–9 (av.)	1941	1943
Total value	—	—	—
Volume index (1938 = 100)	88	73	46
Wheat flour (cwt.)	273,000	315,000	100
Wheat (cwt.)	108,000	498,000	37,700
Barley (cwt.)	200	6,000	59,800
Sugar (000's cwt.)	67	54	40
Tea (000's lb.)	32	35	0·5
Coal (long tons)	4,300	380	660
Crude petroleum (m. gal.)	3·8	1·0	1·5
Cotton piecegoods (m. yd.)	5,843	3,235	2,737
Woollen piecegoods (000's yd.)	396	60	54
Footwear (all types) (000's pairs)	75	7·9	12·1
Kerosene (000's gal.)	1,105	633	948
Chemical manures (000's cwt.)	157	14	125
Iron bars (cwt.)	54,000	198	104
Agricultural implements and tools	—	—	—
All agricultural machinery	—	—	—

Commodity	Value c.i.f. (£000's)		
	1938–9 (av.)	1941	1943
Total value	2,080	1,985	2,267
Volume index (1938 = 100)	—	—	—
Wheat flour (cwt.)	121	345	0·3
Wheat (cwt.)	34	361	63
Barley (cwt.)	0·05	3·4	137
Sugar (000's cwt.)	38	124	74
Tea (000's lb.)	2·2	4·2	0·11
Coal (long tons)	8·7	2·4	7·9
Crude petroleum (m. gal.)	56	60	106
Cotton piecegoods (m. yd.)	107	96	307
Woollen piecegoods (000's yd.)	68	23	30
Footwear (all types) (000's pairs)	7·8	2·0	10·0
Kerosene (000's gal.)	29·4	34·8	74·2
Chemical manures (000's cwt.)	48	14	208
Iron bars (cwt.)	31	0·37	0·09
Agricultural implements and tools	4·0	0·22	0·09
All agricultural machinery	5·0	0·5	0·04

Source. Statistics of Imports and Exports.

Note. Figures exclude military and N.A.A.F.I. stores but include civilian Lend-Lease goods. N.A.A.F.I. stores must be excluded, as military expenditure is given net of N.A.A.F.I. receipts.

island actually increased. The main reason for control of distribution was the expansion of demand which in turn was due to the increased prosperity of many who in pre-war years had not been able to afford it. Finally, there were no reductions in available supplies of such staple items as cheese and olives (exports of cheese which were some 6800 cwt. in 1938–9 (av.) were reduced to 1380 cwt. in 1943).

Probably the most severe cut of all was in textiles. We have seen that imports of cotton piecegoods were reduced from 5843 million yards in 1938–9 (av.) to 2737 million yards in 1943, and similarly, woollen goods fell from 396 to 54 million yards. This fall really did hit the colony, as local production was small in pre-war days and failed to expand to any appreciable extent in wartime.[1] The reduction in imports of footwear from 68,000 pairs in 1939 to 12,000 pairs in 1943 was also another cause of hardship. Some shoes were manufactured to Government order, but they were so shoddy that they remained largely unsold.

Many other consumer goods were in short supply, such as soap, which, despite increases in local production, had to be rationed to 150 drams (i.e. 9 oz.) per head per month in the towns. As in other countries hardware was scarce too. On the other hand, the pre-war consumption of kerosene was maintained, at slightly under 52,000 gallons per month, despite the reductions in imports.

Therefore, although basic supplies of foodgrains, vegetables and oils were assured, there were many shortages of other foodstuffs and manufactured goods. But this analysis does not tell us anything about the reductions in different areas or different classes, and we must now consider the changes of this sort in rough outline.

On the whole, no particular class seems to have suffered undue falls in real income during the war years,[2] and therefore our main task must be to see whether there were any obvious cases of maldistribution involved in the rationing and distribution arrangements. In the first place, the towns probably suffered less than the countryside despite the inevitable advantages the latter had in respect of home-grown foodstuffs. The rationing and allocation systems benefited the towns even in theory. Sugar allocations per head were twice

[1] It was reported in 1944 that the two local weaving factories were producing jointly at the rate of 20,000 ft. of cotton cloth per annum (*Crown Colonist*, March 1944). There was also some hand-loom weaving (*Report of British Goodwill Trade Mission*, p. 55).

[2] See pp. 187–8.

those of the villages in 1943[1]; soap rations were 50% higher in the towns, and imported woollen goods were released to the towns only.[2] In practice, townsfolk were more sure of receiving their allocation than were country areas. Secondly, there was a thriving black market in many areas into which supplies of meat, vegetables and fruit (nominally controlled in both price and distribution) often found their way. This inevitably favoured the richer or more prosperous consumers.

In summary, we can say that overall supplies of cereals and vegetables were not restricted, but many other consumption goods, both foodstuffs and manufactures, did show a sharp decline. Moreover, these hardships were intensified for rural areas by the nature of the rationing and distribution arrangements and for the poorer classes by the uneven working of these arrangements.

§2. Financial Changes

Money

The main changes in money supply may be seen from Table 7. Comments will be made on this table in conjunction with those on Table 8.

TABLE 7. *Money supply (£000's)*

Date	Currency notes in circulation	Index	Total bank deposits (demand and time)	Index	Index all money
Sept. 1939	938	100	1721	100	100
Sept. 1940	1066	114	1639	95	102
Sept. 1941	1644	175	1963	114	135
Sept. 1942	2930	312	3342	194	236
Sept. 1943	3967	423	5327	309	350
Dec. 1944	4918	525	7294 (Sept.)	425	—

Source. Cyprus Government Statistics.

Note. Bank deposits refer to ten commercial banks.

[1] Rations were about 3 oz. per head per week in the towns and 1½ in the villages (*Economic Report*, 1943).

[2] A major complaint in the disturbances of June and July 1944 was that a much greater variety of clothing was allotted to the towns than to the villages (Hansard (Commons), 2 August 1944).

Prices

Table 8 shows the movements of retail prices over the war years. No wholesale price index is available.

TABLE 8. *Retail prices*

Date	Cost of living index	Date	Cost of living index
Aug. 1939	100	June 1943	273
Sept. 1941	166	Sept. 1943	278
Dec. 1941	192	Dec. 1943	235
June 1942	206	June 1944	239
Sept. 1942	228	Dec. 1944	229
Jan. 1943	246	June 1945	233

Source. Cyprus Government Statistics.

Before we compare the price movements and money changes it is interesting to note three facts. First, the main constituent of higher retail prices in Cyprus was not foodstuffs but clothing. When the general index was at its peak figure of 278 in September 1943 clothing prices stood at 702 and food at only 204, although this was partly due to a food subsidy policy, as we shall see later. Secondly, the character of the cost of living index has to be remembered. It represented the cost at official prices of a budget assessed on pre-war standards; but the average consumer had to pay black-market prices for a number of foodstuffs and was unable to buy many of the normal manufactured goods. It is, of course, true that these criticisms apply to cost of living indices in most countries during the war years, but the widespread nature of the black market in foods and the great reduction in imports in Cyprus, unaccompanied by any large-scale home production, made them especially relevant there. Thirdly, the supply of money in circulation increased faster than bank deposits in the early war years. As in other countries this was due to lack of confidence about the military situation at that time.

Owing to the fall in bank deposits in 1940 consequent on the bad war news, and the higher cost of imported goods, prices had increased relatively more than the total money supply by September 1941. But as in other parts of the Middle East this tendency was corrected, and there was no evidence of any unwillingness to hold money in later years.

Incomes

Some efforts were made in Cyprus, as in the Sudan, to keep down the incomes of cultivators, and in the case of grain and olive growers some success was achieved but prices of wines were uncontrolled and the wine producers and vine cultivators both made substantial gains. We have already seen that the gross value of output of wines and spirits was nearly six times greater in 1943 than in 1939. And even though the prices of many agricultural products were controlled, there is little doubt that farmers as a whole prospered.[1] It was estimated that before the war some 82% of all peasants were in debt and that the average debt per head was about £36.[2] Not only did the great wartime rise in prices reduce the real burden of this debt, but the Debt Settlement Board made attempts to reduce rates of interest[3] and peasants' receipts were sufficiently high to allow repayment of capital in many cases. The position of the Co-operative Central Bank reflects these changes, for at 30 September 1939 it had borrowed £18,000 to meet the needs of members for loans, but by 30 September 1944 the deposits of members and members' societies exceeded advances by over £400,000. The Governor, in fact, declared in 1944: 'It is not too much to say that during the past four or five years the rural population has been able to free itself from the indebtedness of a decade ago, one of the principal obstructions to agricultural improvement.'[4]

Information is available on wage changes from several sources. The average daily wage rate of employees on Government work rose in the manner shown in Table 9.

TABLE 9. *Wage rates*

Date	Average daily wage rate (in piastres)	Index	Cost of living index
Aug. 1939	15	100	100
May 1941	24	160	133 (est.)
Sept. 1941	27	180	166
Aug. 1942	30	200	219
Oct. 1942	36	240	235
Jan. 1944	42	280	240

Sources. Commission on Wages and Cost of Living; Ashiotis, op. cit.

Notes. (1) 180 piastres = £1.
(2) Wage-rate figure refers to normal working day.

[1] See Hansard (Commons), 3 March 1943.

[2] Bonné, *Economic Development of the Middle East*, p. 41. Lanitis, *Rural Indebtedness and Agricultural Co-operation in Cyprus*, puts total agricultural indebtedness in 1940 at £2·3 million, which agrees fairly well with the above.

[3] It was reported in the *Crown Colonist* in March 1943 that for some 5000 peasants rates of interest had been reduced from 12 to 5%.

[4] *Cyprus Post*, 16 November 1944.

It must be made clear that these wage rates refer to labour on Government work, which, as we saw in § 1, only averaged about 8000–9000 over the war years, and furthermore, they do not represent wages of unskilled men but are probably more nearly those of semi-skilled. On the other hand, these wages seem to be fairly typical of those paid in private employment or by the Army for similar types of work. Furthermore, they neglect altogether the substantial improvements in working conditions which occurred during the war years, such as leave with pay.[1] It was concluded by the Commission that a daily wage rate of 42 piastres was generally sufficient to meet the increased cost of living except in the case of large families. This latter proviso would, however, have applied before 1939 to wage rates, and therefore is not to be taken as being connected with war conditions.

Other indices of general labourers' wages and compositors' wages show much the same tendencies.

TABLE 10. *Unskilled and skilled wage rates*

Year	Index unskilled labourers (hourly rate)	Index compositors (hourly rate)	Cost of living index (August 1939 = 100)
1939 (Dec.)	100	100	N.A.
1940 (av.)	117	100	N.A.
1941 (av.)	175	157	166 (Sept.)
1942 (av.)	233	202	228 (Sept.)
1943 (av.)	233	253	273 (June)
1944 (av.)	272	360	239 (June)

Sources. Economic Report on Cyprus, 1943; Special information.

These statistics of wage changes have to be treated carefully and their limited nature remembered. They are not averages of all wage rates paid but only of a few samples. The fundamental agricultural nature of the Cyprus economy is such that in 1939 there were only about 10,000 regular wage earners, and about 20,000–30,000 casual wage earners who had no other source of income.[2] There were, in fact, more self-employed men than employees.[3] Although the number

[1] It is probable that changes in earnings were not proportionately greater than changes in rates, simply because working hours were so long before the war. Some workers gained by obtaining more regular employment than before, although even this seems to have been of limited application to rural workers (see p. 195).

[2] These numbers were periodically supplemented by farm occupants unable to obtain continuous employment or adequate income from their primary activity.

[3] *Report of Labour Department*, 1942.

of wage earners increased during the war years, it is obvious that these changes in wage rates did not apply to a very large section of the population. Furthermore, in the case of compositors there was a very strong trade union. Nevertheless, so far as they go, these statistics are in conformity with general impressions[1] on the improved position of workers in Cyprus during the war, and with the general trends which we found in other countries, such as Palestine, where there was a heavy military demand for labour.

Sterling balances

No exact or continuous figures are available, but it was reported in September 1943 that sterling balances were approximately £6 million compared with practically nil before the war, and that they were increasing at the rate of £100,000 a month.

§ 3. Inflation and Controls

The main income-generating factor in Cyprus was military expenditure, but before we examine the ways in which this impinged upon the economy and the steps which were taken to control it, we must examine the relative importance of higher incomes from other sources, such as budget deficits and export surpluses.

The revenue and expenditure figures for the Colony are shown in Table 11.

TABLE 11. *Government receipts and expenditure* (*£000's*)

Year	Budget receipts	Budget expenditure	Surplus (+) deficit (−)	Internal receipts	Internal expenditure	Income creating surplus (+) deficit (−)
1939	1013	1022	− 9	1007	941	+ 66
1940	951	1146	−195	940	1088	−144
1941	1101	1367	−266	1096	1313	−217
1942	1759	1751	+ 8	1492	1691	−199
1943	2280	2160	+120	2184	2090	+ 94
1944	3490	3694	−204	2828	3597	−769

Source. Budget Accounts.

Note. Internal figures exclude grants in aid from and defence contributions to His Majesty's Government, payments of interest on public debt (which is mainly held externally), and contributions to Sinking Funds. No deduction is made for pension remittances to England.

[1] Cf. *Report of Acting Commissioner of Labour*, 1945.

Although there was an income-creating deficit of some size in most years, it was in no way comparable with the military expenditure of about £4 million annually, and in two years public finance was an offsetting item to the growth of incomes. It is clear that we must exclude grants from and remittances to other countries, as these do not represent any absorption from or additions to purchasing power on the island.

The balance of exports and imports of merchandise may be seen from Table 12.

TABLE 12. *Exports and imports (£000's)*

Year	Export (f.o.b.) receipts	Index of volume	Import (c.i.f.) payments	Index of volume	Balance: export surplus (+) import surplus (−)
1938	2478	100	2245	100	+ 233
1939	2423	100	1891	76	+ 532
1940	1526	91	1717	68	− 191
1941	1072	54	1985	73	− 913
1942	1188	50	2257	64	−1069
1943	2180	78	2267	46	− 87
1944	2450	82	4829	51	−2379

Source. Statistics of Imports and Exports.

Notes. (1) Military and N.A.A.F.I. stores excluded, Lend-Lease civilian goods included.
(2) Exports include re-exports.
(3) Volume indices are based on leading items only.

Despite the great reduction in the volume of imports, the contraction of exports and the high prices of imported goods made the balance of trade in merchandise a counter-inflationary factor throughout the war years.

Little is known of private capital or invisible items on current account, but before the war invisible receipts and payments were both approximately equal to £300,000 per annum.[1] With the cessation of tourist expenditure it is possible that receipts declined in wartime. But the major item of receipts was grants from His Majesty's Government, and this factor has already been discounted, in the figures of internal receipts and payments.

Having obtained some idea of the importance of these forces we shall now examine the ways in which military expenditure reacted on the economy, and then finally return to note some of the effects of these less important factors.

[1] *Annual Report on Social and Economic Progress*, 1939.

The initial result of military expenditure was to increase incomes, as a large part of military expenditure, particularly in 1941–2, was payment of wages to labourers on constructional work, etc., and there was no means of imposing any effective upper limit to such wages. This tendency for wages to rise haphazardly was further aggravated by a number of strikes and lock-outs which occurred on the island during the war years.

Farmers' incomes were restricted in the years after 1942 by Government purchasing of large quantities of agricultural products at fixed prices, but although some success was achieved the loopholes for directing supplies into more lucrative black-market channels appear to have been quite large.[1] Finally, there was no control over profits in the wine and spirits trade where manufacturers and merchants made large profits, which were in turn partly recouped by vine growers.

Taxation increases were a partial offset to these higher incomes, as may be seen from Table 13.

TABLE 13. *Internal receipts and all expenditure (£000's)*

Year	Tax receipts	Total receipts	Tax receipts		Total receipts	
			% Govt. exp.	% Govt. and mil. exp.	% Govt. exp.	% Govt. and mil. exp.
1939	863	1007	92	—	106	—
1940	802	940	73	—	86	—
1941	920	1096	70	25	83	31
1942	1103	1492	65	19	88	25
1943	1566	2184	75	27	105	38
1944	2010	2828	56	26	79	37

Source. Financial Reports.

Notes. (1) Tax receipts include customs, excise, property and animal tax, income tax, estate duty, licences and fees.

(2) Grants in aid excluded from total receipts, external payments from Government expenditure.

It is clear from Table 13 that substantial attempts were made to increase taxation and other revenue in 1942 and later years. As in other colonies there was a very difficult obstacle to overcome in tax policy—the tendency for receipts from customs to decline on account of the much lower volume of imports—but the receipts from customs and excise were, nevertheless, increased over the war years (from

[1] See p. 194.

£620,000 in 1939 to £1,069,000 in 1944). The main increases were in direct taxation, however. Income tax was introduced in 1941 and in 1944 yielded £542,000.[1] Estate duty was introduced in 1942, and in 1944 £17,000 was obtained in this way. Finally, Government profits on sales of controlled commodities were quite substantial as miscellaneous receipts, of which they formed a large part, amounted to £728,000 in 1944.

On the other hand, it could not be said that taxation, even at wartime levels, was a really severe burden on all sections of the economy. For income tax only covered about 5000 persons, and land tax, which was the main tax on agricultural incomes, did not increase much during the war.

The main attempt to increase voluntary savings was the issue of Premium Bonds in 1943. 50,000 bonds of £10 each were floated. Interest was paid at the rate of 1% per annum, and, in addition, prizes ranging from £500 to £25 (including redemption of capital) were allotted four times a year. Although the loan was not very popular at first,[2] by April 1944 the bonds had not only been fully taken up but stood at a premium of 20%. The proceeds of the loan were lent to His Majesty's Government at 3% and a second loan was launched in 1944. This was by far the most successful of the Cyprus schemes for voluntary saving, as although Savings Certificates and Bonds were issued it was found that they did not possess nearly the same popularity with the peasants as the Premium Bonds.

Although attempts were made to ensure equitable distribution of goods in short supply, consumer rationing in itself did not impose much limitation on expenditure. Card rationing was confined to the towns, and the only forms of rationing for the rural areas were allocations to traders or co-operative societies, and from traders to consumers, based on a percentage of previous consumption. Sugar, matches, soap, kerosene and edible oils were distributed at regular intervals on a straight system of so much per head of the population; clothing and fuel supplies were issued direct to consumers from Government distribution centres when available. A system of three meatless days a week was also imposed. Bread was not actually rationed but adulterated with raisins and barley.

[1] In 1944 a single man with an earned income of £1500 a year paid 13% and with £10,000 a year paid 62% (corresponding figures for Great Britain were 40 and 69%).

[2] Particularly after the £500 prize at the first draw was won by a manufacturer known to be a friend of the Treasurer!

It is, however, somewhat unrealistic to consider consumers' rationing separately from price control, for the two were linked up closely together in actual administration. Many schemes were introduced for controlling supplies and prices. A Controller of Supplies started work in 1939 but, as in other countries, it was found that attempts to fix prices haphazardly or without control of supplies were ineffective. Gradually schemes were evolved whereby prices of imported goods were controlled by fixing distributors' margins in accordance with pre-war rates; and home industrial, and in some cases agricultural, products were priced according to a rough cost-plus system. In some instances the Government itself took over the wholesale side of distribution; in others it issued instructions to the normal merchants on the desired allocation to districts. The District Commissioners were generally responsible for allocating supplies from the wholesale level to retailers or co-operative societies who then dealt with consumers, but in some cases (cigarettes for instance) the Government itself opened retail shops to ensure supplies. After 1942, the Government requisitioned a proportion of livestock and crops, such as wheat, barley, potatoes, and olives, from farmers at fixed prices.[1] In 1943 it took over the purchasing, transport and supply to urban markets of all fruit and vegetables, for on these extortionate margins had been collected by distributors; as a result many prices were reduced by some 20% in the following six months. Bulk purchasing was extended to many types of imports. Eventually, prices and distribution of all commodities, such as flour, cotton seed, sugar and cloth, together with rents and transport rates, were controlled.

Internal prices of imported wheat and flour involved some difficult problems. They were fixed at the beginning of the war by reference to prices of home-grown supplies, but as import prices rose considerably the Government decided to abolish import duties on flour and introduce subsidies. This subsidy policy was later extended to other commodities, such as cloth and kerosene, but by far the largest proportion of the total amount spent was on bread and flour—particularly imported flour.

It seems fair to say that by 1944 most of these schemes for price and

[1] In 1943, 15,000 tons of wheat (£298,000), 6400 tons barley (£85,000), 590 tons olive oil (£75,000), 3000 tons vetches (£68,000) were the most important purchases out of a total expenditure of £621,000 (*Agricultural Report*, 1943). Physical quantities purchased may be compared with the total volume of output given in Table 4.

distribution control were working reasonably well, but until then they were far from perfect.[1] No statistics are available on black-market prices and operations, but they seem to have been extensive. The main cause of the meat shortage was a large amount of illicit trading. In Nicosia only 120 grocers out of 300 were included in the rationing scheme, but the rest continued to make a living by black-market operations.[2] As we have already seen, there was no control at all over an important sector—prices of wines and spirits—and suppliers did a large trade with military and N.A.A.F.I. purchasers. Finally, the subsidy scheme did ensure cheap bread,[3] but in doing so it absorbed less purchasing power from the population. We shall return to this point when the movements of import prices have been examined.[4]

In the organization of home output the fundamental difficulty was the great reduction in imports. There is no evidence to show that the Cyprus Government failed to check luxury imports, but the closing of the Mediterranean Sea route and the shipping shortage were alone sufficient to explain the drop in supplies of essential imports. Agriculture was handicapped by lack of chemical manures which fell from 151,000 tons in 1939 to 14,000 tons in 1941; industry and transport suffered from coal and acute petroleum shortages (coal imports were only 380 tons in 1941 against 4600 in 1939 and petroleum imports 1·0 million gallons against 3·9 million). Railways had to resort to using wood instead of coal.

There were many other difficulties to be overcome as well as the reduction in imports. The main task in the early war years was to prevent bankruptcy among the carob growers and citrus cultivators. In 1941, £10,500 was loaned by the Government to the citrus growers, and the whole of the carob crop (along with some other minor products) had to be purchased by the Government. Although attempts were made to maintain and increase output of food crops by liberal prices and such measures as propaganda to grow more food, distribution of seeds and feeding stuffs, issues of fertilizers at subsidized prices and (under the Colonial Development and Welfare Act) grants for implementing irrigation schemes, many of the limitations we have found in other Middle East countries soon came into operation. The

[1] It was reported for instance in March 1943 that rationed foods were frequently not available at the controlled prices (Hansard (Commons), 24 March 1943).

[2] *Economic Report on Cyprus*, 1943.

[3] Selected bakeries were also subsidized to supply bread to the poorest classes at specially low prices.

[4] See p. 196.

impossibility of very rapid extensions of the cultivated area,[1] the shortage of agricultural implements, the apathy of the rural population, the shortage of labour in some cases (this was the main reason why the attempted revival of the silk cocoon industry did not meet with great success), and the unwillingness of hired labour to work hard when there were few available consumption goods, all seem to have played their part. The simple facts that agriculture is the predominant industry, and that in the short period the main determinant of output is the weather, are the explanations why rapid increases are impossible in such countries, even though small increases may be recorded.

The cuts in fuel supplies, the absence of any home-produced raw materials (except iron and copper pyrites), the lack of any industrial tradition or high degree of skill, the difficulty of getting any machinery imports, the demands of the military authorities for labour, are sufficient to explain why wartime increases in manufactures were on a small scale.

We have now examined the main ways in which attempts were made to limit the impact of higher incomes, and the tendency to spend out of those incomes, on the price system. We have, so far, only considered these incomes as being due to military expenditure, but we must now see what other causes were operating to push up incomes and prices. The main points we have to examine are whether there was any tendency for exporters' incomes to rise unduly and whether high import prices contributed at all to the inflationary movement. The indices of import and export prices and that of retail prices may be seen in Table 14.

TABLE 14. *Import, export and retail prices*

Year	Import prices	Export prices	Retail prices
1939	100	100	100
1941	266	132	150
1942	302	220	206
1943	541	307	273
1944	473	286	239

Source. Colonial Office Statistics.

From Table 14 it can be seen that there was a tendency for prices of exports, and hence incomes from exports, to rise faster than the

[1] Some 57,000 acres were brought under cultivation from 1940 to 1944.

index of retail prices in 1943–4,[1] but it must be remembered that the index of retail prices refers to controlled prices only, and although no index is available of free prices, the thriving nature of the black market in Cyprus makes it reasonable to assume that export prices were not so very much greater than true retail prices in these years.

Import prices, however, do seem to have played some part in pushing up prices in Cyprus, even though they did help to drain purchasing power from the colony. In the case of wheat and barley, for instance, the internal controlled prices for cultivators were £20 and £13·3 per ton respectively in 1942–3, but import prices of barley rose from £12·2 per ton in 1942 to £45·8 per ton in 1943, and of wheat from £19·7 to £33·2 per ton. To ensure the harvest for 1943–4 it was found necessary to raise home cultivators' prices by 33⅓%. This is a clear case of where internal incomes were pushed up as a result of higher import prices. Even though the subsidy programme did help to stabilize the cost of living index after 1943, this was income-generating expenditure and in 1944 subsidies were running at the rate of £1 million per year. Nor was the effect of import prices in pushing up internal prices, either directly or indirectly, confined to foodstuffs, for import prices of other raw materials and manufactured goods in some cases rose faster than home prices.

The explanation of these high import prices is to be found partly in the supply of goods from high-priced Middle East countries (Syrian wheat for instance), and partly in high ocean freights (coal for instance). In any analysis of the reasons for price increases in Cyprus they must clearly be assigned a role of some importance.

§ 4. Critique of War Organization

There are some obvious reasons why a large measure of price inflation was unavoidable in Cyprus. Military expenditure per head of the population suddenly became high in 1942 and 1943, and war brought many dislocations to the usual economic activities of the island. Some of the normal export mainstays, such as carobs, cupreous concentrates and citrus fruits, were threatened with extinction through the shuttering of European markets and the collapse of the Mediterranean

[1] This conclusion would be reinforced if clothing were left out of the cost of living index.

Sea lines. It can, of course, be argued that these changes increased the spare resources of the colony, but the general upsetting of normal economic life certainly was an additional burden on the administrative machine. The large reduction in the volume of imports of raw materials and manufactured goods bore hardly on an island which had no potential or nascent industrial capacity such as existed in Egypt and Palestine. The fivefold rise in import prices could hardly fail to react on the internal price level, however hard the Government tried to isolate the two. Finally, there were all the usual difficulties met with in primary countries—a small administration, often inexperienced in economic affairs (we have already seen that the total staff available for income tax work was sixteen),[1] a merchant and trading class only too anxious to make profits by any legal or illegal means, a rural labour force not over-anxious to work hard when there was little chance of purchasing consumption goods with its earnings, and a population which was apathetic in the face of exploitation by the trading community,[2] even though it was willing to strike against exploitation by employers.

But are these facts a sufficiently good explanation of the rise in prices which did take place? The administration in Cyprus had certain advantages over that of other colonies and primitive countries; the most obvious one is that an island is not cursed with the everlasting smuggling of goods across frontiers. A small area is also relatively easy to control, as neither concealment of stocks of essential foodstuffs nor transport difficulties are likely to be formidable difficulties. Furthermore, there were not such complications as arose in Palestine through the sharp division into different races. And although harvests were poor in 1941 and not over-successful in 1943, Cyprus is normally self-supporting in most foodstuffs, even if it is very dependent on manufactured imports. Finally, military demands for resources were concentrated mainly on unskilled labour, which has never been scarce in Cyprus.

As in the case of Palestine the main criticism which can be legitimately made against the system of controls devised to minimize the increase in the flow of money demand is that it was only fully developed and applied in earnest after 1942–3. If adequate machinery for requisitioning of crops and control of distribution and prices of

[1] See p. 17.

[2] Out of 1363 cases of alleged profiteering dealt with by the police in 1943, only 178 were reported by the public.

goods, whether imported or home-produced, had been developed before that period it might well have been possible to stabilize the cost of living at a lower level. But it would be unfair to lay all the blame for this at the door of the Cyprus Government; as in other colonies His Majesty's Government was slow to inform them what demands would be made on their resources, even when they could be foreseen. All in all, even if the example of successful controls in the Sudan was not well copied, at least the ineffectiveness of those in Syria and Iraq was avoided.

CHAPTER VII

IRAQ

§ 1. Physical Changes

Man-power

Despite the fact that Iraq is normally viewed as a country which is almost the exact opposite of Egypt in being under-populated and under-cultivated, it cannot be maintained that in Iraq, any more than in most other Middle East countries, there was any real labour shortage on account of war needs. The peak employment of labour by the Allied military authorities appears to have been about 60,000 in 1943, including all categories of labour (skilled, clerical, etc.) employed directly or working for contractors.[1] A large number of these were employed in building and constructional work, but there was also a strong demand for engineering labour. By late 1944 the total number had declined to about 37,000. In addition to this, the Iraq Government Public Works Department employed more men on building work than in pre-war years, and the Iraq Army expanded from 28,000 in 1939 to about 40,000 in 1945. Although there is no accurate census of the population, estimates usually put it at about 4–4·5 millions.[2] Military demands clearly cannot have been very important in such circumstances, although it should be remembered that sections of the population are nomadic tribes, and therefore the main part of the labour supply for military work may well have come from the settled sections only. There were, of course, the usual shortages of skilled labour generally and unskilled labour in particular districts.[3]

Production

The best indication of war demands on productive resources is to be found in the estimated military expenditure of the Allies as shown in Table 1.

The importance of military expenditure in Iraq compared with other Middle East countries may be seen very roughly if we deflate the 1943

[1] *Report of British Goodwill Trade Mission*, p. 11.

[2] *Statistical Handbook of the Middle East*; Worthington, *Middle East Science*, p. 182. The number of males of working age can be put at approximately 1,400,000.

[3] See *Foreign Commerce Weekly*, 18 September 1943.

expenditure per head of the population by the increase in the cost of living index over the war years. In terms of 1939 prices military expenditure per head was about £2·1, which compares with peak expenditures of £2·4 in Egypt and £9·4 in Palestine, calculated in the same way. It is important to note, however, that 1943 was very much a peak year in Iraq, and that military expenditure at a high level in other countries was more prolonged. Furthermore, national output per head was probably even lower than in Egypt in 1939.[1] The main forms which this expenditure took were: military purchases of staple foodstuffs, such as cereals (133,000 tons of barley out of total exports of 169,000 tons in 1943 were on Army account) and dates; employment of local labour on building and engineering work; and personal purchases by troops.

TABLE 1. *Estimated allied military expenditure*

Year	Value (£m.)
1941	8·0
1942	15·4
1943	30·1
1944	10·4

Source. Special estimates.

Note. Expenditure on military contracts and purchases (except oil products) and personal expenditure of British troops included. Figures are net of N.A.A.F.I. and similar receipts and remittances overseas through official channels.

Iraq Government defence expenditure also increased during the war years from £1·9 million in 1939–40 to £3·7 million in 1943–4, and this was an additional drain on internal resources.

The main changes in Iraq exports may be seen from Table 2.

Despite the urgent demands of the Middle East countries and India for grain, and the U.S.S.R. for wool, the principal exports—grains, dates, raw wool—were all much less by volume in 1943–4 than in 1938–9, even though total receipts were higher. In computing the impact of receipts from exports on the Iraq economy—or in adding up the various forms of war contribution—we must be careful not to add together the military expenditure for 1943 and 1944 to the export figures for those years. Exports in 1943 include 133,000 tons of grain (value £4·0 million) and in 1944 they include 94,000 tons (value £2·5 million), and these sums are already included in the figures of

[1] See Bonné, op. cit., p. 36.

military expenditure reproduced in Table 1. To add the value of all exports and military expenditure together would therefore be double counting.

TABLE 2. *Principal exports*

Item	Quantity				Value £000's			
	1938–9 (av.)	1941	1943	1944	1938–9 (av.)	1941	1943	1944
Grain, pulses, flour (000's tons)	273	72	182	182	1086	438	5381	4705
Dates (000's tons)	166	143	72	107	924	1018	1922	2442
Raw wool (000's tons)	6·8	7·0	2·3	3·9	535	965	383	632
Raw cotton (000's tons)	3·0	4·5	2·9	0·6	170	404	410	147
Animals living (000's)	268	390	23	48	216	394	86	266
Hides and skins (000's tons)	1·9	2·5	2·4	1·6	170	192	401	285
Total value	—	—	—	—	3607	3906	9147	9171
Re-exports	—	—	—	—	117	351	343	659
Value of all exports	—	—	—	—	3724	4257	9490	9830

Source. Iraq Government Trade Returns.

Notes. (1) Values are f.o.b. Tons are metric.

(2) Grain exports for 1943 include Army exports of 133,000 tons (£4,014,000) and for 1944 94,000 tons (£2,500,000).

(3) Petroleum exports excluded as Iraq does not receive direct payment for these.

The other main Iraq war contribution was petroleum. As quantities of this were consumed in the Middle East by the Armies, figures of exports through normal channels do not present an adequate picture. Figures of total production were 4·4 million metric tons in 1938, 1·5 million metric tons in 1941 and 4·4 million metric tons in 1945,[1] and so there was no overall expansion of production. The low output of 1941 was part of the general paralysis of the Iraq economy in that year due to revolt and fighting.

Thus war brought new demands on Iraq resources in the shape of Allied military expenditure and local defence expenditure even though the volume of exports was reduced.

As in most other countries of the Middle East, there was no outstanding trend in agricultural production over the war years. Table 3 shows that output remained fairly constant, and therefore in so far as exports of primary products during this period were less than in pre-war years there is no reason to assume that the supply

[1] Shell Transport and Trading Co. 1945, *Annual Report*; *Petroleum Press Service*, November 1945.

of these goods available for the civilian population was much diminished.[1]

TABLE 3. *Agricultural output (000's metric tons)*

Crop	1936–9 (av.)	1942	1943
Barley	583	600	581
Wheat	540	400	390
Millet	120	90	90
Rice (paddy)	250	342	300
Maize	7	10	10
Cotton seed	6·4	4·7	N.A.

Sources. Statistical Handbook of the Middle East; U.S. Department of Agriculture, *Agricultural Statistics*, 1945.

Note. Dates are not included, as it has not been possible to obtain any figures of output.

Industry in Iraq was unimportant before the war. There were a few brickworks and cigarette, textile and soap factories, in addition to cottage industries, in 1939,[2] but these supplied only a very small proportion of domestic requirements of such goods. Nor was there any appreciable expansion in wartime, except for one or two isolated developments, such as a new mill for edible-oil crushing, and in fact in some cases, such as soap, output declined owing to a shortage of raw materials.

Consumption

The overwhelming factor determining the pattern of consumption changes was the reduction in volume of imported goods.

From Table 4 it may be seen that there were substantial reductions in the volume of nearly all types of imports. Staple items of diet, such as tea and sugar, suffered as well as textiles. Essential materials and machinery were also drastically curtailed. These had further reactions, as the output of such industrial products as were manufactured was thereby restricted and this intensified the shortages. The cut in imports also imposed a suspension of capital work, such as flood relief schemes and private building activity, and thereby made more labour available for other purposes, but this was only a minor benefit. It should be understood that the figures of total value mean

[1] There was, of course, consumption by local armies, but this was not large enough to affect the argument.

[2] *Review of Commercial Conditions* (Iraq).

little in view of the abnormal methods of calculation. As a rough estimate, it might perhaps be said that imports were cut by 50% in volume between 1938 and 1943.[1]

TABLE 4. *Principal imports*

Commodity	Quantity			
	1938–9 (av.)	1941	1943	1944
Cotton piecegoods (m. sq.m.)	62·5	32	25·5	21·4
Woollen piecegoods (m. sq.m.)	1·7	0·47	0·33	0·10
Soap (tons)	2,902	1,932	1,945	1,819
Sugar (000's tons)	44·5	40	13·1	29·4
Tea (tons)	3,100*	2,272	2,835	1,471
Coffee (tons)	1,347	1,248	3,339	1,088
Iron and steel (000's tons)	46·7	12	4·2	9·4
Boilers and machinery	—	—	—	—
Paper and cardboard	—	—	—	—
Cement (000's tons)	68	14·6	2·5	7·1
Total imports	—	—	—	—
Commodity	**Value £000's**			
	1938–9 (av.)	1941	1943	1944
Cotton piecegoods (m. sq.m.)	941	664	2,780	3,446
Woollen piecegoods (m. sq.m.)	191	107	191	66
Soap (tons)	85	96	388	480
Sugar (000's tons)	530	826	541	1,034
Tea (tons)	332*	381	1,549	285
Coffee (tons)	52	76	483	158
Iron and steel (000's tons)	906	390	211	286
Boilers and machinery	776	304	123	321
Paper and cardboard	135	204	409	430
Cement (000's tons)	171	58	59	119
Total imports	8,791	6,721	15,679	14,359

* 1939 only.

Source. Iraq Government Trade Returns.

Notes. (1) Iraq imports are not valued c.i.f. Where they are subject to specific duties they are valued c.i.f. plus landing charges; where liable to *ad valorem* duties they are valued at estimated local wholesale prices.
(2) Tons are metric.
(3) Military imports and N.A.A.F.I. stores excluded.
(4) Lend-Lease civilian imports included.

These changes reduced total consumption of sugar, tea, soap and textiles, as local production of soap and textiles can be ignored in this context. Probably the most acute shortage of all was in textiles, for cotton piecegoods were reduced to 50% of pre-war imports by 1941

[1] *Review of Commercial Conditions* (Iraq).

and subsequently remained at this or lower levels. Reductions of the other main commodities, even if more acute at certain times, were never so long sustained.

Of course, consumption reductions varied enormously in their incidence. There is little evidence of any widespread falls in real income, except among the salaried classes, but the distribution arrangements for scarce commodities involved many inequities. In the first place, rationing was not imposed at all until late in the war, and the constant changes in methods when it was imposed gave the speculative traders and hoarders an even better run of success than in most Middle East countries. The poorer classes, both in towns and villages, usually came off worst in such *mêlées*. Secondly, rationing arrangements favoured the towns rather than the villages. Typical of this policy was the sugar-rationing scheme of 1943, which allowed 750 g. per head per month in the towns and only 500 g. in the villages. And even in the rural areas some districts suffered more than others, for some of the remote Kurd villages experienced greater reductions in supply than the rest of the rural population.

§ 2. Financial Changes

The notes in circulation and the volume of bank deposits may be seen from Table 5. Comments will be made on this table in conjunction with those on price changes.

TABLE 5. *Supply of money (£m.)*

Date	Notes in circulation	Index	Bank deposits (all)	Index
Aug. 1939	4·7	100	1·96	100
Dec. 1939	5·2	111	2·02	103
June 1940	5·7	121	2·10	107
Dec. 1940	5·8	123	2·18	111
June 1941	7·3	128	1·84	94
Dec. 1941	10·2	217	3·51	180
June 1942	14·2	302	4·91	252
Dec. 1942	20·7	442	7·40	378
June 1943	28·8	612	10·39	529
Dec. 1943	34·0	725	15·47	790
June 1944	39·8	845	19·84	1010
Dec. 1944	38·8	825	20·60	1050
June 1945	40·5	858	20·53	1047

Source. League of Nations, *Monthly Bulletin of Statistics.*

Note. Bank deposits include savings deposits as well as current and time.

Prices

Changes in wholesale and retail prices are shown in Table 6. Before comparing the relative movements of the money supply and the price levels some points must be observed. First, the accuracy of the price indices in Iraq is even more open to doubt than in most other Middle East countries. It must be appreciated that the cost of living index is not a Government index but is based on Oil Company statistics. It is weighted according to pre-war expenditure by a labourer's family of four, and therefore is subject to all the limitations imposed by the wartime cuts in imports of staple items. Furthermore,

TABLE 6. *Wholesale and retail prices*

Date	Wholesale price index (Dec. 1938–Aug. 1939 = 100)	Cost of living index (1939 = 100)
Dec. 1939	121	N.A.
June 1940	136	N.A.
Dec. 1940	152	N.A.
June 1941	158	N.A.
Dec. 1941	284	N.A.
June 1942	359	N.A.
Dec. 1942	533	305
June 1943	581	323
Dec. 1943	636	405
June 1944	568	358
Dec. 1944	521	375
June 1945	488	369

Sources. Wholesale prices: *Statistical Handbook of the Middle East*; Retail: *Rafidain Oil Co. Index.*

owing to the inadequacy of many rationing and distribution arrangements, black-market and not controlled prices (on which both the wholesale and retail indices are based) were far more the rule than the exception. Finally, the price indices hide enormous disparities in the extents to which prices of individual commodities soared. Some statistics of these disparities and of the ratio of free to controlled prices are given in Table 7.

It can be seen from Table 7 that no simple deductions about price rises of imported as against home-produced goods or of the ratio of free to controlled prices can be made. If we take the controlled prices for February 1944, the price of imported tea was 250% above the level of August 1939, whereas that of imported coffee was only 138%; the price of local wheat rose ten times, that of rice only four times. The ratio of free to controlled price in February 1944 was nearly three in the case of textiles and less than two in the case of wheat; on the other hand, in the case of sugar it was six in December 1943.[1]

TABLE 7. *Wholesale prices of individual commodities (£ per metric ton)*

Date	Imported goods					
	Tea		Coffee		White shirting	
	Price	Index	Price	Index	Price	Index
Aug. 1939	200	100	105	100	0·6	100
Aug. 1941	430	215	180	172	1·5	250
Aug. 1942	445	222	145	139	2·7	450
Aug. 1943	680	340	220	210	9·35	1560
Feb. 1944 (controlled)	700	350	250	238	5·73	950
Feb. 1944 (free)	2500	1250	400	382	16·0	2670

Date	Local produce							
	Wheat		Barley		Rice		Dates	
	Price	Index	Price	Index	Price	Index	Price	Index
Aug. 1939	4·2	100	2·6	100	21·6	100	2·85	100
Aug. 1941	12·75	304	5·2	200	17·0	78	2·8	99
Aug. 1942	22	524	13·5	519	53·5	248	13	457
Aug. 1943	25	595	20·5	787	81	376	26	914
Feb. 1944 (controlled)	25	595	20·5	787	—	—	—	—
Feb. 1944 (free)	40	950	N.A.	—	88	407	22	772

Source. Special information.

Notes. (1) Controlled prices were not operative before February 1944.
(2) White shirting prices are in £ per 40 yd. length.
(3) Wheat and barley prices are producers' prices and do not include costs of collection, tax, cleaning, etc. In the case of wheat this would increase controlled price for February 1944 to £32.

It is clear from a comparison of price and money movements that there was a general tendency for wholesale prices to increase faster than the supply of money up to the end of 1942. Several factors accounted for this, and probably the most important was the revolt of 1941. This started a movement into goods of all kinds, and the accompanying sharp decline in bank deposits in June 1941 (the fall

[1] Special information.

was relatively most severe in current deposits) is a clear illustration of the lack of public confidence at that time. Other causes were the rise in c.i.f. import prices of dollar-area goods, the dismal succession of Allied defeats, the poor harvests in the Middle East in 1941, and the persistent speculative hoarding of commodities in the hope of rising prices.

Despite this tendency for prices to rise faster than the supply of money, it is doubtful whether the inflationary process in Iraq can legitimately be said to have been associated with any very widespread or prolonged distrust of the currency. An essential factor which prevented any headlong flight from the currency was the fixed convertibility into sterling. There is little doubt that if any devaluation of the Iraq dinar had been effected or even rumoured in 1942, the country would have been well on the way to hyper-inflation. During the later war years the tendencies evident in 1941–2 were no longer apparent and there was an increased willingness to hold notes and bank deposits. It is significant in this context that whereas notes of £5 or over formed only 25% of the circulation in 1943, they were 50% in 1945.[1] This, of course, was partly associated with high prices and incomes, but, as in Egypt,[2] there was also a heavy demand for purposes of hoarding or illicit trading.

Incomes

Little information is available on income changes in Iraq, but there is no doubt that the agricultural population—which forms some 60–70% of the total—enjoyed an unrivalled era of prosperity. Before the compulsory requisitioning schemes of 1943 it is probable that the high prices for agricultural produce meant high profits for the speculative dealers rather than the small cultivator. But the prices of £25 per ton for wheat and £20·5 for barley (see Table 7) do represent the prices paid to the cultivators in 1943–4, and thus there is no doubt about their gains in those years, compared with 1939 prices of £4·2 and £2·6 respectively. Furthermore, it must be remembered that only 195,000 tons of wheat and 230,000 tons of barley out of the 1943 crops of 390,000 and 581,000 tons of wheat and barley respectively were purchased by the Government or the U.K.C.C. Therefore, it may well be that cultivators' receipts were more in line with free than controlled prices for those amounts not purchased in this way.

[1] *Iraq Currency Board Report*, 1945. [2] See p. 138.

Generally, we may say that cereal cultivators' prices had risen by 1943–4 about eight times above pre-war levels. Furthermore, in 1943 harvests were very good, and therefore receipts were larger on that account too. The cost of living figures quoted in Table 6 are not an accurate index, but it is undoubtedly true that the cultivator classes in general enjoyed large increases in real income, for although share cropping is the dominant form of land tenure in areas such as the mountain villages, the shares of landlords and cultivators are fixed by time-honoured tradition, and there is no reason to suppose that the smaller cultivators received unduly low shares of the gains. The reductions in indebtedness and the eagerness to invest in the traditional outlets of horses, land and gold are further signs of the general prosperity.

Owing to the rampant nature of black markets the merchants importing goods made very large gains. There was no real attempt to control these gains until 1943, and even then the schemes worked much better in theory than in practice.[1] Army contractors, of course, inevitably gained in the general upswing of activity and prices.

Information on wage changes is extremely scanty, but an index of wage rates paid to unskilled labour by an Oil Company is shown in Table 8.

TABLE 8. *Index of wage rates*

Date	Index	Date	Index
Aug. 1939	100	Dec. 1942	220
Dec. 1939	133	June 1943	220
June 1940	133	Dec. 1943	220
Dec. 1940	133	June 1944	320
June 1941	133	Dec. 1944	320
Dec. 1941	166	June 1945	320
June 1942	180		

Source. Special information from Oil Company.

A comparison of the cost of living index shown in Table 6 with this series apparently shows some fall in real wage rates, but this conclusion should not be pressed too far. For one thing, the two series are drawn up by two different Oil Companies, and owing to the considerable local price differences it cannot be automatically inferred that, because prices rose further in one place than wages in another, there was any general reduction in real wages. In any case money earnings probably went up more than rates, and there was also some extension

[1] See p. 215.

of the pre-war system of providing necessaries of life at concession rates. On balance there is little reason to believe that the bulk of the wage-earning population suffered severe falls in real earnings, even though there were the usual losses among the lower paid salaried workers.

Finally, it must be remembered that even allowing for the increased employment of labour by the military authorities, the wage- and salary-earning population in Iraq is a very small one.[1] Any losses it incurred were far more than outbalanced by the undoubted gains of the agricultural population. The very fact that the inflationary process went so far and so fast in Iraq is an indication that not many people were left behind in the process.

Sterling assets

No complete information is available on changes in sterling assets, as private and institutional holdings were fairly considerable,[2] but a rough indication of the rate of change is to be found in the holdings of the Iraq Currency Board (see Table 9).

TABLE 9. *Iraq Currency Board, sterling assets*

Date	Assets (£m.)	Annual increase
Dec. 1938	5	—
Dec. 1939	6	1
Dec. 1940	7	1
Dec. 1941	12	5
Dec. 1942	22	10
Dec. 1943	36	14
Mar. 1945	43·5	7·5

Sources. Iraq Currency Board Reports; Bank of International Settlements Report, 1944.

§3. INFLATION AND CONTROLS

Our main task here is to trace the reasons why the inflationary process of prices and incomes developed so far in Iraq, but before we do this we must obtain some idea of the relative magnitude of the major causal factors. This is not an easy task in Iraq owing to the complications introduced by the oil concessions and the peculiar way of

[1] In 1939 the total number of Iraqi personnel employed by the Oil Companies was only 3987 (*Statistical Handbook of the Middle East*).

[2] It may be estimated from figures given in *The Economist* (1 February 1947) and Table 9 that these were about £26 million in June 1945, but no earlier figures are available.

assessing import values, and therefore our approach must inevitably be even more rough and ready than in previous chapters.

We have already noted that the peak military expenditure of £30 million was attained in 1943, and that in that year the volume of imports was only about 50% of pre-war levels. These two factors are undoubtedly the two most important points to stress in analysing the nature of the inflationary process in Iraq, but in addition to them we must look at public finance and export and import receipts.

Figures of Government receipts and expenditure are shown in Table 10.

TABLE 10. *Government receipts and expenditure (£m.)*

Year	Budget receipts	Budget expenditure	Surplus (+) deficit (−)	Internal receipts	Internal expenditure	Income creating balance: surplus (+) deficit (−)
1939–40	9·2	8·6	+0·6	6·1	8·6	−2·5
1940–41	9·7	9·8	−0·1	6·8	9·8	−3·0
1941–42	10·2	8·7	+1·5	7·0	8·7	−1·7
1942–43	13·8	11·6	+2·2	11·6	11·6	Nil
1943–44	18·1	15·4	+2·7	14·4	15·4	−1·0
1944–45	18·9	19·0	−0·1	16·7	19·0	−2·3

Source. Statistical Handbook of the Middle East.

Notes. (1) Capital Works Expenditure included in both budget and internal expenditure figures.

(2) Oil Company royalties, advances from Companies and Currency Board contributions are excluded from internal receipts as they do not represent any absorption of purchasing power in the country. Profits on railways, Basra Port and Fao Bar Dredging service are not included in budget receipts, but the magnitude of this error is not large, as total profits of this sort were only estimated to be about £300,000 for 1944–5.

From Table 9 it can be seen that although the budget as a whole showed a surplus during most of the war years, internal receipts usually fell somewhat short of expenditure.

No accurate idea of the contribution of net receipts from trade in merchandise can be gained owing to the peculiar method of calculating import values, but Table 11 shows the published figures for what they are worth.

It must be clearly understood that the apparent import surplus is rather meaningless, in view of the methods of evaluating imports. It is extremely doubtful whether the c.i.f value of imports in 1943 and 1944 could have been more than 1938 values in view of the halving of the volume of imports. On the other hand, the high export figures for 1943 and 1944, it may be recalled, are largely due to military purchases of barley of £4·0 and £2·5 million in 1943 and 1944 respectively, and we are already counting these receipts under military expenditure. On balance, it is probable that payments for imports drained away more than was received in export receipts.

TABLE 11. *Exports and imports of merchandise (£m.)*

Year	Exports (f.o.b.) (including re-exports)	Imports	Balance: export surplus (+) import surplus (−)
1938	3·7	9·4	−5·7
1939	3·7	8·2	−4·5
1940	4·1	8·7	−4·6
1941	4·2	6·9	−2·7
1942	4·7	12·2	−7·5
1943	9·5	15·7	−6·2
1944	9·8	14·5	−4·7

Source. Iraq Trade Returns.

Notes. (1) Imports valued as noted on p. 203.
(2) British military and N.A.A.F.I. imports excluded.
(3) Petroleum exports and most Oil Company imports excluded.

The problem of both visible and invisible items is complicated by Oil Company receipts and payments. Petroleum export receipts should not all be counted as Iraq receipts, as the funds are received by the Oil Companies in London but are not necessarily remitted to Iraq. On the other hand, pre-war import figures appear to have included capital goods imported by the Oil Companies, and although the volume of these cannot have been as great in wartime, the true value of imports is exaggerated to the extent of their value, as they do not absorb Iraqi expenditure. Oil Company royalties[1] have been a standard form of invisible export for some time, but as these have not been reckoned as an internal receipt they must obviously not be included as a further income-generating element. But Oil Companies did have to pay their local employees and purchase local materials, which was another contributory factor.

Other invisible items are not important, but they do include such transactions on current account as port receipts and gold sales, and on capital account there were items such as the borrowing of £1 million sterling in 1938–9 and its repayment in 1943, the two loans of £1 million

[1] Normally about £2 million per annum. The highest wartime figure was £2·79 million (1943–4) and the lowest £1·46 million (1941–2).

from the Oil Companies in 1939 and 1940, transfers of Currency Board profits and investments of private individuals and institutions in foreign assets in the war years.

It is not possible to give any adequate quantitative picture of these various items, but the major factor was undoubtedly military expenditure—at any rate in 1942–4. The higher prices received by exporters, the low volume of imports and the steady 'true' deficit all helped, but in the role of accomplices rather than ringleaders. We shall therefore be justified in mainly concentrating on the problems raised by military expenditure.

The delightfully haphazard way in which different authorities were competing for Iraq products and services in 1942 shows why incomes and prices were likely to rise in a fast and furious manner. The British Ministry of Food was negotiating, via British merchant organizations, for the bulk purchase of the barley surplus; the U.K.C.C. was endeavouring to purchase isolated supplies on behalf of the M.E.S.C.; the Iraq Government was trying to conclude 3-year contracts on behalf of producers with anyone willing to make the highest bid. In fact, there was no registration of cereal stocks at all until 1943, and no Government requisitioning until that date. Similarly, military demands for labour or for commodities of any sort were not adjusted to the local supply position in any way.

As a result, incomes of cultivators, merchants, manufacturers and wage earners were bound to rise to high levels. There was no attempt to keep cultivators' incomes below the rise in the cost of living—rather efforts were devoted to extracting the highest possible prices from the military authorities or from other Middle East countries. Until 1943 there were no standardized fixed prices paid to cultivators for their crops at all. Various laws were passed in 1943 and 1944 regulating margins on imported commodities, but it is extremely doubtful whether they were ever obeyed by more than a fraction of the trading community. Similarly, town rents were controlled on paper but without much practical result. And the usual practice of the military authorities of employing unskilled labour on more highly graded work was instrumental in driving up wages even more than military rates for unskilled labour suggest.

Attempts to limit consumption expenditure by higher taxation or voluntary savings must now be examined. The ratio of internal receipts to Iraq Government and Allied military expenditure may be seen from Table 12.

TABLE 12. *Internal receipts and all expenditure (£m.)*

Year	Receipts	% ratio of receipts to Iraq Govt. exp.	% ratio of receipts to Iraq Govt. and mil. exp.
1939–40	6·1	71	—
1940–41	6·8	69	—
1941–42	7·0	80	42
1942–43	11·6	100	43
1943–44	14·4	95	32
1944–45	16·7	88	57

Source. Statistical Handbook of the Middle East.

Note. Oil royalties, loans from Oil Companies and Currency Board contributions excluded from receipts.

From Table 12 it may be seen that receipts sank to a low proportion of total expenditure in 1943, but after that date the decline in military expenditure and the increase in receipts in 1944–5 helped to improve the situation. There were many changes in rates of established taxes, such as customs and excise, income tax, etc. The emergency customs taxes, introduced in 1940 on staple items such as sugar, tea and piecegoods, yielded £330,000 in 1940–1, although the receipts fell a little in later years. Income tax (including E.P.T. and Surtax) yielded £370,000 in 1939–40 and £1·70 million in 1943–4. Nevertheless, it cannot be said that the burden of taxation was heavy in Iraq. Income tax only applied to a very limited section of the population, for in 1944 there were only 24,000 different payers. Of these 9500 were salary earners, 14,380 lived on profits and unearned income of various categories, and only 120 were limited companies. Nor were rates of taxation high on these incomes; in 1944 a single man with an annual earned income of £1500 per year paid only 10% in taxation, which contrasts with the 40% in the U.K. or the 17% in India at that time. The most vital omission of all was that the agricultural sections were lightly taxed, for they were precisely the people whose incomes had risen so much. Income tax never applied to them at all; and animal and produce taxes, although increased, failed to touch their incomes seriously. Furthermore, this lightness of agricultural taxation had indirect reactions, in that it made higher taxation of other elements appear unjust. Finally, receipts from import duties remained at about £2·3 million throughout the war years, and this was despite the fact that goods are not assessed for tariff purposes on their declared values but on local market prices, which, as we have seen, increased so very much in some cases.

Nor were voluntary savings of any substantial help in restricting consumption expenditure. The Government accumulated reserves out of the steady annual receipts of about £2–3 million from oil royalties, but until 1944 no loans were launched by the Government as anti-inflationary devices. At the end of that year two loans of £1 million—one at 3% interest and the other a Premium Bonds issue with an effective yield of 4%—were launched, but they were really not of much avail in the light of the enormous expansion in money demand which had taken place. Arrangements for Iraqi subscriptions to British War Bonds and facilities for deposits in the P.O. Savings Bank did not produce very substantial results either.[1] It was hard to wean the Iraqi mentality from the traditional view of regarding property or goods as the natural form of investment, but it appears to have been harder still for the Government to try to do so.

Gold sales by the British authorities and diamond sales by the U.K.C.C. were also tried in an endeavour to divert the flow of expenditure from commodities. Gold was sold by tender in Iraq from August 1943 to April 1944, and it is estimated that some £3 million was sold over this period. This must have been counter-inflationary to some extent, but military expenditure was about £15 million over this period, and therefore gold sales were not a very great offset. How far these purchases of gold did represent a true diversion of expenditure from other consumption goods or how far they were bought from hoards of notes is not known. There is no evidence that there were any indirect reactions on prices through wholesale prices falling with gold prices.[2] Nor were diamond sales ever in sufficient quantity to make any real impression on consumption expenditure.

The history of rationing, distribution and price controls and decontrols in Iraq is long and tortuous. Broadly, it may be said that sugar was the only commodity rationed to consumers on a national

[1] Post Office Savings Bank deposits rose from £65,000 in December 1939 to £215,000 in December 1943.

[2] It may be of interest to note that Iraqi appetite for gold was the cause of the suspension of gold sales in Iran, the last of the Middle East countries where gold was being sold. It was realized in June 1944 that gold sold in Iran was being smuggled into Iraq, converted into dinars, and these were then exchanged for sterling which was smuggled back into Iran. British liability to convert 60% of all Iran sterling balances into gold at world prices meant that the whole process was no longer a means of reducing gold outlay (cf. p. 20).

basis until 1944, although there were special arrangements for distribution of scarce goods, such as soap, utility cloth, vegetable oils and rice, to selected classes, such as Oil Company personnel and Government servants. In January 1944, schemes were introduced for rationing of tea, coffee and textiles to the whole population, but the textile scheme suffered many vicissitudes during the year. By the end of 1944, ration cards had been issued to a large proportion of the population in preparation for further attempts to establish a sound system. Thus consumers' rationing really played little direct part in curbing inflationary tendencies. It applied to a small number of commodities, and even there only in the last stages of the war. As in other countries the schemes tended to favour the towns rather than the rural areas, for not only were rations greater in the towns (the combined tea and coffee ration in June 1944 was 90 g. per head per month for the urban population and 60 g. for the rural),[1] but they were also more sure of getting them. The history of the attempts to apply textile rationing in Baghdad is a sorry one, but the plight of many country districts was even worse, and from the point of view of assuring grain supplies it was more vital to distribute consumption goods to rural than to urban areas.

Nor was direct price control much more effective than rationing in checking the inflationary movement. Import licensing was introduced in 1941, and by 1943 this was extended to cover a wide range of commodities imported by land as well as by sea. In 1942–3 a large number of measures were introduced for registration of stocks and control of prices either by ceiling prices or by percentage mark-up on import prices, but the only results were that supplies disappeared from the markets, and, apart from short intervals when it was feared that the Government might really carry out its threats of enforcing controls, prices travelled gaily upwards. Some success was achieved in early 1944 when, along with the rationing drive, a large number of commodities had maximum retail prices fixed, but these measures only applied for a few months, as most price controls were discontinued from October 1944, in anticipation that the war would end soon and be followed by a flood of imports. Nor were the attempts to control prices of home-grown products much more successful. Requisitioning at fixed prices was only applied to cereals in 1943, and even then did not apply to more than about half the barley and wheat

[1] Equivalent to about 3 and 2 oz. respectively.

crops.[1] The cupidity of the cultivators was only matched by the profit-making capacity of the merchants.

The fundamental difficulties of applying rationing and price controls in Iraq were the inefficiency and incompetence of the administration, the lack of any adequate control of supplies and the apathy of the population. The constantly changing organization of the departments and personnel concerned with supply, the multiplicity of regulations[2] issued to subordinate officials, and the venality of many sections of the administration[3] were alone sufficient to explain why rationing was not likely to work. Even apart from this, Iraq was at the mercy of the Allied Supply authorities for the provision of such staple goods as sugar and textiles, and by 1943–4 stocks of textiles were so low that the failure of any consignment of textiles to arrive was sufficient to upset any rationing scheme, however well planned. Inside the country merchants of all classes were only too keen to hoard scarce goods or sell them to one another, and retailers were only too anxious to give short weight or adulterate official rations. Although the Iraq Government did attempt to deal with these practices in the case of some commodities by conferring monopoly rights of distribution at the merchant level on specific British firms (e.g. for sugar) and by selecting retailers for distribution to consumers, there were a number of commodities (such as footwear or vegetables in 1943) for which prices were fixed without any control over distribution whatever, and this, of course, invited trouble. The long land frontiers made smuggling of commodities of all types an easy as well as a profitable and time-honoured livelihood. Finally, the application of complicated and constantly changing regulations to a population partly nomadic and neither understanding nor caring to understand them raised many more obstacles.

In view of the great reduction in the volume of imports (see Table 4), it was inevitable that the limited success of the Iraq Government in controlling incomes directly or controlling expenditure out of incomes by the usual measures of taxation, savings, rationing and price control would lead to a large price-inflation. For in 1943 cotton piecegoods were reduced to less than half pre-war figures, and sugar to one-third; and basic materials, such as iron and steel and cement, also

[1] The Government had a legal monopoly of wholesale trading over all the crops, but it was never fully enforced.

[2] The changing allocations and methods of rationing tea and coffee in the first six months of 1944 are an example.

[3] A typical example is given on p. 218.

suffered heavy reductions. As textiles, sugar and tea are staple goods on which the Iraqi spends a large proportion of his income, any reductions of such magnitude inevitably had inflationary results.

There were other indirect reasons why the reduction in the volume of imports was so important. Agricultural production in Iraq is undoubtedly strictly limited in the short period by fundamental difficulties of climate, water supply, the chaotic state of land rights in some parts of the country, the habit of shifting cultivation, and by the ancient methods of wooden ploughs and hand sowing, but nevertheless the cut in imports did react on productive capacity in at least two ways. First, the reduction of imports of machinery and spare parts was of importance, particularly for the irrigation pumping systems. Secondly, and probably more vital still, there was the fact that the lack of consumption goods made the cultivator unwilling to produce. It is true that the 1943 grain surplus was very large, but this was a reflexion of high prices, and it is at least open to argument that the supply of subsidiary products, such as vegetables, available for the townsfolk would have been larger if more consumption goods had been available for the rural population.

In similar manner the lack of imports made it difficult even to maintain the low level of industrial production, let alone raise it. Materials and machinery were rigorously cut down, and new road vehicles or spare parts for old were practically unobtainable. Railway stores also were very much reduced, and this was particularly serious in view of the heavy military demands.

To some extent this lack of imported supplies and the consequent results were the fault of the Iraq Government. Until 1941, there was no import licensing and no attempt was made to lay in stocks of essentials, private merchants being allowed to import those goods which were most profitable to themselves rather than those which were most needed by the community. The lack of consumption goods available to rural areas was due to official internal distribution arrangements and to the failure to control stocks as well as to global reductions in imports.

In all these ways, the reduction in the volume of imports presented fundamental and inescapable problems for a country without the power to manufacture substitutes at home and unable for one reason or another to impose adequate controls.

§ 4. Critique of War Organization

There were clearly many reasons why some degree of inflation was inevitable in Iraq. The military revolt of 1941 brought trade to a standstill and paralysed the economy. Then came a large volume of military expenditure which at its height was roughly of the same order of magnitude per head of the population, expressed in terms of 1939 prices, as in Egypt. The unique opportunities for high export prices for the staple grain, date and wool products[1] helped in the process, and the inevitable cut in imports of essentials tore further gaps in the price structure of the economy.

The nature of the country and the structure of economic life explain why any such upheavals were bound to be accompanied by financial upheavals too. The administration was small and often untrained in economic affairs; there was, for instance, no staff of competent assessors to deal with income tax. Furthermore, it was often corrupt. Between February and August 1944 it was found that some £1,187,000 of textiles had been sold against coupons in Baghdad, but only £940,000 of coupons had been issued there up to that date. Part of the explanation is to be found in purchases by non-Baghdad residents, but the illegal distribution of coupons by Government employees played no small part. Moreover, this administration had to deal with a country of 116,000 square miles and with extremely long frontiers, which were a paradise for anyone with smuggling tendencies. Information was scanty about the normal ways in which economic affairs were conducted. It was impossible to impose adequate rationing when not even the overall size of the population was known, and even if it were the wanderings of nomadic tribes would be quite likely to make the information for particular areas out of date by the time it was wanted. Finally, the tendency for many sections of the population who had acquired cash to hoard goods on the slightest fear—or fear of fear—of shortage, or conversely to dishoard in anticipation of Government action,[2] inevitably created instability in the system. When prices were already tending to rise because of the reduction in supply such habits pushed them up still further.

[1] A striking contrast with the problems of citrus growers in Palestine and Cyprus.

[2] When the 'Bill for the Organization of Economic Life' was being debated in 1943, wholesale prices of many commodities fell or rose daily on the anticipation that the bill would or would not be passed.

But similar problems to these were faced and overcome in other Middle East countries without such large price- and income-inflation. What are the further factors which explain why prices rose so much further than in Egypt or Palestine? One obvious point is that when local production capacity is allowed for the impact of the fall in imports was not so severe in these countries as in Iraq. But military expenditure in both these countries was longer sustained than in Iraq, and in Palestine higher per head of the population. It was also directed to large-scale purchases of manufactured goods and not simply to unskilled labour and staple crops, which should have been easier to provide without derangement of the economic system. Nor is there the same overwhelming long-term problem in Iraq of the pressure of population on the land which always faces the Egyptian Government, or the embittered antagonism of Jews and Arabs which bedevils administration in Palestine.

The obvious answer is the hesitancy of the Iraq Government to impose controls soon enough or efficiently enough to check the growth in the volume of money demand. There was no import licensing until 1941, and yet no effort to build up stocks; price and distribution controls were virtually non-existent before 1943, and rationing (except for sugar) before 1944. It is true that the administrative machinery was not adequate enough to enforce these controls fully, even when they were applied, and that therefore they were not very successful in practice, but this argument cannot be applied to the methods of encouraging savings, for the loans which were floated at the end of 1944 were outstandingly successful. The £10 Premium Bonds stood at a premium of £2 on the first day after they were launched, and were, in fact, fully subscribed by the second day. There is little doubt that similar loans could have been floated earlier in the war years by the Iraq Government if the will and the vision had been there. It is also very probable that the British Government could have raised loans, although it might have been necessary to pay higher interest rates than those paid on the 1944 bonds. Finally, other methods, such as subsidization of essential prices or differential rationing of consumer goods to encourage grain cultivators, were never tried; in fact, rationing definitely favoured the urban population rather than the cultivators.

There is little doubt that, as in Egypt, there was no great desire to restrain the inflationary process in its early stages. This was, of course, closely connected with the parallel facts that Iraq was not officially at war until 1943 and even after that date she was not liable for the military expenditure which took place. In such circumstances, there was little incentive for the Government to tax for a budget surplus or encourage voluntary savings; nor could it be expected that public response to such moves would be encouraging. Many could argue that it was high patriotism to do nothing to check the inflationary movement. The cultivators, landlords and merchant classes behind the Government were making large profits and at the same time could always claim that in so doing they were building up the sterling assets of the country. The Government itself was obviously better occupied in seeing that cereal growers got high prices for their crops rather than in restricting the level of incomes and consumption expenditure.

CHAPTER VIII

SYRIA AND THE LEBANON[1]

§ 1. Physical Changes

Man-power

As in the other countries of the Middle East, the main wartime demand for man-power was the direct employment of labour by the Allied military authorities. The peak figure was reached in late 1943, and this was of the order of 30,000 men. The greater part of these were unskilled labourers for work on such projects as the Tripoli-Haifa railway extension, but there was, of course, the usual demand for skilled fitters, carpenters, and electrical workers, and, in addition, a considerable proportion were employed as Army drivers. By 1945 the total number still employed was less than 19,000. In addition to direct War Department employment private contractors on work for the Services used about 4000–6000 in the peak year 1943, although this number was rapidly reduced in 1944 and 1945. There was no further drain on man-power due to expansion of local Armed Forces, for these were negligible. As the total population of the two countries in 1942 was estimated at 3·9 million (Syria 2·9 million and the Lebanon 1·0 million),[2] the diversion of man-power to war demands cannot be said to have been serious. This conclusion is reinforced when it is recalled that unemployment was heavy in the towns during the blockade of 1941.[3] Nevertheless, as elsewhere, there were shortages in particular trades and areas.

Production

The first form of war demand to consider is estimated military expenditure. The figures are set out in Table 1.

If military expenditure in 1942 is deflated to 1939 prices by the cost of living index it can be seen that very roughly military expenditure was of the order of £1·7 per head of the population. The major part of this expenditure was wage payments of civilians employed by

[1] Unless otherwise stated, financial statistics are in £ sterling.

[2] *Statistical Handbook of the Middle East.* On the basis of the Lebanon Census of 1944 the number of adult males of working age in both countries may be put at about 1,100,000.

[3] See *Foreign Commerce Weekly*, 12 September 1942.

the military, and personal expenditure of troops, but in addition there were, of course, Army consumption of local foodstuffs[1] and purchases of a few manufactured and processed goods, such as matches,[2] beer,[3] jam and canned fruit. The exact size of the military contracts for these goods is unknown, but it is reasonable to assume that they account for the major part of the increased production shown in Table 4.

TABLE 1. *Estimated Allied military expenditure (£m.)*

Year	Expenditure	Cost of living index (Aug. 1939=100)
1940	7·1	Dec. 162
1941	6·8	June 248
1942	20·4	June 340
1943	23·2	June 457
1944	18·9	June 559

Source. Special estimates.

Notes. (1) Expenditure of French and British military authorities included.
(2) All types of military expenditure inclusive of personal expenditure of troops (but net of N.A.A.F.I. receipts, remittances overseas through official channels) are covered.

The second form of war demand was the expenditure of the Office des Céréales Panifiables (hereafter called O.C.P.). This organization was formed in 1942 with a complete monopoly over the purchase, trading and transport of cereals, and in 1942, 1943 and 1944 bought up very large stocks from Syrian producers. In 1943, for instance, some 380,000 tons of cereals were bought at a cost of £12·9 million. In so far as these cereals were used for supplying the Armies or other populations of the Middle East or for building up stocks in Syria and the Lebanon, there was, *pro tanto*, a drain on current local resources and at the same time more purchasing power was created locally. The exact proportions in which purchases were disposed of is not known for every year, but in 1943 some 80,000 tons were exported and 75,000 tons put to stock, which contrasts with a net annual average export of 450 tons of wheat and wheat flour in 1935–8.

Thirdly, there was some local defence expenditure by the two Governments, but as there were no Armed Forces of any size this was not very important. In 1943, the peak year, Defence and Police

[1] In 1944 alone, Syria and the Lebanon produced 20,000 tons of fresh vegetables to meet Army requirements in the Middle East. A considerable amount of dehydration was also done.

[2] 1 million boxes were delivered to the Services in 1943.

[3] Production was 288,000 bottles a week by September 1943.

expenditure of all types, which included some civil as well as purely military items, amounted to £1,280,000.

Fourthly, we have to consider the exports, excluding the purchases of the O.C.P. These are set out in Table 2.

TABLE 2. *Principal exports*

Commodity	Quantity (tons)		Value f.o.b. (£m.)	
	1938–9 (av.)	1942–3 (av.)	1938–9 (av.)	1942–3 (av.)
Silk (all forms)	—	—	0·23	0·81
Barley	30,700	2,350	0·13	0·10
Citrus fruit	28,500	420	0·21	0·006
Lentils	19,346	1,226	0·175	0·03
Chick peas	10,800	108	0·07	0·007
Wool	3,047	3,140	0·30	0·63
Cement	45,700	15,385	0·06	0·13
Volume index (1938 = 100)	102	17	—	—
Value of exports	—	—	3·7	3·15
Value of re-exports	—	—	0·1	Nil
Total value	—	—	3·8	3·15

Source. Recueil de Statistiques de la Syrie et du Liban.

Note. O.C.P. exports, military stores and petroleum re-exports excluded.

The figures in Table 2 tell their own story without any need of comment—there was an overwhelming fall in the volume of exports of all types, even though prices did increase sufficiently to make exporters' total receipts in 1942–3 nearly as great as in 1938–9. This fall in volume obviously relieved the pressure of wartime demands on domestic supplies.

From this brief and sketchy picture of the demands on Syrian and Lebanese resources during the war we must turn to examine the principal changes in domestic output. Before doing so, it is necessary to add a word of warning that the statistics of output are of very dubious character and are much more of the nature of estimates than calculated totals. In fact, the majority of the statistics of Syria and the Lebanon are subject to even wider margins of error than those of other Middle East countries.

The main changes in agricultural output may be seen from Table 3.

From Table 3 it seems that wheat output[1] increased above pre-war levels, although it should be remembered that 1943 was a record crop

[1] The *area* under wheat cultivation also expanded considerably, as it increased from 501,000 hectares in 1935–8 (av.) to 645,000 hectares in 1942. (1 hectare = 2·47 acres.)

year in nearly all the Middle East countries. Output of other staple cereal crops was roughly maintained at pre-war levels, but vegetable production increased somewhat.

TABLE 3. *Agricultural output (000's metric tons)*

Commodity	1935–8 (av.)	1942	1943
Wheat	487	508	624
Barley	320	249	330
Millet	75	72	44
Maize	23	33	22
Vines	171	594	292
Melons and water melons	161	63	327
Olives	78	179	134
Potatoes	41	71	N.A.
Onions	41	41	40
Chick peas	14	13	19

Sources. Statistical Handbook of the Middle East; Recueil de Statistiques de la Syrie et du Liban.

Notes. Millet figure is 1936–9 (av.) and not 1935–8 (av.). Vine figure is 1938 only and not 1935–8 (av.).

Manufacturing on an organized factory scale has never been important in Syria and the Lebanon, and the largest industry from the point of view of employment has always been hand-loom weaving in which some 20,000 workers were engaged before the war. Nevertheless, there was some expansion of output in a number of light industries, as may be seen from Table 4.

TABLE 4. *Industrial output*

Commodity	1938–9 (av.)	1940	1941	1942	1943
Cotton yarn (tons)	1302	1950	2145	1960	2350
Flour (000's tons)	183	245	210	245	288
Soap (tons)	2275	N.A.	1500	2000	4500
Jam (tons)	185	215	180	600	700
Canned fruit (tons)	2415	1835	1341	6000	6000
Beer (000's litres)	2400	1820	3434	4793	7032
Tobacco manufactures (tons)	1408	1700	1700	1800	1900
Cement (000's tons)	170	90	68	172	N.A.

Sources. Statistical Handbook of the Middle East; Recueil de Statistiques de la Syrie et du Liban.

Note. Tons are metric.

From Table 4 it can be seen that apart from the recession of 1941, which was part of the general freezing of activity in that year, there was a wartime expansion of output in these industries. How far this expansion took place at the expense of other industries, and how far it was really an addition to national output as a whole, it is difficult to determine. But it is known that production of other goods, such as cotton piecegoods and silk cocoons,[1] expanded over the war years, although continuous output statistics are not available. There is no reason to believe that there was any reduction in services of all kinds, and it seems fairly safe to conclude that the increase in output to satisfy military demands was not achieved by cutting down other sectors of the economy.

Consumption

As with the other Middle East territories the main determinant of cuts in overall consumption was the reduced volume of imports, of which particulars are shown in Table 5.

It is clear that there were great reductions in such staple consumption goods as sugar, rice and cotton piecegoods, as well as in vital raw materials. In fact, in 1941 the volume of imports sank to a lower proportion of the pre-war level than it did in any other Middle East country in any one of the war years.

With the sparsity of information about pre-war consumption habits, stocks in 1939 and expansion of home-produced foods, it is not possible to make any accurate estimates of the reductions in supplies available of even the main items in normal consumption. Instead, we must content ourselves with a few broad generalizations.

Flour and bread were rationed in both Syria and the Lebanon after 1942, and monthly rations varied nominally between 10 and 13 kg. per head per month. How this compared with average pre-war consumption figures is not known accurately, but it is believed to have been rather less.[2] But it must be emphasized that it was only a nominal ration, and many people simply did not see this amount in practice unless they could afford to pay the high prices of the black

[1] In 1944, factory cloth output was about 3600 tons, or equivalent to 40% of pre-war imports (see p. 226). Silk cocoons purchased by the Ministry of Supply were 700,000 kilos in both 1943 and 1944; paper production expanded from almost nil in pre-war years to 1100 tons per annum by 1944.

[2] See p. 236.

market. Furthermore, there was, in Syria at any rate, the usual discrimination between town and country.

TABLE 5. *Principal imports*

Commodity	Quantity			
	1938–9 (av.)	1941	1942	1943
Cotton piecegoods (000's tons)	9·0	1·5	2·9	1·4
Sugar (000's tons)	34·0	18·4	24·1	10·5
Tea (tons)	161	81	291	122
Coffee (tons)	1,575	2,532	3,051	2,928
Rice (000's tons)	18·8	17·8	0·7	7·4
Sesame (tons)	1,244	120	1,030	227
Coal (tons)	135,000	16,000	38,600	32,000
Timber	—	—	—	—
Iron and steel bars (tons)	21,167	13	1	169
Hides and skins raw	—	—	—	—
Volume index	100	24	53	50
Total value	—	—	—	—

Commodity	Value c.i.f. (£m.)			
	1938–9 (av.)	1941	1942	1943
Cotton piecegoods (000's tons)	1·13	0·41	1·76	2·14
Sugar (000's tons)	0·32	0·56	1·1	0·31
Tea (tons)	0·02	0·01	0·13	0·04
Coffee (tons)	0·05	0·20	0·30	0·31
Rice (000's tons)	0·20	0·34	0·03	0·26
Sesame (tons)	0·02	0·002	0·04	0·02
Coal (tons)	0·19	0·06	0·20	0·18
Timber	0·28	—	0·08	0·19
Iron and steel bars (tons)	0·09	—	—	—
Hides and skins raw	0·16	0·09	0·02	0·002
Volume index	—	—	—	—
Total value	8·3	4·4	11·8	12·5

Source. Recueil de Statistiques de la Syrie et du Liban.

Notes. (1) Petroleum (pipe-line) imports, military and N.A.A.F.I. stores excluded. (2) Tons are metric.

In the case of sugar there was a definite drop in consumption as the two countries are very dependent on imports. Despite official rationing of the commodity the incidence of the cut was extremely uneven, as supplies were so often not available at controlled prices. There were occasional distributions of rice when available, but on what principle is unknown. Tea was in reduced supply at various stages of the war, and here again the shortage was intensified by speculative hoarding.

Textiles were normally the most important manufacture imported in pre-war years. Although piecegoods were reduced drastically in the war years it is not clear how far civilian consumption declined as a whole owing to the existence of some modern mills (which were turning out cloth at the rate of about 3600 tons per annum in 1944) and a large domestic hand-loom industry which, despite its unbelievably primitive methods and the lack of imported yarn, did expand output in wartime. Probably more important than the fall in total supplies available was the lack of any control whatever over distribution. Other types of manufactured goods normally imported, particularly pharmaceutical products for instance, were in very short supply too.

§ 2. Financial Changes

Money and Prices

The changes in the supply of notes and the level of bank deposits are apparent from Table 6.

TABLE 6. *Supply of Money (£S. m.)*

Date	Notes in circulation	Index	Bank deposits	Index	Index all money
Aug. 1939	43·0	100	18·8	100	100
Dec. 1939	47·9	111	32·7	174	131
June 1940	56·5	131	37·3	198	152
Dec. 1940	81·0	187	50·4	268	212
June 1941	100·0	232	31·6	167	213
Dec. 1941	105·6	246	44·8	237	244
June 1942	144·8	336	66·9	354	342
Dec. 1942	193·4	448	120·8	643	509
June 1943	219·2	510	141·2	748	582
Dec. 1943	272·5	632	219·5	1165	796
June 1944	285·5	662	205·0	1090	793
Dec. 1944	340·3	789	188·0	1000	855
June 1945	367·8	855	202·2	1077	922

Note. £S. 8·83=£1 sterling.

Table 7 shows the movements of price indices during the war years. Several points must be observed in connexion with these tables. The fluctuations in the level of bank deposits are a clear indication of the various 'crises of confidence' which took place. The great fall between December 1940 and June 1941 can be ascribed very largely to the Allied blockade and subsequent invasion.

The accuracy of the wholesale and retail prices is open to doubt, as neither index was a very true picture of conditions even in pre-war days—the wholesale index referred to fifty-seven commodities only, and its method of compilation was not above suspicion. One retail index was compiled primarily by the Oil Company to measure the

TABLE 7. *Price indices*

Date	Wholesale	Retail (Oil Co.)	Retail (Beirut)
Aug. 1939	100	100	100 (Jan.–June)
Dec. 1939	134	—	110 (Jan. 1940)
Dec. 1940	205	162	—
June 1941	N.A.	248	—
Dec. 1941	484 (Jan. 1942)	288	233 (Jan. 1942)
June 1942	631	340	275
Dec. 1942	761	368	365
June 1943	860	457	419
Dec. 1943	901	522	500
June 1944	913	559	537
Dec. 1944	1088	629	594
June 1945	961 (May)	605	561 (May)

Source. Oil Company information.

Note. Controlled prices were used where they existed, in the compilation of these indices.

TABLE 8. *Free and controlled prices (per long ton)*

Commodity	Unit	May 1943	Aug. 1943	Oct. 1943	Dec. 1943
Wheat:					
Controlled	£	39·1	39·1	39·1	39·1
Free	£	181·2	90·6	73·6	67·9
Ratio	—	4·6	2·3	1·9	1·7
Barley:					
Controlled	£	27·7	27·7	27·7	27·7
Free	£	62·2	67·9	50·9	N.A.
Ratio	—	2·3	2·5	1·8	—
Sugar:					
Controlled	£	N.A.	N.A.	N.A.	87·2
Free	£	N.A.	N.A.	N.A.	152·9
Ratio	—	—	—	—	1·7

Note. Prices for wheat and barley are those paid to producers.

cost of living for its own employees, and the other is only representative of conditions in Beirut. Both retail and wholesale indices are subject to the limitation that they do not take black-market prices into account. In some ways this limitation is less serious here than in other countries, in that nominally controlled prices were the exception rather than the rule, but on the other hand where they did exist the character of the black market was virulent, as Table 8 shows.

From Table 8 it seems reasonable to assume that in 1943 black-market prices were roughly double the official prices; the high ratio of wheat prices in May 1943 is largely explained by the doubts about the size of the new harvest at that time.

Even when all these various snags and faults in the price indices are taken into account, there is still a wide difference between the proportionate rises of wholesale and retail prices. This is largely to be explained by the sale of such types of bread and flour as appear in the retail price index at subsidized prices, whereas there was no subsidy policy as a whole on cereals,[1] and by the fact that house rents did not increase as much as the general price levels.[2]

TABLE 9. *Gold and commodity prices*

Date	Equivalent market price of gold sovereign (in shillings)	Index of gold prices	Price index			
			Retail		Wholesale	
			Jan.–June 1939 = 100	Jan. 1943 = 100	Aug. 1939 = 100	Jan. 1943 = 100
Jan. 1943	97*s.* 5*d.*	100	379	100	790	100
Mar. 1943	124*s.*	127	403	107	837	106
Apr. 1943	125*s.*	128	403	107	845	107
May 1943	129*s.* 6*d.*	132	401	106	867	110
June 1943	135*s.*	138	419	111	860	109
July 1943	116*s.*	119	440	117	852	108
Aug. 1943	98*s.*	101	416	110	860	109

Source. Special estimates.

It is instructive to compare the relative movement of prices and money in Syria and the Lebanon with that which occurred in other Middle East countries such as Palestine and Egypt. Of all the Middle East countries Syria and the Lebanon came nearest to a flight from the currency. From August 1939 to June 1942 official wholesale prices rose by 531% whilst the supply of money increased by only 242%, and although the money supply did tend to increase faster than the price level in later years there is little doubt that in 1942 the stage had been reached at which the overriding aim was to hold as little paper money as possible. The distrust of the local currency is clear from other signs, such as the tendency of gold prices and local prices to move together. This was largely due to the traditional habit of making transactions with reference to gold prices. Table 9 brings out the point.

[1] See p. 236.

[2] In the Lebanon, the official maximum permitted increase from 1939 to 1944 was 100%, but it is not known how far this was observed in practice.

It seems that at this stage of the war commodity prices were following gold prices up and down, even though the amplitude of the fluctuations was not so great;[1] but it must be added that no such correlation is observable in later years. This was in large part due to the free convertibility of £S. into sterling introduced at the end of May 1943,[2] which was probably more instrumental than any other single factor in preventing hyper-inflation on the Hungarian model in Syria. Nevertheless, it is interesting to note that even after the free convertibility was introduced capital was exported to Egypt on a considerable scale and the £E. was quoted at a substantial premium on the free market in Syria.

Incomes

The most important point to consider is how far the incomes of cultivators rose. It is not possible to produce any comprehensive and cast-iron evidence on the subject, but there is little doubt that, generally speaking, the rises in income were large enough to leave them substantially better off in real terms than they were before the war. First, official wheat prices had risen some 7–8 times above pre-war prices by mid-1943, whereas the cost of living had only risen by about 4½ times. And official prices were certainly not the only ones received by Syrian cultivators. Free prices in Syria were always substantially higher than controlled, and for those fortunate enough to live near the Turkish frontier and possessed of the smuggling tendencies not altogether rare among Syrians there was the opportunity of another lucrative market. Nor is it legitimate to assume that the cost of living index represented the true rise for the average cultivator. The main constituent of the index is cereals, and cereal prices rose more than most items in the index, and therefore, for this reason alone, it probably overestimates the rise in the cost of living for cultivators, even when the fact that other goods were often only obtainable at black-market prices is taken into account. Secondly, farmers gained through the expansion of output which brought in more returns than before. Thirdly, the real burden of indebtedness was reduced by the general rise in prices, but the value of any savings held in gold, the

[1] The main cause of the fall in gold prices in August 1943 was the fear that it might not be possible to store some of the wheat crops earmarked for export before the rains came. Other commodity prices were subsequently adjusted to the fall in gold prices.

[2] The price of the gold sovereign fell from £S. 64 to £S. 57 the day this was announced.

normal method of holding assets, was not impaired. Finally, there is no reason to believe that these gains were entirely absorbed by the larger landlords in view of the traditional nature of the share-cropping arrangements. During the 1943 harvest even labourers working for a money wage were reported to be earning £6S. per day with food, which represented a real income beyond the wildest dreams of their miserable poverty in pre-1939 days.[1]

It is impossible to determine the extent of the rise of wages in the towns generally, but the example of the wages earned by daily paid general labour of an Oil Company may be quoted.

TABLE 10. *Weekly wage rates (in £S.)*

Period	Wage rate	Index	Cost of living index
1939–30. xi. 41	12·5	100	100 (Aug. 1939)
1. xii. 41–28. ii. 42	19	152	288 (Dec. 1941)
1. iii. 42–31. viii. 42	21	168	340 (June 1942)
1. ix. 42–31. xii. 42	28	224	368 (Dec. 1942)
1. i. 43–30. ix. 43	31	247	457 (June 1943)
1. x. 43–31. iii. 44	37·5	300	522 (Dec. 1943)
1. iv. 44	40	322	559 (June 1944)

Source. Oil Company information.

This comparison of wage rates and the cost of living index definitely shows a tendency for real wage rates to fall. In the case of black-coated workers the fall was undoubtedly greater, for whereas industrial workers generally had received increases of the same order of size as the Oil Company employees, salaries of these grades had only doubled by the end of 1943. On the other hand, it must be remembered that the unemployment of 1940–1 disappeared with the inflationary movement of 1942–3 and therefore real wage rates of such workers probably increased. For many others—particularly those working for the Armies—there were chances of working longer hours and much more regularly than in pre-war days, which undoubtedly pushed up earnings more than rates.[2]

Finally, the flagrant nature of the gains obtained by all types of dealers in home produce or importers of goods, is too well known to

[1] Some account of this is given in *International Labour Review*, vols. XXVIII and XXIX.

[2] This view is confirmed by the *Report of the British Goodwill Trade Mission*, which states (p. 38) that 'in the Lebanon...wages in some factories had increased as much as 800% during the war and...wage increases were less urgent than other forms of social legislation'.

need emphasis. Few statistics are available, but when it is known that it was not infrequent for imported goods to be changing hands in the customs sheds at ten times the c.i.f. value the kind of thing that happened is easily seen. Even in the case of exports of cereals controlled through O.C.P., working expenses and dealers' margins were sufficiently high to make f.o.b. prices some 35–40% above the already high prices paid to cultivators.

§ 3. Inflation and Controls

Two of the factors tending to swell incomes in Syria and the Lebanon—military expenditure and O.C.P. purchases—have already been outlined, and we shall now discuss the way in which the process developed. Before this, however, we must turn aside to assess the importance of other subsidiary factors.

The Budget receipts and expenditure of Syria and Lebanon are somewhat tangled owing to the existence of a common budget, individual budgets for the two republics, and some minor budgets for various special districts. In Table 11 the receipts and expenditure for the three major budgets are added and the minor ones are neglected. It can be seen that public accounting in no way contributed to the inflationary process.

Table 11. *Budget receipts and expenditure (£m.)*

Year	Receipts	Expenditure	Balance
1939	3·7	3·3	+0·4
1940	3·9	2·8	+1·1
1941	3·7	2·9	+0·8
1942	6·7	4·9	+1·8
1943	10·8	7·6	+3·2

Source. Recueil de Statistiques de la Syrie et du Liban.

Nor do exports of merchandise (excluding O.C.P. exports) account for any increased receipts after payments by importers have been deducted. Table 12 shows the substantial adverse balance recorded over the war years.

Nor, on balance, did invisible items contribute to Syrian inflation. The main items to consider on current account are remittances from émigrés, which were estimated to amount to a total of about £9·4 million between 1939 and 1943 (inclusive).[1] These clearly did contribute to expenditure power inside the country, but, on the other hand, official gold imports in 1943–4 were about £5 million. On capital account the influence was definitely anti-inflationary, as capital exports between 1939 and 1943 (inclusive) were put at about £12 million.[2] It is possible that this anxiety of some sections of the community to hold their wealth in assets overseas caused distrust of the £S. and contributed to the internal speculative movement, but, on the other hand, gold imports probably had the opposite effect and therefore indirect reactions of this sort cannot be said to be very important one way or the other.

TABLE 12. *Exports and imports of merchandise (£m.)*

Year	Value of imports (c.i.f.)	Volume index	Value of exports (including re-exports) (f.o.b.)	Volume index	Import surplus
1938	8·0	100	3·4	100	4·6
1939	8·5	101	4·2	103	4·3
1940	6·5	60	2·2	39	4·3
1941	4·4	24	1·3	16	3·1
1942	11·8	53	2·7	21	9·1
1943	12·5	50	3·6	13	8·9
1944	10·6	N.A.	5·3	N.A.	5·3

Sources. Recueil de Statistiques de la Syrie et du Liban; Statistical Handbook of the Middle East.

Notes. (1) O.C.P. exports, military and N.A.A.F.I. imports and exports and petroleum imports (through pipeline) and exports excluded.
(2) Private bullion included; gold imported for official sales excluded.

From this discussion it is fairly clear that the major factors promoting income increases were military expenditure and the purchases of the O.C.P. We have seen the magnitude of military expenditure in Table 1, and it may be recalled that in 1943 it reached a peak level of £23 million. The exact effect of O.C.P. expenditure cannot be recorded, as the proportions of purchases sold to the Army authorities and to other Middle East countries are not accurately known,[3] but in 1942 and 1943 the disbursements due to external sales or accumulation of stocks were estimated to be about £10 and £12 million respectively. These statistics must be treated as approximate, but they do serve to put the major income-creating factors in perspective.

[1] Special estimate. [2] Ibid.

[3] Working expenses of O.C.P. were covered entirely by receipts from internal sales of wheat and barley.

We now have to show how incomes rose as a result of this expenditure. There is little doubt that the direct result of O.C.P. purchases of grains was to grant a huge bonus to cultivators. Pre-war prices of wheat in Syria had been of the order of £4·5 per ton. By 1942 costs of wheat from overseas had risen to £24 a ton (c.i.f.), but O.C.P. fixed wheat purchase prices at £39 a ton. Continuous statistics of f.o.b. prices for Syrian wheat are not available, but they were £54 per ton in October 1943. Similarly, barley purchase prices were fixed at £27. 15*s.* per ton and maize at about £31 in 1942. These payments pushed up incomes and correspondingly expenditure, with the natural result of large price rises all round. There were, also, more complicated reactions than this simple analysis suggests, for Syria is very much a wheat-minded country, and the sight and rumour of a sight of a large rise in wheat prices probably added to the speculative fever. On the other hand, it must be remembered that these prices, once fixed, were maintained throughout 1942 and 1943,[1] and this policy certainly helped to cure the speculative rush to hold stocks in anticipation of further price rises. It is difficult, on balance, to assess the liability of O.C.P. in respect of the income- and price-inflation. Probably the fairest judgement is to say that it did add impetus to the spiral initially, but eventually it was a stabilizing rather than a destabilizing influence.[2]

It is needless to add that no measures—or at least no effective measures—were ever taken by the local Governments to check the rise in cultivators' incomes by direct methods of control. The effects of military expenditure were similarly untrammelled.

We must now examine the contribution of taxation in checking consumption expenditure.

Although the budget surplus was sufficiently large to make some contribution towards offsetting military expenditure, it cannot on any account be maintained that taxation laid any heavy burdens on the population. Proceeds of direct taxation in the Lebanon rose from £136,000 in 1939 to £500,000 in 1943, but even then an employee earning a fixed salary or wage[3] was only taxed at 3%, however large

[1] A marked contrast with the policy adopted by the Bengal administration when scarcity arose in 1943.

[2] This analysis, of course, neglects completely such results as the benefit to the whole of the Middle East from having an assured supply of Syrian wheat on the one hand, and the disadvantages of the high Syrian prices for countries like Palestine (see p. 119) on the other.

[3] Taxation on incomes from professions or trade is based on rental values of the buildings occupied.

his income or however small his family. Similarly, in Syria direct tax receipts rose from £550,000 in 1939 to £1·2 million in 1943, but a man earning £1500 per annum paid only 4% (if in receipt of a salary) or 5% (if in trade).[1] Most important of all, income tax did not touch the thriving agricultural interests. The major part of revenue was provided from customs and other indirect taxes, but these again did not hit the agricultural community very hard.

TABLE 13. *Government Receipts and all Expenditure (£m.)*

Year	Tax receipts	Total receipts	% of Government and military expenditure	
			Tax receipts	Total receipts
1940	2·9	3·9	29	39
1941	2·6	3·7	27	38
1942	4·9	6·7	19	26
1943	7·2	10·8	23	35

Source. Recueil de Statistiques de la Syrie et du Liban.

Note. Budgets of Intérêts Communs, Syria and Lebanon Governments only included (i.e. district budgets excluded).

Voluntary savings in the form of contributions to public bonds were negligible in both countries except for lottery loans of about £1 million raised in the Lebanon in 1943, but gold sales did play a more important part in checking the inflationary tendencies than in any other Middle East country. Between August 1943 and April 1944 some £5 million of gold bars and sovereigns were sold (at prices around 100*s.* per gold sovereign)[2] through the banks to dealers. In the last quarter of 1943, in fact, military expenditure was more than covered by receipts from gold sales. There is little doubt that this gold was passed on to the small cultivators for whom it was an acceptable medium of hoarding, one sign of this being the heavy demand for gold at harvest time. Moreover, gold coins had hardly passed out of usage as a normal method of payment before the war, and the habits of fixing commodity prices by reference to gold prices still persisted. Thus, in addition to the absorption of purchasing power which would otherwise have been spent on goods for consumption or hoarding and the provision of an incentive for the cultivator to increase production, it is not improbable that gold sales, by

[1] Income tax was only imposed in Syria in 1942.

[2] King's head sovereigns carried a premium of 10% over bar gold and of 2·5% over queen's heads (the latter is said to be due to Moslem anti-feminine prejudices).

keeping gold prices in check, were an indirect means of restraining the rise in wholesale prices. It is certain that much more gold could have been absorbed by Syria, if it had been available, as demand was far more insatiable than in any other Middle East country where the policy was tried.

Rationing and direct methods of price control contributed little to keeping the inflationary movement at bay in Syria and the Lebanon. In Syria consumer rationing was limited to flour, bread and sugar. The Ravitaillement services received stocks of cereals from the O.C.P. which were issued to the towns regularly, but only in bulk allocation (lasting for several months) to the villages. Distribution to bakers in the towns was controlled, but consumers were not tied to individual retailers, although they were issued with ration cards in, for instance, Damascus. In 1943 monthly rations were 13 kg. per head (70% being wheat) in the towns and 12 kg. in the villages; this compares with a rough figure for pre-war consumption of 12·15 kg. in the towns and 15·20 kg. in the villages, which brings out the favourable treatment accorded to the towns. Sugar was distributed in bulk to the towns and issued to the public through special depots where coupons were deposited. Distribution in the village was supervised by the Elders.[1]

Arrangements were somewhat different in the Lebanon, as the whole population, rural and urban, had ration cards,[2] and special depots were set up in both towns and villages for distribution of both cereal and sugar rations to the consumer. Rations of cereals were 10 kg. per head per month in the towns and 11 kg. in the villages. There was also some restriction of supplies to hotels and a system of restaurant tickets.

Attempts were made from time to time to allocate scarce supplies and materials to firms and traders. Imports of newsprint and rubber were centralized through one agency; L'Office Pharmaceutique had control of imported and locally produced pharmaceutical products; in 1944 Advisory Boards were set up to allocate supplies of vehicles and parts, iron and steel, textiles and paper. Retail prices of some basic foods, such as cereals and sugar, in addition to other consumer goods, such as kerosene or benzine, had percentage margins or ceiling prices fixed from time to time.[3] We have already seen that wholesale prices

[1] The head of the family drew the rations for the whole family and signed for it—or left his thumbprint, if illiterate!

[2] The only country in the Middle East to be so rationed.

[3] Some types of bread in certain areas were subsidized, but the losses thus incurred were compensated by surcharges on other types.

were fixed for cereals, and some imported raw materials were also subject to price control.

Nevertheless, there were many defects in rationing and price control arrangements. In the first place they did not extend to more than a few commodities and therefore could not possibly have much effect on consumption expenditure. Secondly, the schemes often did not work in practice, the main trouble being inadequate control of supplies. We have already seen that speculative hoarding of cereal supplies produced a crisis in 1942 which even a determined effort failed to break.[1] After 1942 supplies from producers were assured by O.C.P. purchases, as the attempts to secure all surpluses over farmers' requirements for personal consumption, seed and fodder were on the whole fairly successful, despite the widespread hoarding and smuggling tendencies.[2] Nevertheless, the rationing schemes in both Syria and the Lebanon had many irregularities even when the supply situation improved; the number of ration cards never corresponded with the number of consumers in the towns, and in the villages

[1] See p. 14. For the historically minded the following quotation may not be without interest: 'The inclemency of the season had affected the harvests of Syria; and the price of bread, in the markets of Antioch, had naturally risen in proportion to the scarcity of corn. But the fair and reasonable proportion was soon violated by the rapacious arts of monopoly. In this unequal contest, in which the produce of the land is claimed by one party as his exclusive property, is used by another as a lucrative object of trade, and is required by a third for the daily and necessary support of life; all the profits of the intermediate agents are accumulated on the head of the defenceless consumers. The hardships of their situation were exaggerated and increased by their own impatience and anxiety; and the apprehension of a scarcity gradually produced the appearances of a famine. When the luxurious citizens of Antioch complained of the high price of poultry and fish, Julian publicly declared that a frugal city ought to be satisfied with a regular supply of wine, oil, and bread; but he acknowledged that it was the duty of a sovereign to provide for the subsistence of his people. With this salutary view, the emperor ventured on a very dangerous and doubtful step, of fixing, by legal authority, the value of corn. He enacted that, in a time of scarcity, it should be sold at a price which had seldom been known in the most plentiful years; and, that his own example might strengthen his laws, he sent into the market four hundred and twenty-two thousand modii, or measures, which were drawn by his order from the granaries of Hierapolis, of Chalcis, and even of Egypt. The consequences might have been foreseen, and were soon felt. The Imperial wheat was purchased by the rich merchants; the proprietors of land, or of corn, withheld from the city the accustomed supply; and the small quantities that appeared in the market were secretly sold at an advanced and illegal price. Julian still continued to applaud his own policy, treated the complaints of the people as a vain and ungrateful murmur, and convinced Antioch that he had inherited the obstinacy, though not the cruelty, of his brother Gallus' (Gibbon, *Decline and Fall of the Roman Empire*, vol. II, ch. XXIV, pp. 509–10; Bury edition).

[2] Numerous methods were employed such as the barter of rice, which was in very short supply, for wheat.

supplies were very spasmodic. It is true that these deficiencies were not so obvious by the end of 1944, but even then the schemes did not work really well.

Other foodstuffs and manufactures were never even as effectively controlled as cereals, for speculative hoarding was rampant at all stages of the distributive process, whether the goods were imported or not. Various measures were tried, such as the attempt to start co-operative marketing of vegetables in Beirut in 1943, the prohibition of forward transactions in 1943 and the suspension of Army buying of eggs in 1944 when supplies were cornered, but none of these was ever of much avail. If the war news took a good turn stocks were dishoarded and prices began to fall, but if the war news was bad hoarding increased, and nothing the Government said or did had more than a momentary effect on the upward surge of prices.

In Table 5 we saw that the reduction in the volume of imported supplies was very large. During the blockade period of 1940–1 imports were only 24% of the 1938–9 level by volume, and even over the next two years they only reached the 50% mark. This was clearly a vital factor making for an inflationary price rise. Speculative hoarding of imported goods aggravated the shortage of supplies and led to cumulative price rises simply because, as prices rose, more and more people expected them to rise further, and as a consequence more and more supplies were hoarded and therefore prices did rise further. There were further reactions too. The shortage of imported raw materials and machinery severely limited internal production. Farm tractors are a good case in point, for unlike some Middle East countries the opportunities for using them were plentiful, particularly in the Djezira,[1] and when some did arrive in 1944 excellent results were achieved.[2] Similarly, it proved possible to grow very satisfactory potato crops from U.K. seed potatoes when they were available. Industrial production, small as it was, nevertheless suffered from the lack of raw materials such as coal or cotton yarn and the absence of machinery for textiles or soap making. Finally, the lack of common consumer goods always makes the task of grain-extracting authorities much more difficult. In so far as this only meant that less cereals were available for export then, of course, this was, *pro tanto*, a deflationary influence in Syria, but in so far as it reduced current

[1] See Keen, *Agricultural Development of the Middle East*, p. 83.

[2] A system of leasing by O.C.P. to individual farmers was adopted.

internal supplies or cast doubts on their future availability and thus led to more speculative activity, it added impetus to the spiral.

It should not be imagined, however, that the lack of imports was the only reason holding back home production. Quite apart from the inherent limitations of water supplies and strip cultivation in agriculture and antiquated techniques in both industry and agriculture, little positive effort was made by the local Governments—except at the insistence of the Allied authorities—to try to increase output. The alleged rationing of scarce raw materials among the most needy firms and industries never really worked; the Advisory Boards to regulate supply and distribution of vehicles, iron and steel, and paper were only formed in 1944, and even then their history was very chequered. Even though imports were so restricted and local resources and techniques so limited, there can be little question that greater determination and will-power could have done something to improve the supply situation.

§4. Critique of War Organization

Enough has now been said to show the character of the price-inflation in Syria and the Lebanon and the reasons why it took place. It is quite clear that the major factors responsible for the very great price rises in these two countries were the complete absence of many of the controls normally employed and the nominal character of those actually imposed. It is true that there were various difficulties peculiar to these two countries; the blockade of 1941 which reduced imports to a low level sooner than in other Middle East countries; the invasion of that year and the disturbances of later years; political squabbles between two independent Governments; the division of authority between Syrian, Lebanese, French and British administrators; the corruption and inefficiency of minor officials; the grasping nature of merchants well versed in the arts of dodging laws; the semi-feudal condition of the mass of the population and the nomadic habits and lawless character of others all made the imposition of any controls on Western lines a Herculean task. Nevertheless, there can be little doubt that the Governments could have pursued more thorough and more energetic policies if they had been so minded. Even in respect of imports in 1943 and 1944 licences were more often than not granted to importers with scarcely any regard for the quotas fixed by the

Allied Supply authorities. As in Egypt or Iraq, the real rulers of the country were a small clique of great landowners and merchants who were prospering from the inflationary process and had little reason to want any controls or policies which would check it.

It was the unwillingness of the Syrian and Lebanon Governments to deal with the impact of war rather than their inability to do so which is the real key to the financial changes between 1939 and 1945.

CHAPTER IX

NIGERIA

§ 1. Physical Changes

Man-power

In Nigeria direct recruitment for the Army made some inroads on man-power resources. Exact figures for recruitment from Nigeria are not available, but the total force raised from the West African colonies was about 160,000 men,[1] and of these it is probable that some 90,000–100,000 men came from Nigeria. Many Africans were also employed on behalf of the Armies in various capacities, such as road, camp and airfield construction, and the peak figure of men so employed was about 44,000 in 1942–3.[2] In addition, men were conscripted for service in the tin mines of the Jos plateau. The scheme started in October 1942 in full earnest and carried on for 19 months, the peak figure of conscripts at any one time being about 20,000 (in the early months of 1944). The total number of individual labourers conscripted over the whole period was about 92,000, which was larger than originally planned for the reason that many did not complete the authorized 16-weeks period of service.[3]

How did these main demands fit in with the man-power supply in Nigeria? Total population was put at 20·6 millions in 1938,[4] but it had probably increased to about 22 millions by 1945. In the light of this it seems reasonable to conclude that the overall drain on Nigerian man-power was not large,[5] for it must be realized that the peak demand for labour for war purposes cannot be obtained by simple

[1] Colonial Office Information.

[2] The average number of men employed in 1942–3 by the Nigerian Public Works Department, which carried out nearly all the construction work for the combatant services, was 38,000, but it is estimated that the peak figure was 15% greater. No figures of African labour performing domestic services, etc., for the Services are available.

[3] There was also some expansion of non-conscript labour in the tin mines. Average total employment expanded from 45,000 in 1939 to 71,000 in 1943, and of the latter only about 16,000 were conscripts.

[4] 1938 Annual Survey.

[5] Cf. *Nigerian Gazette*, 20 June 1940: 'So far as African personnel is concerned our reserves of man-power are almost inexhaustible.' Also Governor's Speech to Legislative Assembly, 15 March 1943: 'There has been no serious shortage of labour other than skilled labour during the year, but the supply and distribution of labour has had to be kept constantly under review.'

addition of the figures above, as the individual maxima occurred at different stages of the war. Furthermore, local road and airfield construction was quite frequently arranged to take place in the season when least labour was needed for farming.

Nevertheless, as in the case of so many primitive countries there were certainly shortages of particular categories of labour, and some districts had heavier drains than others. The situation was complicated, not only by the heavy demands for men with, for instance, mechanical aptitude or building skill, but also by the limited areas and races from which men could be obtained. Men from many tribes were quite unsuitable as soldiers; many had not the physique to do the work in the tin mines and others could not stand the climate. Other difficulties, such as a very heavy turn-over,[1] were inevitable with a population normally used to extremely low wages or more often to none at all.[2] Another complication was that the pre-war annual inflow of casual labour from French territory was no longer possible when this was under Vichy control.

Production

Complete statistics of military expenditure of all types throughout the war years are not available, but some idea of the sums involved can be gained for the years 1943–5. In both 1943–4 and 1944–5 expenditure (including pay of native soldiers, wages of native employees, purchases[3] by individual non-native soldiers and Services purchases and contracts) was of the order of £3·5–4·0 million.[4] The main constituents of these sums were the disbursements to individual soldiers or employees and their dependents, but the sums spent by the military authorities on local foodstuffs, such as rice, guinea-corn, vegetables and dairy products, were far from negligible. There was also some demand for local products, such as rope, twine and timber.

[1] The difficulties of persuading men to return to road work after pay-day are well described in *Crown Colonist*, October 1944.

[2] The total wage-earning population was put at 182,600 in 1938 (*Labour Conditions in West Africa*, Cmd. 6277, App. 3). The use of hired labour in the cocoa-producing areas is rapidly extending, however. (See *The Native Economies of Nigeria* (ed. Perham), vol. I, p. 91.)

[3] Excluding N.A.A.F.I. purchases.

[4] It is highly probable that expenditure was somewhat higher than this in 1942–3 when military needs were more pressing. A pointer to this is that Public Works Department expenditure on account of Services work was £1·76 million in 1941–2, £1·77 million in 1942–3, £0·93 million in 1943–4, and £0·43 million in 1944–5 (*Annual Report*, 1944–5).

Nigerian Government expenditure was not unnaturally small in relation to these sums. In 1938–9 military and defence expenditure was £310,000, and by 1943–4 it had reached a level of £405,000. In addition to this military expenditure, which after 1941 took the form of a contribution to His Majesty's Government, there were in 1943–4 other items such as War Measures (cost of Civil Defence, War administration, etc.) £187,000, and Nigerian Supply Board Administration £156,000. Finally, there was a gift of £100,000 by the Nigerian Government to His Majesty's Government in 1941.[1]

The contribution made by Nigerian exports can be seen from Table 1. It can also be seen that although there was no obvious trend in the exports of the staple products of palm kernels, palm oil, ground nuts, and cocoa, there was a general increase in rubber and all types of mineral products. The cocoa figures are rather deceptive, however, as large quantities had to be burned or otherwise disposed of owing to shortages of shipping in 1942–3. Rubber and minerals production, particularly tin ore, extraction of which was stepped up by the labour conscription policy, were contributions of some importance to the Allied war effort, after the loss of Malayan and Netherlands East Indies sources in 1942.

In previous chapters we have tried in a rough and ready manner to relate the increase in goods produced on military account or export account with the all-round increases in internal production and output, and thereby obtain some idea of whether there was much *prima facie* evidence for believing that internal stocks or supplies of these goods for home consumption were likely to be adversely affected. In the case of Nigeria it is more difficult to make any such deductions, as figures of total output, as distinct from figures of exports, of many products do not exist. By the nature of the case it is impossible to tell whether a reduced supply of palm oil marketed by native producers is due to weather conditions, diminished willingness to work, devotion of more time and energy to growing food crops, or increased domestic consumption. But the problem is obviously most difficult in the case of native foodstuffs production. It is known that the Armed Forces were supplied with quantities of cereals, vegetables, eggs and meat,[2] and although it is thought that production of foodstuffs did increase

[1] This did not add to the real war contribution. Cf. p. 266.

[2] The Governor reported in his 1944 Speech that in the preceding year the Civil Supply Officer had purchased, on behalf of the Army and the Mines, 4200 tons of maize, 7000 tons of millet, 10,000 tons of guinea-corn and 2300 tons of rice.

TABLE 1. *Principal exports*

Commodity	Quantity 1934–9 (av.)	1941	1942	1943	1944
Tin ore (000's tons)	11·4	18·4	16·5	17·5	18·2
Palm kernels (000's tons)	323	378	344	331	314
Palm oil (000's tons)	133	128	151	135	125
Ground-nuts (000's tons)	217	247	194	142	156
Cocoa (000's tons)	93	105	60	87	70
Raw cotton (000's centals)	177	229	415	160	97
Benniseed (000's tons)	13·5	8·8	22	12	4
Rubber (000's lb.)	5346	4603	14,935	16,499	21,085
Columbite (tons)	Nil	Nil	Nil	831	1975
Wolfram (tons)	Nil	Nil	Nil	84	44
Coal (000's tons)	44	54	73	80	188
Hides, cattle and goat untanned (000's cwt.)	124	125	133	119	113

Commodity	Value f.o.b. £000's 1934–9 (av.)	1941	1942	1943	1944
Tin ore (000's tons)	1815	3490	3208	3441	3824
Palm kernels (000's tons)	2527	2283	2458	3117	3637
Palm oil (000's tons)	1483	1047	1427	1587	2030
Ground-nuts (000's tons)	2202	2140	1688	1475	2013
Cocoa (000's tons)	1978	1769	1042	1542	1338
Raw cotton (000's centals)	394	619	1127	437	264
Benniseed (000's tons)	103	83	189	137	44
Rubber (000's lb.)	97	245	664	794	1071
Columbite (tons)	Nil	Nil	Nil	156	342
Wolfram (tons)	Nil	Nil	Nil	17	10
Coal (000's tons)	41	51	68	94	247
Hides, cattle and goat untanned (000's cwt.)	613	563	600	596	580
Total exports	12,340.	13,124	13,696	14,320	16,203
Re-exports	188	658	828	831	987
Grand total	12,528	13,782	14,524	15,151	17,189

Source. Nigeria Trade Reports.

Notes. (1) Military and N.A.A.F.I. stores, bullion, specie, notes excluded.

(2) Average for 1934–9 taken, owing to very wide fluctuations in the volume of exports in pre-war years. Although there was a fall in average value of some items between 1934–9 (av.) and 1941, the change was not so great between 1939 and 1941, as the 1934–9 (av.) figure is somewhat inflated by the high prices of 1937.

(3) Tons are long; 1 cental = 100 lb.

on the whole and that native consumption of home-grown foods was roughly maintained, no concrete evidence is available. In the case of rice, for instance, it proved possible to supply both locally-stationed military forces, ships in harbour and the Gambia from time to time. Imports were heavily reduced,[1] and it is highly likely that home production increased, but what the net effect of these reactions was on home consumption of rice it is impossible to tell. Similarly, there was some increase in sugar and vegetable (onions and potatoes) output.[2]

In the case of cocoa, exports are no guide at all to total output because of the destruction of surpluses and local utilization for cocoa butter. The total amount of main intermediate crops marketed in 1942–3 was 111,000 tons as against 82,000 tons in 1939–40,[3] but this increase should be mainly interpreted to be the result of weather conditions rather than a deliberate attempt to push up output. There was a definite increase in coal output, as it rose from 323,000 tons in 1939 to 668,000 tons in 1944–5,[4] which was sufficient to make the colony virtually independent of imports and provide an export surplus. Increases in current tin, columbite and wolfram output were the necessary pre-conditions of increases in exports.

There was also some expansion of light industries in Nigeria during the war. Timber production increased from 1·7 million cubic feet in 1939 to 4·1 million cubic feet in 1943.[5] Rope production increased from 8400 yards in 1940 to 4 million yards in 1944. Jam and preserve making, tanning of hides,[6] the manufacture of building materials and crude cotton piecegoods also increased. With the exception of the last named all these activities were encouraged with the primary object of meeting local military requirements.

Consumption

No clearly defined picture of changes in basic home-grown foodstuffs can be given in Nigeria, but general impressions are that on the whole there was little change,[7] for although output in some lines

[1] See Table 2, infra.

[2] Potato output increased from some 600 tons in 1940 to 1300 tons in 1943 (*Crown Colonist*, January 1945). Governor's Speech, 1945.

[3] *Report on Cocoa Control in West Africa* 1939–43, Cmd. 6554.

[4] Colliery Department, *Report*, 1939 and Department of Labour, *Report*, 1944.

[5] Forestry Department, *Report*, 1944.

[6] A modern tanning factory was started at Apapa in 1944 with an estimated initial output of 1000 hides per month. *Crown Colonist*, April 1944.

[7] See, for instance, *West African Review*, April 1943, or Governor's Speech, 1945.

probably fell, there were usually compensating factors.[1] It is possible to see what reductions took place in a wide variety of consumption goods, however, simply because the colony is normally heavily dependent on current imports. Stocks of imported goods were never large in peacetime, and home production, even when it expanded in wartime, made little difference to the overall supply situation.

The main changes in imports can be seen in Table 2.

TABLE 2. *Principal imports*

Commodity	Quantity			
	1934–9 (av.)	1941	1942	1943
Rice (cwt.)	199,000	3600	9700	50
Other cereals (000's cwt.)	53	40	44	72
Fish (000's cwt.)	202	2	2	0·3
Sugar (000's cwt.)	149	24	39	34
Unmanufactured tobacco (000's lb.)	2812	2142	1894	2825
Coal (000's tons)	31	33	21	14
Cotton piecegoods (m. lb.)	261	145	205	203
Cotton yarn (000's lb.)	1014	360	515	439
Bicycles (no.)	17,128	2189	5568	8211
Corrugated iron sheets (000's tons)	10·1	1·0	1·8	0·5
Illuminating oil (m. gal.)	3·1	1·7	0·4	2·4
Matches (000's gross)	232	117	132	88
Buckets and pails (000's doz.)	331	4·1	8	3

Commodity	Value £000's c.i.f.			
	1934–9 (av.)	1941	1942	1943
Rice (cwt.)	110	4·1	8·8	0·09
Other cereals (000's cwt.)	49	38	50	54
Fish (000's cwt.)	348	9	6·8	3·3
Sugar (000's cwt.)	110	37	62	56
Unmanufactured tobacco (000's lb.)	140	156	153	269
Coal (000's tons)	52	135	81	58
Cotton piecegoods (m. lb.)	2355	1832	3394	4725
Cotton yarn (000's lb.)	64	32	57	52
Bicycles (no.)	65	12	34	49
Corrugated iron sheets (000's tons)	182	24	52	13
Illuminating oil (m. gal.)	73	47	11	83
Matches (000's gross)	28	27	32	38
Buckets and pails (000's doz.)	60	6·7	9·3	6·0
Total	9001	6505	10,489	12,418

Source. Nigeria Trade Reports.

Notes. (1) Military and N.A.A.F.I. stores excluded.

(2) Re-exports are deducted from illuminating oil figures but are negligible for other items.

[1] It is significant that the quantity of palm oil marketed for export did not increase so much as the quantity of palm kernels in some areas (Governor's Speech, 1945).

About rice, cereal and sugar consumption, it is possible to say little because there was probably some expansion of home-grown crops to meet the decline in imports. In the case of dried and preserved fish there is little doubt that the reductions in imports did hit the ordinary consumer, as it was a frequent article of consumption before the war.[1] But the greatest general reduction was undoubtedly in manufactured goods. Cotton manufactures reductions were by far and away the most important, but those of bicycles, illuminating oil, matches and buckets were all significant. It is true that there was some local use of palm oil and cotton-seed oil instead of illuminating oil, but these did not make any appreciable difference to the overall picture. On the other hand, the reduction in coal imports was largely compensated by increased home production.

There is little available evidence on the distribution of these cuts in consumption of manufactured goods. There are no plain criteria, such as a pronounced reduction in real income[2] of any particular sections of the population or a rationing system which deliberately favoured the towns against the rural areas. Nevertheless, it does seem to be true both from the known data about the efficiency of the distribution schemes and the evidence of private observers that on the whole the coastal towns suffered less than the up-country areas.[3] As the distance from the importing centres and the main seat of Government became greater, it became more and more impossible to maintain any control over the activities of a hoard of middlemen unused and unwilling to abide by regulations which contravened their own inclinations.

[1] Cf. Cmd. 6277. Similarly, the reduction in imports of condensed and unsweetened milk (from 7513 cwt. for the average of 1934–9 to 6480 for the average of 1940–5) was also important.

[2] It will be seen in § 2 that evidence suggests that the peasant farmers did not obtain sufficient price increases for their crops to compensate for higher costs of consumption goods in the same way as wage earners obtained increases in pay. On the other hand, it must be remembered that these are the very classes who do not depend so much on purchases of consumption goods, as they grow their own food and often weave their own cloth, or produce simple household utensils.

[3] This view has been confirmed since the above was written in *Enquiry into the Cost of Living and the Control of the Cost of Living in the Colony and Protectorate of Nigeria*, Colonial no. 204, p. 9.

§ 2. Financial Changes

Money and prices

It is impossible to give any accurate statistics of the money supply, as published figures only relate to the four West African colonies as a whole and no break-down is available for Nigeria. However, it is not unreasonable, in view of the size of Nigeria in relation to the other three colonies, to assume that the total of notes and currency issued in Nigeria must have increased roughly in the same proportion as the whole, and therefore figures of the total issues are shown in Table 3.

Table 3. *West Africa—note and currency issues (£m.)*

Date	Currency	Notes	Total	Index
30. vi. 39	10·0	1·7	11·7	100
30. vi. 40	11·0	1·6	12·6	108
30. vi. 41	11·4	2·1	13·5	116
30. vi. 42	14·3	3·4	17·7	152
30. vi. 43	18·3	5·6	23·9	204
30. vi. 44	20·4	5·9	26·4	226
30. vi. 45	22·1	7·6	29·7	253

Source. West African Currency Board Reports.

No official figures are available of the relative increases[1] or absolute figures of bank deposits, and therefore the validity of Table 3 as a true indication of the expansion of the supply of money is obviously very limited.

Information on price movements is similarly very limited. The cost of living index shown in Table 4 applies only to conditions in Lagos, and, as the office of Government Statistician was abolished in 1935, it is hardly likely that it can be a very accurate indication of what really happened there.[2]

The Report of the Committee on Cost of Living in Lagos (1942) found that up to April 1942 the prices of manufactured goods had in general risen further than the cost of foodstuffs (e.g. household equipment prices had gone up 88% since 1938, low-quality clothing 67% and all foodstuffs only 53%). Rents appeared to have been

[1] A special estimate puts the increase at about 200%.

[2] The findings of the 1945 Commission published in Col. no. 204 are that although 'there is not one cost of living problem but many' it is possible to generalize very roughly by saying that the price level doubled between 1939–45. Thus the official index would appear to be too low (op. cit. p. 17).

kept down, as the recorded increase was only 2·85%.[1] Of course, discrepancies between these margins varied somewhat in the later war years, but the relative increases appear to have remained of the same order of magnitude. Away from the coast, however, it seems probable that manufactured goods were subject to even greater price increases relatively to foodstuffs, owing both to the greater reduction in supplies and the activities of intermediary traders, but concrete statistical evidence is not available to prove this.

TABLE 4. *Cost of living index (Lagos)*

Date	Index
1. ix. 39	100
1. iv. 42	147
1. iv. 43	159
1. x. 43	174
1. iv. 44	161
1. ix. 44	165
1. iv. 45	176

Source. Nigerian Government Statistics.

Incomes

Generally, wage rates and earnings of the lowest paid workers appear to have very roughly doubled over the war years. Wages of unskilled workers in Government public works were put at 16*s*. 6*d*. per month in 1939,[2] whereas in 1942 they varied between 30*s*. and 40*s*. a month.[3] These increases were achieved by flat-rate increases,[4] which obviously favoured the very low-paid classes relatively to those in higher grades. It is also probable that further gains were made by those in the coast towns through increased chances of earnings, for lack of opportunity to do more than intermittent work was one of the principal reasons for their exceptionally low standard of living before the war.

[1] This explains why the general index rose much less than some of the component indices, for rents in towns were a formidable proportion of expenditure before the war (cf. Cmd. 6277). Some doubt was thrown on the figure of 2·85% by later evidence, however (see Col. no. 204, p. 9 and p. 29). Exploitation by landlords appears to have been very common. (Ibid. p. 202.)

[2] Cmd. 6277, p. 136.

[3] The 1942 Cost of Living Enquiry Committee reported that 54% of the casual labourers employed by the Government earned between 30*s*. and 40*s*. monthly in February 1942.

[4] Graded, however, according to district conditions (Hansard (Commons), 30 September 1942).

In other occupations, too, wages appear to have risen to a similar degree. The pay of soldiers was increased from 1*s*. a day in the early war years to 2*s*. a day in the latter part. In the coal mine at Enugu earnings were about 5*s*. per week in 1939,[1] and although average weekly wages were only put at 6·74*s*. per week in 1944,[2] it is probable that average earnings over longer periods had further increased through more regular work. Whereas costs of male domestic servants were usually about 25*s*. to 30*s*. a month before the war, in 1943–4 they were more usually 50*s*. to 60*s*.[3]

This evidence is scanty and should not be taken at more than its face value, but it does suggest that real earnings of some large sections of the wage-earning population did not fall appreciably during the war years. There were, of course, some clerical and skilled grades of labour who did not obtain such large increases in salaries or wages, but it should be remembered that in West Africa before the war there was a very sharp cleavage between the clerical and manual class wage earners, the former enjoying a very high and somewhat inexplicable advantage,[4] and therefore any reduction in real earnings did not mean such a heavy burden as we might at first think. But wage and salary earners only form a small proportion of the Nigerian population, for even including Army personnel it is unlikely that they numbered more than about 400,000 in 1944–5. The much more important point is what happened to the incomes of the peasant farmers, and to this question we must now turn.

It is unfortunately not possible to make any straightforward deductions from the prices paid for the main cash crops—groundnuts, palm oil, palm kernels, cocoa—because the prices paid by the European purchasing firms and organizations are so different from the prices received by the farmer. Between the European firm and the peasant producers there exists a whole chain of intermediaries, and about the ramifications of their activities very little is really known.[5]

In the case of the cocoa farmers it is probable that some hardships were suffered, as cocoa-purchasing prices were on the whole kept *below* 1939 prices until the 1943–4 and 1944–5 seasons.[6] Whether

[1] Cmd. 6277, p. 58. [2] Department of Mines, *Report*, 1944.

[3] Further evidence of broadly similar changes in rates in different towns is given in Col. no. 204, p. 42.

[4] Cmd. 6277, p. 22.

[5] A general description is given in the *Cocoa Commission Report*, 1937, Cmd. 5845.

[6] See p. 254.

the prices actually received by growers were more or less than proportionately reduced is not known, and how far the somewhat larger crops compensated for these losses is not known either, but the general truth of the argument that reductions in real income were caused by the stabilization of export prices and the rise in prices of imports, such as cloth and footwear, is not really open to doubt. In the case of palm- and ground-nut products the position is not so clear, as between 1939 and 1943 buying prices per ton increased from £5. 4*s*. 0*d*. to £9. 8*s*. 9*d*. for palm oil, £3. 15*s*. 9*d*. to £8. 2*s*. 6*d*. for palm kernels, and £3. 15*s*. 9*d*. to £9. 0*s*. 0*d*. for ground-nuts.[1] It is not known whether farmers' prices increased in the same proportion, but it is highly probable that farmers did have quite a substantial share in these gains. As a whole it is probable that farmers did suffer an involuntary loss on the terms of trade and that the effect on real income was intensified still more in some instances by voluntary reduction in output. It is essential to remember that hoards of cash are quite worthless in the eyes of the African peasant and therefore, if it is not possible to obtain the goods he requires, he will not normally try hard to produce larger crops and thereby add to his cash holdings.

There are four more important points to stress in this analysis. The first is that farmers normally grow food as well as cash crops—cocoa, in fact, started in the first place as an adjunct to subsistence farming,[2] and in many areas a large amount of simple work, such as weaving of cloth or construction of farm implements, is also carried on. Therefore, over a large sector of his needs the farmer is insulated from the gyrations of the price system.[3] Secondly, some agricultural wage earners are partly paid in kind (e.g. the plantation workers in the Cameroons), and the same argument applies again. Thirdly, as in so many other backward countries, heavy indebtedness is a widespread characteristic of the economy. It does not normally take the form of mortgaging land but rather of securing advances on crops, often from the various middlemen at rates of interest from 50 to 100% per annum.[4] In so far as these debts are not completely repaid when crops are sold, but drag on from year to year—and this state of affairs is by no means uncommon—then the general rise in prices during the war obviously benefited the agricultural community by reducing the

[1] Hansard (Commons), 21 July 1943.

[2] See Cmd. 5845.

[3] It may be noted that there were no widespread free—or cheap—meal facilities in the towns at any time before or during the war years.

[4] Cmd. 5845.

real burden of indebtedness.[1] This argument, of course, applies to many other classes in West Africa, as prolonged indebtedness to traders and similar people in the towns is also common. Finally, there was always another resource which could be utilized to prevent standards falling too far, and that was more intensive use of women and child labour. It must not be forgotten that to many Africans a family is as much an asset as it was to the Lancashire cotton worker 100 years ago.

Sterling balances

No exact figure is available for Nigerian balances, but the holdings of the West African Currency Board shown in Table 5 give some idea of the rate of increase over the war years, as it may reasonably be assumed that the largest share of these is on Nigerian account. Other West African holdings of sterling appear to have been about £61 million in 1945, as £91 million was estimated to be the total amount in mid-1945.[2] No comparable figure for 1939 is available, however.

TABLE 5. *West African Currency Board Balances*

Year (at 30 June)	Amount (£000's)
1939	12,075
1940	12,960
1941	14,927
1942	16,954
1943	23,323
1944	25,981
1945	29,508

Source. West African Currency Board Annual Reports.

§ 3. INFLATION AND CONTROLS

We have seen that there was a general tendency for incomes to rise throughout the colony, and we must now examine the causes and results of this movement.

Military expenditure clearly played an important part in contributing to higher incomes, but internal Government finance tended to impede the income creation process. Table 6 shows Budget Receipts

[1] This did not apply, of course, in cases where interest was paid in real terms; and this procedure is not uncommon in the cocoa areas, for instance. See *The Native Economies of Nigeria* (ed. Perham), vol. I, p. 98.

[2] *The Economist*, 1 February 1947.

and Expenditure as stated and the same figures adjusted to exclude transactions involving external receipts and payments.

TABLE 6. *Government receipts and expenditure (£m.)*

Year	Budget receipts	Budget expenditure	Surplus (+) deficit (−)	Internal receipts	Internal expenditure	Income creating balance: surplus (+)
1939–40	6·1	6·5	−0·4	6·1	5·2	+0·9
1940–41	7·27	7·25	+0·02	7·27	5·6	+1·7
1941–42	7·97	7·0	+0·97	7·97	5·3	+2·6
1942–43	9·0	9·0	Nil	9·0	7·0	+2·0
1943–44	10·9	10·0	+0·9	10·9	7·7	+3·2
1944–45	11·4	10·1	+1·3	11·4	8·4	+3·0

Source. Reports on Accounts and Finances.

Notes. (1) Grants from His Majesty's Government excluded from internal receipts.

(2) Defence contributions and gifts to His Majesty's Government, interest and sinking fund payments excluded from internal expenditure. No deduction is made for pensions and gratuities paid to overseas recipients.

In addition to the surpluses shown in Table 6 the Railway Budget also showed substantial annual contributions to the Reserve.

There was a great increase in receipts from exports which was only partially offset by increased payments for imports.

TABLE 7. *Imports and exports of merchandise (£m.)*

Year	Exports	Imports	Balance (export surplus +)
1939	10·5	6·7	+3·8
1940	11·6	7·5	+4·1
1941	13·8	6·5	+7·3
1942	14·5	10·5	+4·0
1943	15·2	12·4	+2·8
1944	17·2	15·6	+1·6

Source. Nigeria Trade Reports.

Notes. (1) Bullion, specie, notes excluded.

(2) Military and N.A.A.F.I. stores excluded.

(3) Civilian Lend-Lease stores included. If received through credit Lend-Lease channels, Government charged consumers at normal rates and held balances in suspense account.

Trade in merchandise was clearly an income-generating factor of some importance in Nigeria in the years 1939–41, as exporters' receipts were substantially increased, while payment for imports did not rise. The reactions of the reductions in the volume of imports and the increases in import prices on internal conditions will be discussed later.[1]

Little is known about invisible items on current account and private capital transactions, but it is believed that they did not show much movement in either direction from pre-war figures,[2] which normally showed a substantial excess of payments over receipts due to pensions, remittances, debt charges, etc.[3]

Military expenditure and higher export receipts were therefore the main causes of the income-generating process. Now we have seen in other countries how crucial was the mechanism by which this movement worked. In the Sudan, where there was a definite attempt to isolate producers' incomes from high export prices, it proved possible to hold down internal prices far better than in any other Middle East country; in Syria and Iraq, where controls were negligible, prices rose higher than elsewhere. In some respects Nigeria was able to avoid the worst consequences of this type. The various purchasing authorities for cocoa[4] deliberately limited prices paid for crops, both to prevent any diversion of effort from oil seeds, and also to restrict the growth in internal purchasing power.[5] Purchasing prices (per ton naked ex scale port of shipment),[6] were, for instance, £15–16 for best quality in 1939–40 but only £10–11 in 1942–3. By this means a surplus of £1·17 million[7] from sales was accumulated by 1943 which was obviously far less likely to affect the internal price level than it would have done if it had been in producers' hands. Although prices for oil-seeds products were not so effectively restrained,[8] gains were not on the scale seen in many other countries. The very fact that Nigeria is so highly dependent on a few staple exports and that purchase of those exports is normally confined to a few firms are the main reasons why it was possible to prevent incomes from increasing rapidly.

Control over incomes due to military expenditure obviously could

[1] See p. 259.

[2] *The Economist*, 3 November 1945.

[3] Cf. Hailey, *African Survey*, p. 1351.

[4] Initially the Ministry of Food and then the West African Cocoa Control Board. This was superseded later by the West African Produce Control Board responsible for bulk purchase of all the staple exports.

[5] See Cmd. 6254.

[6] I.e. prices paid at buying stations to producers for unbagged produce.

[7] This figure is the share of the total surplus imputed to Nigeria. A further £1·530 million was added by the 1943–4 and 1944–5 results (see *Statement on Future Marketing of West African Cocoa*, Cmd. 6950).

[8] See p. 251.

not be so effective. For although many of the workers on road building, etc., were employed by the Government Public Works Department, and not by the military authorities, which should have made it easier to limit their wages, and although local agreements were sometimes reached between military purchasers and Government officials on prices to be paid for foodstuffs, there were many channels through which the stream of expenditure seeped into the system. In the nature of the case it was difficult to limit personal expenditure of troops or their dependents, and we have seen[1] that this was much the most important constituent of military expenditure. Whether this was fully realized is open to doubt, as the normal determinants of Nigerian prosperity under peacetime conditions are the volume of staple exports and the average prices they fetch, but, in general, the authorities do not appear to have realized that in war it was not sufficient merely to control these receipts. The rise in the cost of domestic services and the increased incomes of soldiers' dependents, for instance, had little to do with higher export receipts, but they were closely associated with military expenditure.

There were substantial increases in taxation and other receipts which did offset military disbursements to some extent. In 1943–4, for instance, total receipts were £10·9 million or about 95% of combined internal and military expenditure, and in 1944–5 they were £11·4 million or 94%. Income-tax (including companies tax) receipts rose from £99,000 in 1939–40 to £1,370,000 in 1944–5, and this was a noteworthy increase. But it must be remembered that it only applied to a small section of the population, and despite the large rise in yield, rates were not really high by wartime standards on those whom it did touch.[2] Native direct taxation ('Jangali') did not change so much during the war years, but this is not surprising in view of the complexity of the system.[3] Despite the reduction in the volume of imports, the sheet anchor of public finance continued to be customs and excise receipts which expanded from £2·48 million in 1939–40 to £5·2 million in 1944–5, but here it is doubtful how far such classes as subsistence farmers were affected, more particularly as the quantity of imported goods was so reduced. It is probable, however, that such measures as the successive raising of customs duty on tobacco and

[1] See p. 242.

[2] Maximum rate in June 1943 was 10*s.* in the £ on individuals (Hansard (Commons), 30 June 1943). There was no surtax.

[3] See Hailey, op. cit. p. 576ff.

the excise duty on cigarettes made some inroads into the surplus purchasing power of the trading classes.

It did not prove more possible to interest many people in Nigeria in voluntary saving than in the other primitive countries, and despite the various attempts to persuade people to buy savings certificates and the like, little difference was made to the amount of purchasing power available for consumption expenditure. By 1944[1] some £378,000 had been contributed to Nigerian Savings Certificates, and between 1939 and 1945 Post Office Savings Bank deposits increased from £210,000 to £1,180,000,[2] but these were not large sums in relation to the general expansion of incomes.

Nor was rationing of consumers in the strict sense of any importance in West Africa. Even in the towns there was no attempt to distribute essential goods on Middle Eastern, let alone Western, lines, with the single exception of salt, for which a form of rationing was devised for a limited period. Controls over distribution and prices were not really much in evidence before 1942,[3] but with the formation of the West African Supply Centre in January of that year and the general keying up of the war effort, controls were introduced which in time spread to most imported commodities. The Nigerian Supply Board was established and many restrictions were imposed on importers, such as licensing of all imports, declarations of stocks of principal consumer goods, directives on channels and methods of distribution and bulk purchasing of scarce goods.[4] All essential goods were price controlled by a system of margins; wholesale prices were usually determined by landed costs plus 20% and retail prices landed costs plus 30%. These prices appear to have been fairly well observed in the case of importing houses, but in Lagos they were more often broken than observed, and up-country the threats of fines and publication of convictions were very empty for the simple reason that no African could ever be induced to give evidence against offenders.[5] There was little real check on the activities of the strings of native or Syrian intermediaries.[6]

[1] Governor's Speech, 1944.

[2] See Col. no. 204, p. 35.

[3] See Evans, *African Affairs*, October 1944.

[4] For details see *Memo. on Organization and Control of Wartime Trade and Production*, 1943.

[5] 'It should be noted that in general price control is only effective in so far as sales by the principal importers are concerned' (*Memo. of Director of Supplies*, Col. no. 204, p. 121).

[6] Offences were particularly flagrant in the distribution of bicycles and bicycle parts which were heavily reduced in supply. See Table 2 and Governor's Speech, 1945.

The Food Control Section of the Supply Board was mainly responsible for bulk purchasing of supplies for the Forces and the mining communities and for the supply of native foods to the town markets. Despite the many subsistence sections of the Nigerian economy the latter function was of considerable importance for the large towns. On the whole, there appears to have been little reduction in the supply of foods, and the main trouble was the withholding of supplies by the larger intermediaries. Local attempts were made to combat this by price regulation, but in general they met with very little success for just the same reasons as the controls over imported goods failed up-country. The most interesting and certainly the most successful experiment was the 'Pullen' scheme in Lagos. Quantities of local foods, such as yams, gari and rice, were bulk-purchased and then supplied to selected retailers to sell in special markets at or below controlled prices. Retailers were obliged to keep lists of controlled prices by their stalls, and if they were caught selling at higher prices they were promptly removed. These schemes did undoubtedly have some success for a time in steadying the ordinary market prices, and they provide an interesting example of how the usual wartime problems of distribution in primary economies can be dealt with. Essentially, the method was not to attempt to feed all Lagos but to put sufficient food into the markets to make competition work and cut out collusion, agreed or tacit, between sellers.

Before 1945 no actual subsidy policy was adopted in Nigeria to stabilize prices, but in the case of sugar, flour, and condensed milk an agreement was reached between the Government and the Association of West African merchants to secure lower prices of these commodities by partially foregoing duties and profits respectively. This was probably highly desirable from the point of view of the real incomes of the poorest classes of consumers, and it also probably allayed agitations for higher wages,[1] but at the same time it was quite clearly a factor tending to push up internal prices generally by reducing the amount of expenditure on imports. On this occasion it does seem that the Government slipped into the old fallacy of regarding lower prices, instead of control of incomes, as the essential aim in an anti-inflationary policy.

We have surveyed the income-generating process in Nigeria and

[1] Whether increases in wages would have made much difference to total purchasing power in view of the small number of wage earners is very doubtful, however.

the measures taken to limit its direct impact on the economy, and therefore we must now ask what steps were taken to increase the supply of foodstuffs and other consumption goods. The most important point in this context, as in so many other countries, was the reduction in the volume of imports. Not only were the supplies of foodstuffs, piecegoods, kerosene, lanterns, hardware, etc., reduced to a small proportion of pre-war levels (and it was particularly the cheaper varieties which were severely curtailed as they had formerly come from the Continent and Japan), but there were also reductions in iron and steel which handicapped peasant construction of farm implements,[1] and there were virtually no imports of tin-mining machinery which necessitated the adoption of industrial conscription to bolster up output.[2] There are other secondary points to note about imports, for not only were supplies much reduced[3] but they were also more irregular. The submarine sank ships but it also made others arrive weeks late or at unexpected ports, and this threatened disruption of an economic structure which at best is hardly stronger than a doll's house. The essential system of trade on the coast is for the same firms and the same ships to handle the staple exports and imports. But if an incoming ship is late this threatens disaster, for crops will not keep under poor storage conditions (and often no more exist) in a tropical climate, as the Allied Armies found to their cost during the war. Even if a ship is not late but diverted to another port, complications are nearly as bad, because the lines of communication run from the interior to the ports but not from port to port. It is obvious that when such interruptions of normal shipping were frequent the whole balance of the economy would inevitably be upset.

Another related problem is how far the increased costs of imported goods contributed to the expansion of prices and incomes. Table 8 shows the movements of import and export prices.

It is certainly true that import prices rose faster than internal prices, but, in view of the small number of wage earners in the country and the lack of any very close relationship between the cost of living

[1] The skill of village artisans seems to be much lower than in, for instance, India.

[2] Cf. *Annual Report, Department of Labour*, 1944: 'As new mining machinery was not available and could not easily have been imported if it had been available the only alternative was to introduce a limited form of National Service.' In view of the supply position of tin in 1942 this attitude of the Allied Supply authorities is quite inexplicable.

[3] Even if demand could have been heavily curtailed (e.g. by rationing) prices would still have risen, as the heavy overheads of landing cargoes at West African ports were spread among fewer ships.

index and wage rates in the early war years, it is doubtful whether the impetus given to the upward movement of incomes was very important. The counter-inflationary effect of the additional payments which had to be made to foreign exporters for a given volume of imports was more than sufficient to outweigh it.

TABLE 8. *Import and export prices* (1939 = 100)

Year	Import prices	Export prices
1940	134	116
1941	146	113
1942	166	123
1943	222	138
1944	242	163
1945	223	180

Source. Colonial Office information.

Firm attempts were made to increase peasant output of foodstuffs and other goods over the war years as well as that of oil and oil seeds by propaganda, demonstration plots, issues of seeds, guarantees of markets and prices, provision of transport and storage facilities. The Department of Agriculture ran farms to produce food for military camps; the Veterinary Department organized the supply of hides, skins, and dried meat; the Forestry Department arranged rubber collecting and timber felling. The Government helped mineral production by organization of labour supplies—in the case of tin by compulsion.[1] Small local industries were encouraged by propaganda, assurances of markets and credit facilities. In Lagos a Labour Advisory Board and Employment Exchange were opened. Some control of skilled labour in essential work was also imposed.

But there were many factors limiting local expansion. The lack of imports of iron and steel and tin machinery has already been observed; in a few cases labour migration to military work, or to other districts, hindered production;[2] in all, the small-scale operations, the absence of storage facilities, efficient transport or credit facilities and the low standard of skill and education of labour imposed severe limitations on short-term development. And not only was it a question of the

[1] Police action was also taken to prevent work in gold mines.

[2] The 1942 benniseed crop was reduced to nearly 50 % of the 1941 crop, mainly as a result of labour migration. At the same time men flocked into Lagos, increasing the overcrowding and the level of unemployment (by 1945 there were some 20,000 unemployed in Lagos).

inability of the country to produce more; it is also highly probable that producers were in some areas unwilling to work harder or increase output. How far this was due to higher prices being offered it is difficult to tell, although it is significant to note that rather more and not less cocoa was produced in response to lower prices. More probably the shortage of consumption goods with the consequent lack of any inducement to a community unused to saving in money terms was the major explanation. Nor were these difficulties of unwillingness to work confined to producers only, for it was found in the tin mines that the output per head of conscript labour was some 20% less than that of free labour. And matters were not made easier by the diminished effectiveness of European supervision. This was partly due to officials being conscripted or seconded to other duties and partly to the strain of serving longer periods under unhealthy conditions before going on leave.[1]

§4. Critique of War Organization

It is not difficult to find grounds for criticism in the organization of the war economy in Nigeria. Too much attention was paid to receipts from exports and too little to those from military expenditure. Taxation was not really stiff, judged by wartime standards, even on the higher income ranges. Voluntary savings were not an important offset to military expenditure. Rationing of native populations was virtually non-existent, and although it is possible to plead the usual difficulties of operating rationing successfully in a primitive country, on examination they seem to be rather less formidable than in many other countries where rationing of essential commodities in the towns was found practicable. An important characteristic which distinguishes West Africa from many other primary producing countries is the high proportion of population dwelling in towns. In 1931 some 29% of the Nigerian population was living in towns of over 5000 inhabitants.[2] This should have made it far more easy to ration large sections of the population for essential goods than it was in the Middle East countries. Nor was price control very effective away from the coastal areas and the 'Pullen' markets. It seems difficult

[1] This difficulty seems to have been prevalent in East Africa also. See Orde Browne, *Labour Conditions in East Africa* (Col. no. 193).

[2] Hailey, op. cit. p. 1426. This, of course, does not mean that all these people were employed in urban occupations.

to believe that measures such as the power to commandeer stocks of traders and merchants at controlled prices could not have been adopted and operated often enough to persuade hoarders to disgorge their stocks. We have also seen the doubtful character from an anti-inflation viewpoint of the 1943 agreement to reduce import prices of sugar, flour and condensed milk. There were obviously very great difficulties to overcome in providing the necessary facilities for expansion of cash crops or foodstuffs and in persuading the peasants to co-operate, but there was at least one factor which should have made things easier. It is commonly argued that the heavy indebtedness common to colonial territories destroys all incentive among producers.[1] In so far as the real burden of this was reduced during the war years this should have helped the campaign to increase production. Finally, import control by licence did not work very satisfactorily in the early war years.[2]

But after all, even if some controls did not work well in Nigeria and others were misconceived, the overall result was not so very bad. The Lagos cost of living index is far too untrustworthy as a price indicator for the whole country, but the general character of the price movements was obviously very different from the experiences of the Middle East countries (with the exception of the Sudan). And this was achieved despite many handicaps. The war threw an immense strain on an economic system built up on a fusion of modern European methods of trading and commerce with the age-long habits of native subsistence farmers. The decreased volume of imported consumption goods and the erratic way in which they arrived might well have upset the whole balance of domestic production. Then there were the difficulties inherent in so many primitive economies—a mixed population of many different races, abilities and creeds; a large country about whose economic life very little is really known; an administration never adequate in peacetime and seriously depleted in war;[3] and a merchant class not unwilling to take advantage of the old-established ignorance of consumers and the new-found opportunities of war. On the other hand, the war did not touch Nigeria as heavily as many of the other countries. In view of the (largely unknown) differences in national income per head it is difficult to state dogmatically that

[1] See, for instance, Fabian Society, *Co-operation in the Colonies*, Ch. x.

[2] Cf. Hansard (Commons), 4 August 1942.

[3] The province of Bornu, for instance, which is approximately equal in area to Ireland, is administered by a Resident and four District Officers (Col. no. 204, p. 5).

military expenditure bore less heavily on the population than in other countries, but the general impression that it must have done appears to be valid. Further, the main Allied demands were for the resources which Nigeria could most easily supply—man-power and normal export products (except cocoa). The general fall in imports was not as heavy as in the countries of the eastern Mediterranean, nor was it likely to be felt so keenly as in Trinidad or Palestine, where imported food supplies were so vital. Finally, the centralized nature of the export trade and the comparative absence of old-established smuggling customs made it relatively easy to control producers' incomes.

To summarize, it may reasonably be argued that local Government policy bore some responsibility for such gaps in war economic organization as did occur. A good example is the decision to put the Public Works Department on a care and maintenance basis in 1940, which was hardly a hall-mark of foresight. But there was no wild movement of prices, no very obvious maldistribution of resources, and no very clear evidence of excessive hardship among any appreciable fraction of the population. The indictment, if it can be so called, is therefore hardly a formidable one.

CHAPTER X

TRINIDAD

§ 1. Physical Changes

Man-power

The great problem which the Trinidad Government had to face in wartime was the construction of the American Defence Bases. This affected the man-power supply in several ways. The most important was the employment of labour on constructional work, for over the greater part of the years 1942–3 about 24,000 men were employed by the American authorities and some 4000–6000 by subcontractors, making a total of 28,000–30,000. Even in the latter period of the war when actual construction work was finished, labour was needed for maintenance purposes on a large scale.[1] But this simple total is rather deceptive, for it only represents the average number engaged on any one day, and therefore conceals the fact that some workers only worked for 1 or 2 days a week, earning sufficient during that time to keep themselves for the rest of the week. Furthermore, it also neglects the fact that others not lucky enough to be engaged waited near the precincts of the bases from day to day in bright anticipation. Therefore, on both counts, the reduction in labour available for other purposes was greater than the above figures suggest.

There were other indirect reactions too. Many men were employed by the American authorities, performing various personal services, and even if men did not obtain employment many womenfolk did, and thereby earned sufficient to enable their husbands and families to perform less regular work or in some cases to live in complete idleness. For instance, there was a heavy decrease in the supplies of labour available for work in the northern sugar belt in the early months of 1943, and although this coincided with the intensification of work on the U.S. Navy base, this was many miles away and there was no evidence of any mass migration. The real explanation of the shortage of labour seemed to be the extra services performed for the U.S. troops stationed in the area.[2]

From what sources was this labour force drawn? In the first place

[1] Some 9400 men were still directly engaged in December 1944 (*Industrial Adviser Report*, 1944).

[2] See Trinidad Council Paper, no. 1/1944.

the population was increasing owing to both immigration and natural causes. Between 1 January 1941 and 31 March 1943 alone there were some 10,500 immigrants;[1] and although accurate figures of population are not available after 1931 it was put at 502,000 in 1942,[2] which represents a 21% increase over the 1931 figures. This, however, exaggerates the natural rate of growth, for there was a certain amount of immigration in pre-war days as well as in wartime.

In the second place, there was some unemployment at the beginning of the war which disappeared completely by 1942–3.[3] Here, again, the exact amount is not known, but it is doubtful whether it can have been very large if under-employment is excluded. Thirdly, the sugar plantations suffered a heavy loss of labour, and this was the point at which the American demands undoubtedly hit the island economy hardest. Before the war some 25,000–30,000 men were employed on the estates during the reaping season, but by 1943 only about 17,000–18,000 were working there, and even in 1944 only 21,000.[4] How far this reduction in numbers was due to direct employment in the bases, and how far to indirect reactions of one sort or another is not known, but there is no question that American war demands in some form or other were entirely responsible. There were also other changes in the sugar industry, for the number of cane-farmers was reduced from about 20,000 in 1937 to about 11,400 in 1943,[5] and although this change cannot be attributed purely to American influences with such certainty, it was undoubtedly bound up with them. It is important to emphasize that these man-power drafts did really constitute a bottleneck in the sugar plantations and were the main cause of the large reduction in output which took place.

Other sources, such as the cocoa industry, also supplied labour. Accurate statistics of the labour force are not available, but the number is known to have been much reduced below the figure of 17,500 labourers and 10,000 planters in 1940.[6] The asphalt industry also showed a reduction from 600 in 1938–9 to 380 in 1943. On the other hand, there is no evidence of any drain of labour from the

[1] Council Paper, no. 1/44.

[2] *Foreign Commerce Weekly*, 28 November 1942. This figure includes Tobago but excludes U.S. Forces. It implies about 170,000 males of working age.

[3] *The Economist*, 4 July 1942.

[4] *Industrial Adviser Report*, 1944. Similarly figures of acreage reaped fell from the 1937 peak of 31,000 to 20,000 in 1943 (Council Paper, no. 1/44).

[5] For various reasons these figures do somewhat exaggerate the change; see Council Paper no. 1/44.

[6] These figures are from *Labour Conditions in West Indies*, Cmd. 6070.

oil industry (about 13,100 in 1938–9 and 13,600 in 1943–4), or from the Government Public Works Departments which employed about 7000 men throughout the war. The number employed in minor industries is not known, but as output expanded, or at least remained steady in many of these,[1] it is improbable that the labour force was affected very much.

To summarize, there is little doubt that war demands[2] did leave Trinidad short of labour.[3] Although this does not mean that everyone was doing a full week's work judged by Western standards, it does mean that, given the willingness and ability to work of the ordinary labourer, the main limitation on expansion of output as a whole was the size of the labour force available.[4] The crucial point is that it was only possible to satisfy war demands for labour by reducing output in other directions.

Production

It is not possible to give a complete statistical picture of the impact of American war demands on Trinidad resources, as only partial details of American expenditure are available. It is known, however, that the total wages bill paid out to local labour engaged on the construction of the bases during the period 1941–4 was about £6 million.[5] This figure does not include expenditure on local raw materials, but this was not an important factor, as most of these were specially imported. No figure is available of expenditure by American military and constructional personnel, but as the number of these rose to about 50,000 in 1942–3 this must have been heavy. If we assume expenditure of 5*s.* per head per day, and this does not seem excessively high when American military rates of pay are recalled, this would give us a peak rate of expenditure of £4·56 million per annum. Furthermore, this does not include any bulk purchases of food by the Army authorities, but this is not a serious omission, for, as in the case

[1] See p. 268.

[2] There was also some recruitment for the Armed Services, particularly the Caribbean Force and the R.A.F., but this was not an appreciable problem compared with the main demands.

[3] All Trinidad Government reports bear the same imprint in 1943 about the labour shortage, e.g. forestry work and coffee reaping were both hindered through labour shortage.

[4] Cf. *Development and Welfare in the West Indies*, 1943–4 (Colonial no. 181): 'More employment was available than labour but this demand could have been met by an increased work effort by the labourers employed.'

[5] *The Times*, 25 February 1947.

of raw materials, much of this was imported. It can easily be surmised, therefore, that military expenditure per head of the population stood at a high level compared with that of the other countries reviewed in this survey.[1]

In addition to American military expenditure there were also the demands of the British military authorities and the defence expenditure of the local Government. Figures of British military expenditure are not available, but they are not thought to be large, as a major garrison was never stationed in Trinidad. Local expenditure on defence purposes increased as shown in Table 1.

TABLE 1. *Local defence expenditure* ($000's)

Year	Naval and military services	Special war services	Total
1939	332	40	372
1940	993	498	1491
1941	1287	320	1607
1942	1283	1701	2984
1943	1310	2281	3591
1944	1313	2667	3980

Source. Council Papers.

Notes. (1) £1 sterling = $4·8 (Trinidad).
(2) Naval and military services include contribution to His Majesty's Government (about $1,250,000 annually for 1941 and succeeding years).
(3) This total rather exaggerates the real problem as Special War Services include, for instance, subsidy expenditure which did not represent a drain on real resources. Subsidies amounted to $350,000 in 1943 and $720,000 in 1944, the two years when they were important.

In addition to the contributions shown in Table 1, there were four large interest-free loans from the Trinidad Government to His Majesty's Government between 1940 and 1943, which amounted to a total of $9·2 million, and a large number of miscellaneous gifts. It is doubtful whether these loans and gifts added to the drain on resources, however, for much the same quantity of goods would have been exported to the United Kingdom in their absence. The real effect was in reducing the growth of the sterling balances.

Trinidad contributions of exports may be seen from Table 2.

[1] In addition to military outgoings other American authorities incurred various items of expenditure. Net expenditure by non-military agencies from July 1940 to June 1946 (excluding purchases of supplies and materials which enter into the Trade Accounts) was £578,000 (Special information).

TABLE 2. *Principal exports*

Commodity	Quantity			
	1934–9 (av.)	1942	1943	1944
Unclassified raw materials	—	—	—	—
Sugar (000's tons)	120	85	54	55
Molasses (000's gal.)	3242	1400	Nil	Nil
Rum (000's proof gal.)	100	320	165	556
Cocoa (m. lb.)	30·7	10·1	8·0	10·6
Copra (m. lb.)	12·5	0·08	0·2	2·2
Asphalt (000's tons) crude and dried	64	12	12	17
Asphalt (cement) (000's tons)	14	5	16	14
Bitters (000's proof gal.)	11·5	30·6	56	51
Exports	—	—	—	—
Re-exports	—	—	—	—
Total	—	—	—	—
Commodity	**Value f.o.b. ($m.)**			
	1934–9 (av.)	1942	1943	1944
Unclassified raw materials	26·6*	34·4	29·3	39·9
Sugar (000's tons)	5·29	5·3	3·6	4·1
Molasses (000's gal.)	0·17	0·11	Nil	Nil
Rum (000's proof gal.)	0·07	0·19	0·21	0·68
Cocoa (m. lb.)	2·2	1·2	0·97	1·4
Copra (m. lb.)	0·24	0·004	0·017	0·24
Asphalt (000's tons) crude and dried	0·85	0·19	0·20	0·28
Asphalt (cement) (000's tons)	0·20	0·20	0·53	0·58
Bitters (000's proof gal.)	0·11	0·25	0·47	0·44
Exports	28·8	43·1	36·7	49·3
Re-exports	2·1	4·1	5·3	4·8
Total	30·9	47·2	42·0	54·1

* 1939 only.

Source. Customs Returns.

Notes. (1) Figures relate to Trinidad and Tobago.

(2) Exports include ships' stores and bunkers.

(3) 'Unclassified raw materials' are almost entirely oil products. Oil export figures have not been published in detail but the Governor declared in 1943 that the value of all exports less oil was $11·8 million in 1941. Total exports were later revealed to have been $40·3 million in 1941 and therefore petrol exports must have been $28·5 million compared with unclassified raw materials valued at $28·7 million.

(4) Detailed export figures do not include re-exports but these were negligible for the items listed.

(5) Average of 1934–9 is taken on account of heavy fluctuations from year to year.

From Table 2 it can be seen that the sharp decline in sugar, molasses, cocoa and copra and the expansion in rum exports were the principal features. Oil products retained their overwhelming predominance.

As might be expected the trend in export figures was closely bound up with figures of local production. Total crude-oil production was 2,583,000 metric tons in 1938 and expanded fairly steadily to 3,079,000 metric tons in 1945.[1] Sugar production reached a peak at 155,000 tons in 1936–7 (av.) but fell to the very low figure of 71,000 tons in 1943, and was only 74,000 tons in 1944. Similarly, output of cocoa, which in 1937 occupied more than half the total crop acreage (and twice that devoted to sugar), was vastly reduced during these years. These were by far the most important changes in output during the war years, but there are a number of other items to consider. There was an intensive effort to grow more food, and some success was achieved in greater production of rice, sweet potatoes, yams, Indian corn, etc.[2] Local production of such copra products as margarine and edible oil was increased after the embargo imposed in 1941 on exports of copra and coconuts. There was also some attempt to expand a few manufactured products such as matches, textiles and paper, but the contribution which these made towards implementing imports was not important.

Thus, in brief, the principal contributions to war were the supply of labour and local services to the American authorities and the maintenance of food and oil production. These were mainly achieved at the expense of the sugar and cocoa industries.

Consumption

Changes in overall consumption were closely associated with the reductions in imports, as those normally cover such a wide range of consumers' requirements.

The types of reduction which occurred can be seen from Table 3. Wheat-flour imports remained fairly constant but rice imports suffered a definite reduction, although in this case increased home production partly compensated for the fall. Boot and shoe and cotton piecegoods imports remained fairly static. Raw materials, such as iron and steel, were scarce, and all types of machinery, particularly sugar machinery, were curtailed.

[1] *Shell Transport and Trading Report for* 1945; *Petroleum Press Service*, November 1945.

[2] Total acreage under food crops in 1944 was estimated to be 2½ times that of 1939 (*Report on Agriculture*, 1944). Rice production was estimated to be 9500 tons in 1942 or 50% more than 1939 output (*Blue Book*, 1942).

TABLE 3. *Principal imports*

Commodity	Quantity			
	1934–9 (av.)	1941	1942	1943
Wheat flour (000's cwt.)	615	772	597	711
Rice flour (000's cwt.)	385	397	297	253
Condensed milk (000's cwt.)	69	73	82	109
Preserved fish (000's cwt.)	60	66	68	56
Iron and steel (tubes and pipes) (000's tons)	20*	21	11	8
Machinery:				
Oil mining (tons)	712*	962	508	205
Oil refining (tons)	587*	1090	254	192
Sugar (tons)	1165*	236	312	242
Soap (000's cwt.)	31	27	3	7
Cotton piecegoods (m. yd.)	10·3	9·1	13·1	10·8
Boots and shoes (all types) (000's doz. pairs)	57	62	49	60
Total imports	—	—	—	—

Commodity	Value c.i.f. ($000's)			
	1934–9 (av.)	1941	1942	1943
Wheat flour (000's cwt.)	1,654	2,396	2,301	3,308
Rice flour (000's cwt.)	894	1,390	1,410	1,471
Condensed milk (000's cwt.)	468	1,230	1,786	2,626
Preserved fish (000's cwt.)	422	960	1,390	1,262
Iron and steel (tubes and pipes) (000's tons)	2,703*	3,577	2,133	1,660
Machinery:				
Oil mining (tons)	680*	786	517	291
Oil refining (tons)	288*	484	229	109
Sugar (tons)	364*	128	149	139
Soap (000's cwt.)	170	180	32	101
Cotton piecegoods (m. yd.)	990	1,546	3,305	2,932
Boots and shoes (all types) (000's doz. pairs)	514	949	1,349	1,883
Total imports	29,133	57,485	55,094	59,788

* 1939 only.

Source. Customs Returns.

Notes. (1) Transhipments, military stores, excluded. Civilian Lend-Lease goods included.

(2) No deduction is made for re-exports in respect of individual items, but these were negligible for the above commodities except in the case of machinery ($168,000, $148,000, and $25,000 for all types in 1941, 1942, and 1943 respectively).

Whether there was any reduction in overall consumption it is difficult to tell. Although there were reductions in imports of individual commodities, the reduction in total volume does not appear to have been great—and such reductions in foodstuffs as took place were largely compensated by increased home production. There is little doubt that real incomes of some classes of workers increased,[1] and although the supply of imported consumption goods was not sufficiently large to allow a proportionate increase in consumption, the diversion of resources to war equally did not entail much reduction in consumption of home-produced goods and services. In fact, consumption of these expanded in some directions. There was a large increase in gambling; and consumption of rum, for instance, rose from 367,000 to 1,034,000 proof gallons between 1939 and 1943. This was, of course, partly due to military demands, but there can be little doubt that the local population helped in the process. Nor is there much evidence to show that any particular income or economic class suffered much worse reductions in real income than others, for the system of cost of living bonuses which was applied to the poorer classes' incomes from the early stages of the war was gradually extended to the middle classes,[2] and thus the discrepancies between lower paid salaried workers and wage earners or cultivators which we have so often found in other countries were not present to the same degree.

§ 2. Financial Changes

Money and prices

Owing to the mixture of currency and banking systems in the West Indies[3] it is unfortunately impossible to present any accurate statistics on changes in currency, note circulation and bank deposits in Trinidad. Table 4 shows the expansion of the note circulation as recorded in the *Annual Reports* by the Commissioners of Currency, but it must be emphasized that it is only a very rough guide to the sort of changes which took place.

On the one hand these figures do not include many notes which do circulate in the island (e.g. those of Barbados or British Guiana are legal tender), and on the other hand they include some which do not, such as those in circulation in the Windward and Leeward Islands.

[1] See p. 274. [2] See *Review of Commercial Conditions* (Trinidad).
[3] See Clauson, *Economic Journal*, April 1944.

Finally, there are no figures available of aggregate bank deposits in the territory, and there is therefore no means of knowing the proportion of the total money supply represented by notes or the importance of the expansion.

TABLE 4. *Notes in circulation* ($000's)

Date	Total	Index
31. xii. 39	1,265	100
31. xii. 40	2,125	168
31. xii. 41	7,084	558
31. xii. 42	15,433	1,225
31. xii. 43	22,864	1,800
31. xii. 44	22,602	1,790

Source. *Commissioners of Currency Reports.*

Nor are the statistics of prices very adequate. The changes in the official cost of living index are shown in Table 5.

TABLE 5. *Cost of living index*

Date	Index	Date	Index
Aug. 1939	100	Dec. 1942	162
Dec. 1939	109	June 1943	168
June 1940	119	Dec. 1943	180
Dec. 1940	123	June 1944	180
June 1941	131	Dec. 1944	179
Dec. 1941	134	June 1945	180
June 1942	144		

Source. *Trinidad Gazette.*

Note. No wholesale price index exists.

This index suffers from the usual faults. The accuracy of the weighting at the base date (1935) is not above suspicion; there were many changes in consumption patterns in the war years; and above all only controlled and subsidized prices are covered. It is highly probable that the weighting underestimated the importance of services such as laundry or boot repairing and overestimated imports during the war years, and as the rise in price of such services was often greater than that of imports,[1] the true rise in the cost of living is not brought out by the index. More important still, the controlled price

[1] See Council Paper, no. 1/44.

very often did not represent the price normally paid. In the case of rice, for instance, black-market prices were often more important than controlled prices.

Incomes

Rather more information is available on income trends in Trinidad than on money and price changes, for the increases in wage rates in the principal industries are available.

In the sugar industry, statistics of labour costs in field work are available and are shown in Table 6.

TABLE 6. *Average wage payments per unit of work in sugar industry*

Period	Wage costs (in cents)	Index
1939: Jan.–June	55	100
July–Dec.	49	89
1942: Jan.–June	79	144
July–Dec.	73	133
1943: Jan.–June	86	157

Source. Council Paper, no. 1/44.

These figures are a fairly accurate index of wage rates, as the normal method of payment is a specific rate for a given task or unit of work, and therefore changes in productivity do not affect the validity of the statistics as an index of wage rates. It is possible that there was some reduction in the number of tasks performed per week,[1] which would, of course, mean that earnings increased proportionately less than rates. But on the whole this does not seem to have been very frequent, and, generally speaking, the number of tasks usually performed seems to have remained at about three or four per week[2] throughout the war years. If we compare the rise in rates and earnings with the cost of living index it seems fairly clear that there was some fall in real rates and earnings up to 1943, even if it was not large.

In the case of sugar-factory workers the same conclusion seems to hold. Unskilled helpers or labourers received average daily earnings of about 60 cents in 1939–40. By 1942 these were more usually about 80 cents and by 1944 more usually about 100. Skilled fitters and

[1] See Col. no. 181, p. 12.

[2] Making a total of 16–20 hr. work per week. There was certainly no increase in the number of hours worked.

turners, on the other hand, secured increases of the order of 80–100% between 1939–40 and 1944,[1] which were at least large enough to compensate for the increases in the cost of living as shown by the index.

In the oil industry, average daily rates moved as shown in Table 7.

TABLE 7. *Average daily rates (index)*

Year	Unskilled	Semi-skilled	Skilled	Cost of living index
1939	100	100	100	100 (Aug.)
1942	137	132	134	144 (June)
1944	152	146	146	180 (June)

Source. Industrial Adviser Reports.

It would appear from this table that there were sharp falls in real wage rates. It is probable, however, that in the oil industry relative increases in earnings were greater than rates—earnings were often 50% or more above current rates in the war years. Further, the oil companies provided some of their workers with various commodities at subsidized prices. Therefore the fall in real earnings, if any, was not large.

Nominally, the wage rates paid to those fortunate enough to obtain employment on the defence bases were based on those paid by the Trinidad Public Works Department,[2] which were generally higher than those on the estates. General labourers received about 80 cents a day before the war, whereas the usual wage per task on the estates was 50–60 cents, and normally only one task was performed each day. This percentage difference was roughly maintained during the war years, and therefore even if American rates had really kept pace with Trinidad Government rates there would have been a strong incentive for workers to move from the estates. In actual fact, earnings were considerably higher than these nominal rates for two reasons. First, the American authorities exacted more work from their employees than had been customary before, and thus even if rates were not higher—and that is a matter of some doubt—earnings certainly were. Secondly, any man with the slightest pretence to special proficiency

[1] *Industrial Adviser Reports.*
[2] See *Caribbean Islands and the War*, U.S. Govt. 1943.

was upgraded[1] and thus became entitled to higher rates. Thus it was reported that in mid-1942 casual labourers on the U.S. bases were earning 115 cents a day compared with normal earnings in sugar of 80 cents a day or in Government Public Works of about 95 cents a day.[2] There is no doubt whatever that workers on construction of the bases were able to earn sufficient to give them a far higher real income than before the war, if they were willing to do so.

The class which probably did lose most by the war changes was the sugar planters, and this was because output was reduced owing to labour shortage—some 229,000 tons could not be harvested in 1943[3]—and prices did not rise sufficiently to offset these losses.[4] But all in all, it is highly questionable whether those people who could be regarded as war economic casualties formed any appreciable proportion of the community.[5] The fact that work was readily available for those who wanted it (including women) enabled families in need of a greater income to obtain it, and on balance it seems right to conclude that the workers were in the main better off as a result of the war.[6]

Sterling balances

No detailed information is available, but an estimate has been made[7] that Trinidad sterling balances stood at £19 million at 30 June 1945. It seems probable that this balance accumulated almost entirely between 1939 and 1945, for it is significant that investments held by the Commissioners of Currency increased from $1,245,000 at 31 December 1939 to $23,047,000 at 31 December 1944.[8]

§ 3. Inflation and Controls

Before we discuss the ways in which American expenditure pushed up prices in Trinidad we must examine the importance of the other factors which we have found to have varying degrees of importance in the different countries surveyed.

[1] Similar events took place in other West Indian territories (see Richardson, *Review of Economic Conditions, Policy and Organisation in Bermuda*).

[2] *Crown Colonist*, July 1942.

[3] *Review of Commercial Conditions* (Trinidad).

[4] The basic rate per ton increased by 86% between 1938 and 1942 (*Blue Book*, 1942).

[5] It is significant that nutritional deficiencies among children were thought to be less marked in 1944 than in 1940 (Col. no. 181, p. 8).

[6] Further details which have become available since the above was written (see Hansard (Commons), 19 February 1947) largely confirm this conclusion.

[7] *The Economist*, 1 February 1947.

[8] *Reports* for 1939 and 1944.

The Trinidad budget when adjusted for external items showed a surplus in all years except 1940, and was therefore on balance an offsetting influence to the inflationary movement. Table 8 shows the details of budget receipts and expenditure and internal receipts and expenditure.

TABLE 8. *Government receipts and expenditure* (*$m.*)

Year	Budget receipts	Budget expenditure	Surplus (+) deficit (−)	Internal receipts	Internal expenditure	Income creating balance: surplus (+) deficit (−)
1939	13·4	13·0	+0·4	13·3	12·0	+1·3
1940	15·5	20·5	−5·0	15·4	17·0	−1·6
1941	18·9	16·8	+2·1	18·9	13·5	+5·4
1942	23·4	21·2	+2·2	23·4	17·5	+5·9
1943	29·2	28·9	+0·3	29·2	22·7	+6·5
1944	29·2	31·2	−2·0	29·2	26·9	+2·3

Source. Government Accounts.

Notes. (1) Grants from Colonial Department and Welfare Fund excluded from internal receipts.

(2) Loans and contributions to His Majesty's Government, Sinking Fund and interest payments excluded from internal expenditure. No deduction is made in respect of pension payments ($629,000 in 1939 and $808,000 in 1944).

The value of exports and imports of merchandise may be seen from Table 9.

TABLE 9. *Value of imports and exports* (*$m.*)

Year	Value of imports (c.i.f.)	Value of exports (including re-exports) (f.o.b.)	Balance: export surplus (+) import surplus (−)
1939	34·8	37·4	+ 2·6
1940	45·1	46·2	+ 1·1
1941	57·5	47·3	−10·2
1942	55·1	47·1	− 8·0
1943	59·8	42·0	−17·8
1944	68·9	54·1	−14·8

Source. Customs Returns.

Notes. (1) Exports include ship stores and bunkers, exclude military stores.

(2) Imports include civilian Lend-Lease goods, exclude transhipments and military stores.

During the years in which the dangers of an inflationary boom were most acute it can be seen that there was a very substantial import surplus, and thus the payments overseas were much more than sufficient to compensate for the receipts of exporters.

At the same time, however, it is not improbable that higher prices of imported goods may have helped to push up internal prices and wages. Table 10 shows the relative changes in import prices and the cost of living index over the war years.

TABLE 10. *Import prices and internal prices*

Year	Import prices index	Cost of living index
1939	100	100 (Aug.)
1940	126	119 (June)
1941	132	131 (June)
1942	184	144 (June)
1943	197	168 (June)
1944	213	180 (June)

Source. Colonial Office information.

It can be seen that after 1941 there was a permanent lead of import prices on domestic prices, although it must be remembered that the accuracy of the index of the latter is rather problematical. Import prices rose not only because of the general rise in world prices but also because of the diversion of purchases from peacetime sources of supply to the higher cost countries of the North American continent.[1] Increased c.i.f. rates were also influential, particularly when Canadian and American goods had to be hauled by train to Florida and shipped from there in order to save the longer sea voyages from the normal ports. The importance of high import prices lay in that the main items entering into the cost of living index were imported, and therefore the controlled prices on which the index was based were largely dependent on c.i.f. prices. In a territory where there is a large wage-earning population the index is one of the main standards by which incomes are adjusted, and this was so in the case of Trinidad,[2] although, of course, wages also rose because of the increased demand for labour. As the subsidy policy adopted in 1942 was a means of checking the effects of the rise in import prices, however, it would not be wise to ascribe too much importance to this problem in the later war years.[3]

[1] In 1936–9 (av.) 37 % of imports (by value) came from Great Britain and 34 % from Canada and the U.S.; in 1944 11 % came from Great Britain and 59 % from Canada and the U.S.

[2] The oil companies, for instance, automatically increased hourly rates by ½ a cent for every 5 points rise in the index.

[3] See p. 279.

We must also consider the current invisible items and private capital movements. Little is known about the latter, but the former probably added to the inflationary pressure on balance. We have already deducted the amounts of Government gifts and contributions to His Majesty's Government and interest payments from the figures of Budget expenditure, and so these must not be counted again as an out-payment. The volume of private gifts increased during the war years, but in so far as they were made in kind they were clearly no help in reducing the pressure from disposable incomes internally. It is also probable that stocks of goods for export, paid for but not yet shipped, were larger at the end of the war period than at the beginning and therefore represented an additional source of income. And even though receipts from tourist traffic were negligible during these years the development of Trinidad as a base in Transatlantic Air Services was a new form of invisible export.

The ways in which American expenditure raised incomes and consumption outlay in the island were simple. It has already been shown that the nominal rates agreed upon were in practice not observed, and this alone was sufficient to push up incomes to much higher levels than before; but subcontractors had a further incentive to raise wages, as they were paid on a cost-plus basis. There were also reactions which can best be described as psychological. American habits of tipping in dollars and generally regarding the dollar as the lowest unit of account produced similar reactions among the local inhabitants. Many charges were thought of in terms of dollars—a taxi driver would ask for a dollar however short the distance; a boot repairer would exact a dollar however trifling the repair. Such indirect impacts as these which cannot be fully brought out by statistical evidence—at any rate within the limits of the information available—must be regarded as important in producing the wartime inflationary boom in prices and incomes in Trinidad.

Taxation policy was not so inhibited by the usual limitations of public finance in colonial territories as was found elsewhere. It can be seen from Table 8 that although it never proved possible to offset American expenditure to any appreciable extent in Trinidad, there were still substantial increases in receipts.

One obstacle to the expansion of indirect taxation in Trinidad was that many import duties were specific and not *ad valorem*, and therefore receipts did not increase automatically through the rise in import prices. Total customs and excise receipts did, however, increase from

\$7·3 million in 1939 to \$12·3 million in 1944. Income-tax rates were raised considerably during the war years,[1] and yields rose from \$1·4 million in 1939 to \$7·3 million in 1944. A number of emergency taxes were imposed in 1940, and by 1943 they brought in \$2·8 million, of which \$2·3 million was E.P.T. (normal rates were 80% of profits above the base level) and \$430,000 a special levy on oil. Despite these various increases, however, there is little doubt that those who benefited most from American war expenditure were not badly hit, for they both enjoyed the fruits of the subsidy policy, which aimed at keeping down prices of essentials, and in large measure escaped the extra burdens of income tax.

Voluntary savings were not a substantial offset to the inflationary potential despite the various types of securities issued under the War Loan Ordinance. Savings Certificates and 3% debentures were issued, and over the war period absorbed some \$167,900 and \$1,769,000 respectively. 2% short-term certificates were also issued in 1944. Generally speaking, however, the response was disappointing to the Government, for neither the wealthier business men nor the main companies showed themselves eager to subscribe. On the other hand, it must be recalled that substantial contributions were made from all quarters to the British Government in the form of gifts, loans and subscriptions to securities.

Various measures were adopted during the war for the control of distribution and prices of essential commodities. A Food Controller was appointed in 1942, and he was responsible for regulating food imports, encouraging the production of food locally and organizing the general distribution and marketing of all foodstuffs. But we have seen that there were never any very reduced supplies of essential commodities, and, in general, rationing was little used even as a means of securing equitable distribution, let alone as an anti-inflationary policy. The usual types of arrangements for limiting the number of wholesale traders and linking retailers to members of the selected band were adopted in the case of a number of commodities, but in general policy did not go much further than this. More efforts were devoted to price control of essentials by direct control of prices (by margins or ceiling methods), either alone or in conjunction with subsidies. In the cases of staple foods such as flour, rice, condensed milk, pickled meats and copra products, subsidies were granted by

[1] In 1943, 85% of income received was paid out by those in the highest income class (Hansard (Commons), 30 June 1943). There was no surtax.

the Government and a Price Control Committee excercised powers of price fixing. But how far these prices were observed in practice is another story. In many cases—rice is a good example—fixing of controlled prices appears to have been a signal for supplies to disappear and only reappear via illegal channels at high prices.[1] On the other hand, the subsidy policy does not always seem to have been subject to the limitations as an anti-inflationary policy which we found in other countries, for when the policy was inaugurated in late 1942, there was an immediate rise in foreign exporters' prices for the main commodities affected.[2] Thus Government expenditure to some extent subsidized foreign exporters rather than home importers and was not therefore entirely a means of contributing to internal outlay. But the later extension of bulk purchasing prevented further occurrences of this sort, and, of course, at the same time introduced the inflationary element of subsidy methods. Expenditure of this sort was $720,000 in 1944.

Efforts were made to increase home production of foodstuffs and some types of manufactured goods, and these, of course, reinforced the material available to dam the flood of extra purchasing power. Sugar cultivators were compelled to devote large areas to short-term crops of vegetables, such as peas and beans, and home acreage of other staple foods, such as rice, was also largely increased. All in all, some 10,000 acres were converted to food crops by 1942.[3] Guaranteed prices were offered to producers, and adequate storage and marketing facilities assured by the opening of some thirty Government depots.[4] Similarly, encouragement was offered to producers of edible oil, margarine, soap and allied products in order to expand production, and this also met with some success. A Fish Marketing Scheme, by which the Government purchased fish as soon as it was landed and then transported it to licensed wholesalers, was started in 1943.[5] Subsidies and guaranteed markets or prices to sugar and cocoa growers, however, were designed to meet post-war economic requirements rather than wartime emergencies.

Far more important than these various changes was the fact that the volume of imports of many staple commodities was not substantially

[1] See Council Paper, no. 1/44.

[2] See Governor's Speech, 1943. It is possible that some rise would have occurred anyway as the U.S. went more and more on to a war footing.

[3] *Blue Book*, 1942.

[4] See *West India Royal Commission, Statement of Action Taken*, Cmd. 6656.

[5] Col. no. 181, p. 39.

reduced. For this meant that not only was there a large supply of consumption goods to absorb purchasing power, but also that the difficulties of speculation and hoarding by importers, lack of normal raw materials or capital equipment for home production,[1] and unwillingness of workers to produce when there was no opportunity of obtaining the goods they wanted were not nearly so applicable as in the other countries with which we have dealt. The tremendous importance of this point must be remembered throughout any analysis of the inflationary tendencies in Trinidad during the war years.

§ 4. Critique of War Organization

In addition to the maintenance of imports at a level commensurate with pre-war years the Trinidad Government had other advantages in its favour. There was no serious drain of man-power for the Services, as His Majesty's Government's policy in the early war years was against recruitment of large contingents from the West Indies.[2] Nor were difficulties of enforcing controls so acute as in some countries, for the territory was fairly small and did not possess all the disadvantages of long land frontiers adjacent to other countries with higher internal price levels. It is also possible that the mass of the population was more amenable to normal methods of propaganda to encourage production, and that it more easily understood the complications of maximum prices for essential goods, than in some countries.

As against these points there were also some very definite disadvantages. The most obvious is that the island did incur a labour shortage as a result of American demands, and in this respect the situation which developed was more akin to that in Great Britain than to the state of the other primary countries considered in this survey. It is possible to argue that man-power resources were not distributed very well, but it is not possible to argue that more men could have been made available for war purposes without reducing still further the output of some goods and services.[3] There were also difficult indirect problems associated with American expenditure, for there

[1] There were of course particular shortages, e.g. feeding stuffs and some types of machinery (see Table 3).

[2] Cf. *The Economist*, 14 March 1943.

[3] The Secretary of State for the Colonies declared: 'There is an all round shortage of labour in Trinidad at the moment' (Hansard (Commons), 7 July 1943).

was little chance of taking any effective steps to limit the incomes of the principal recipients by direct means or to restrict their consumption outlay by suitable taxation. Furthermore, the general psychological atmosphere associated with this expenditure ('one dollar for anything'), and the prevailing attitude among the Americans, both individually and collectively, that controls were only introduced to be broken, made it impossible to secure stout enforcement of such controls as were introduced. Finally, there were the usual limitations of a small administration unused to dealing with such problems, a population composed of a mixture of races with varying standards and habits of consumption and a hard core of traders only too eager to seize any opportunity which might come or be induced to come their way.

Nevertheless, there are some obvious gaps which do not seem to be fully explained by these points. Import controls were far from stringent in the early war years; bulk buying of essential imports was not introduced until the weaknesses of trying to combine an unholy mixture of Government and private trading in imports were demonstrated. Furthermore, the co-ordination of the various controls was far from satisfactory. In fact, a special committee had to be appointed in 1945 to inquire into the many complaints about the functioning of the Control Board, which had been established in 1940 as a central advisory body on all matters of supply. It was found that import control had not functioned as it should have done (some import licences had been arranged by collusion between the Board and private importers), that the cost of administering the Bulk Purchasing Department had been unduly high, and that the general arrangements for dovetailing the controls had been poor.[1] For instance, there had been cases where the Food Controller or the Bulk Purchasing Department had refused to supply the Price Control Committee with information on foodstuffs costs, and at least one case in which the Price Control Department refused to fix a wholesale price high enough to allow the Food Control to dispose of goods to distributors without incurring losses. Similar gaps to these could be given in other fields of Government policy and control—it is very difficult to argue that direct tax receipts could not have been further increased, or that public land could not have been sold in small lots to the newly prosperous workers, for example.

[1] 'The various Departments and the Price Control Committee appear to have functioned as a loose agglomeration of bodies lacking any controlling and co-ordinating direction' (Council Paper, no. 8/1945).

There is one very clear-cut reason why anti-inflationary measures were not enforced more fully, and that is the simple one that no classes suffered heavy involuntary falls in real income, for even the plantation workers could have reduced their losses if they had been prepared to work harder. This does not mean that everybody was enjoying a high standard of living as a result of the process, for poverty was still very widespread at the end of the war as well as at the beginning. But there is no reason to believe that the movement of prices and incomes associated with the diversion of resources to the war effort was anything but a healthy—and probably desirable—development.

CHAPTER XI

CONCLUSIONS

In this chapter we shall deal with three broad topics. First, some observations of a general nature will be made on the changes in prices and incomes which took place in the countries under review. Secondly, the relations between these changes and the relative war efforts will be examined. Thirdly, some of the lessons of wartime experiences for possible future developments of primary economies will be explored.

Under the first of these headings we shall start by discussing the fundamentally rigid structure of primitive economies. The normal analysis of changes in investment and activity is based on the idea that if an attempt is made to increase the level of investment there will tend to be an increase in the value of the national output. If the increase in the rate of investment takes place when there is a reserve of unemployed labour, then the increased value of national output will be largely due to an increased volume of output; if there is no reserve of unemployed labour the increased value will be mainly due to a rise in the general price level. What Lord Keynes called a 'true inflation'[1] will only take place when reserves of unemployed labour have been exhausted.

These are the bare bones of the argument, but they are no more than that, and in the general analysis of price-inflation they are sombrely clothed with cautious provisos. It is generally recognized that specific bottlenecks will occur in any upswing of activity, and that these will tend to cause price and income changes in some sectors of the economy before reserves of labour as a whole are exhausted. Further, the difficulties of defining the point of full employment with any precision are well known, and it is therefore customary to argue that there is no black and white distinction between an economy which has a reserve of unemployed labour and one which has not, but only a grey borderland where, it is admitted, one cannot be dogmatic about the relative contributions of higher prices and higher volume to an increase in the value of national output.

In the case of primitive economies the difficulties of defining full employment are even greater than in advanced countries. The general characteristic of many primitive economies is that there is very little unemployment in the way that we understand the term, but a great

[1] *General Theory*, p. 303.

deal of under-employment. This makes it quite impossible to point to any concrete statistical evidence of figures of personnel unemployed, but at the same time we do know perfectly well that there is frequently a large amount of labour in countries of the type dealt with in this survey which simply has not sufficient to do. The evidence we have seen in the detailed chapters makes it quite clear that nowhere, with the possible exception of Trinidad, were wartime demands for labour sufficient to make serious inroads on the general reserves of labour. Indeed, His Majesty's Government did not intend that this should happen; it was not desired to recruit a large Army from India, and the Cabinet decision in 1939 was that colonial man-power should not in general be used for the Armed Services. The real point at which this policy is open to criticism is that too little and not too much use was made of these reserves of labour, for there can be little doubt that the Allied war effort as a whole was weakened by the failure of the supreme planners to devise means of employing the populations of these countries to greater capacity.

If, therefore, the explanation of the wide price and income changes which took place is not to be found in heavy general demands on labour reserves, we must ask how far it can be found in bottlenecks and obstacles to expansion of output. It is here that we come to grips with the rigid structure of the economies of these countries. We have pointed out from time to time that many primitive economies consist of two main sections: internal activity supplies the basic foodstuffs and simple manufactures, and external trade is the means of obtaining all capital equipment, and many raw materials and manufactures. Of course there are exceptions to this broad generalization, for Trinidad imports most of her foodstuffs and exports oil, and Palestine exports some manufactured goods but imports a large proportion of her cereals. Nevertheless, such examples do not upset the general picture. Now any disruption of this normal pattern of economic activity is liable to generate great changes in prices and incomes. For the output of primitive agriculture is notoriously inelastic. In India and Egypt this is fundamentally due to the pressure of an expanding population on an area of cultivable land which is not merely strictly limited but is in constant danger of shrinkage through soil erosion. The opportunities for expansion of output through more extensive cultivation are obviously very limited in such circumstances. The population problem, although its presence is marked in Palestine and the Lebanon, is not so acute in other Middle East countries; but soil erosion is common to all. Nor is this all, for difficulties arise also through the system of land tenure and the primitive techniques employed which militate against any sudden changes in output and which no Government can hope to alter in the space of a few years.[1] And if by any chance a poor harvest intervenes, then any attempts to increase output are rendered quite ineffective. Similarly, the output of manufactures in most primitive countries is subject to very severe limitations, and such goods as are produced are often made by high-cost, uneconomic methods. It is often claimed that the shortage of skilled labour is a very important factor in this connexion, but it is doubtful whether it is the fundamental point. The real thing is that educational standards are normally so low that it is impossible to supplement the supply of skilled and semi-skilled labour by intensive short courses as was done in Britain during the war. If Britain had had to rely on the pre-war engineering industry for all her skilled and semi-skilled labour in the war factories, her war output would have been limited to much lower levels than those actually achieved. Quite apart from labour problems, a sharp limit to potential output is set by such factors as the primitive processes often employed, the lack of adequate storage, poor transport and power facilities, and the inadequacy of the arrangements for the supply of credit.

Now these limitations alone are sufficient to explain why it was difficult to expand the overall volume of domestic output very appreciably in these countries in wartime, but when the vast reduction of imports which many of these countries had to face is recalled, it is quite clear why bottlenecks occurred at such early stages in so many industries. For we have said that all capital goods are imported. The importance of the reduction in agricultural machinery was not always very great, as in many countries the majority of cultivators have never seen or heard of tractors and similar machines. In some countries, however, as the 1944 harvest results in Syria showed,[2] the lack of such implements was a handicap. But even if the fall in imports of agricultural machinery should not be over-emphasized, there is little question that the reduction of imports of machinery for industrial purposes, of which textile machinery for India and Egypt or tin-mining machinery for Nigeria are obvious examples, made it difficult even to maintain pre-war standards of output, let alone improve on them. And such difficulties became still more acute when changes in

[1] These points are treated fully, in so far as they affect Middle East countries, by Keen, op. cit.

[2] See p. 238.

the nature and type of output were required, for although old machinery can always be used more intensively to produce more of the normal types of output, such measures are of little use when new products are required to meet war demands or to replace imports. There were also many reductions or cessations of imports of essential raw materials. Egyptian agriculture is very heavily dependent on imported fertilizers, but they were extremely short during the war years. All the Middle East countries need coal for railway use and other industrial purposes, but it was impossible to procure it in anything like adequate quantities.[1] The sharp fall in imported consumption goods common to all the countries under review in this survey was perhaps the most serious blow of all, for at the very time when the incomes of the inhabitants of these countries were vastly increased through Allied demands for their products and services, the supply of many of the goods which they normally purchased was curtailed or in some cases cut off altogether. Even apart from this direct reaction, the lack of imported consumption goods was itself an additional impediment to domestic production. The ability to expand internal production was very limited for the various reasons listed, but there is little doubt that the willingness to do so was also limited when the usual foodstuffs, textiles, footwear, hardware and kerosene were either not available at all or only to be bought at fantastically high prices.

Thus the fundamental rigidities of primitive economies—limited (and non-expansible) supplies of land and capital equipment and excessive dependence on imports of various kinds—made it inevitable that any large expansion of incomes would spend itself on higher prices all round rather than on a greatly increased volume of output even though there was rarely any general shortage of labour. This tendency was reinforced by another characteristic of these economies—

[1] We are not directly concerned here with the reasons why the Allied authorities curtailed imports of capital goods and raw materials to the primary producing countries so severely. Indeed they may never be fully known. But this does seem to have been a clear case of administrators concentrating on fulfilling their own bit of the war production programme without adequate consideration of the broader economic issues involved. The war effort gained immensely by the division of functions between some of the principal Allies—the differing degrees to which the labour force was mobilized for Armed Service and for production purposes in the United Kingdom and U.S.A. and Canada, for instance. How much more it could have gained if the semi-employed natives of so many primary producing countries could have been given the tools and materials to work with cannot now be determined. But the conclusion that in this way some of the Allied war potential was never fully mobilized seems, nevertheless, inescapable.

that of excessive instability of prices. For the working of an economy consisting of a large number of small producers and a narrow oligarchy of merchants is not altogether unlike that of an organized commodity market. The essential characteristic of such markets is that there is no rigidity in prices, for no one has both the power and the will to restrain price movements by suitable variations in stocks and/or output. Those who have the power to do so usually prefer to vary their stocks in such a way as to add impetus to the price fluctuation, i.e. if there is a chance of prices rising owing to a poor crop prospect the speculator will often add to his stocks in the hope of forcing up prices still further and thus making a capital gain rather than reduce his stocks to prevent a large price rise from taking place. Those who sell or purchase these commodities for 'real' purposes might very well have the will to prevent these excessive price fluctuations, but they normally form such a small section of the market that individually they are quite powerless to do so. Now similar situations to this are characteristic of the economies of many primitive countries. The many small cultivators of India and the Middle East are *individually* quite unable to prevent rises or falls in grain prices, and the merchant and trading classes are only too glad to seize any opportunity of exploiting prospective shortages to their own advantage without any regard for the consequences to society. But in some ways the situation is even worse than in the organized markets of the West, for the habit of varying holdings of stocks in a way likely to add impetus to incipient price movements is not confined to merchants and traders but quite frequently spreads through all classes of society. Small-scale producers hold on to their stocks in the hope of rising prices; Governments encourage them in these habits both by example and precept,[1] and even if stocks are not held in the hope of sales later at a higher price the expectation of scarcity, or, perhaps better, the idea that other people expect scarcity, is sufficient to make consumers (or producers in their role of consumer) desire to lay in supplies. In this context, however, it must be emphasized that primitive economies should not be judged by twentieth-century standards as we know them, but more nearly by the habits of our ancestors in the seventeenth or eighteenth century who, unable to rely on a distributive mechanism which habitually creaked and often broke down altogether, frequently laid in large stocks of essential foodstuffs to guard against all eventualities. Irregular supplies or even famine are not so much a thing of the past

[1] We have seen illustrations of this in the case of India (p. 69) and Iraq (p. 212).

in the Middle East and India that consumers have forgotten these elementary precautions. Finally, not only is this excessive instability of prices characteristic of internally produced crops, but also of the great range of imported manufactures where the many intermediaries, merchants, wholesalers and retailers alike, thrive in times of shortage.

Thus the rigidity of economic structures highly dependent on imports and the endemic instability of the price system in these countries go far to explain the underlying characteristics of the war-time changes in prices and incomes. Any sudden shock to the economic system threatens the whole mechanism with collapse in such circumstances, and when a large increment in demand for the goods and services of these countries is associated with a sudden short fall of imported goods, the strain is doubly severe. Of course the picture we have drawn of the fundamental characteristics of these economic systems does not fit all of them equally well. In Trinidad, the situation was much more akin to that in Western countries, where labour reserves were exhausted, than to the Middle East countries. In Nigeria it is doubtful whether the tendency for price instability is so marked as in India. Nevertheless, our general description is not so very wide of the mark. The reasons why price and income changes were not on such a large scale in these two colonies as in most of the other countries are to be found in the smaller burdens laid on them (the volume of military expenditure was not high in Nigeria and the reduction in imports was not very severe in Trinidad), and the Government measures introduced, rather than in any underlying differences.

This brings us to another point. It is clear from the description of events in individual countries that the local Government could do a great deal, if it wished, to curb the pace of the inflationary movement. We have seen from time to time that these Governments were handicapped in many ways: they had little experience of economic controls at all, and still less of wartime controls;[1] they often did not know the current or future magnitude of military expenditure and in fact some were not at war themselves; administrations were

[1] It must not be forgotten that the experience of economic controls in the 1914–18 war was of invaluable help to the administrators of 1939–45 in Great Britain. The crudity of views held in the earlier period is recalled by Keynes (*Treatise on Money*, vol. II, p. 170ff.), particularly in the following passage: 'he [the President of the Board of Trade] suggested that the line of escape from rising prices must be found in rising wages, whilst the general opinion at that time was that prices should be kept down but consumption left uncontrolled' (p. 171n.).

frequently small, not infrequently corrupt, and provided with little information about the economic life of the population. But these handicaps were in one form or another common to all, and it is difficult to explain the varying degrees of Government attempts to curb prices and incomes solely by reference to them. There appear to be two other major explanations why some Governments were more successful than others in limiting the upward surge of prices. First, there was unquestionably some woolly thought on the subject. We have seen how in India a good deal of heated argument was wasted on the subject of whether the new rupees created were backed by sterling assets or not. Another good example was the reply given in the House of Commons in 1942 *à propos* rationing of scarce goods in Jamaica.[1] Probably more important than these points, however, was the failure in most countries to grasp that the essential thing was to concentrate on limiting incomes. Where the great majority of the population does not work for a weekly wage the dangers of an upward rise of wages in response to any increase in prices due to higher indirect taxation are neither very widespread nor very acute. There is no semi-automatic relationship between prices and wage levels under such conditions,[2] and therefore any policy which aims at pushing up prices by taxation is almost wholly beneficial as a weapon against inflation. Where it is difficult to lay heavy taxation on the agricultural community, or to persuade it to hold cash or bonds, or to block the channels of consumption expenditure, the only alternative is to control incomes. Most of these Governments took steps towards this policy by requisitioning of crops at controlled prices, or in some cases by direct exchange of consumption goods in short supply for crops, but few adopted it soon enough or thoroughly enough.

It cannot, however, be claimed that muddled thinking is a sufficient explanation of the inaction of some Governments. The other main reason why they did not take adequate action to limit the movements of prices and incomes is that they were unwilling to do so. Now this unwillingness is not, after all, surprising. There was no impelling sense of urgency in those countries which were not at war; whether at war or not it did not take much knowledge of economics to realize

[1] 'The problem is one of price, not of supply, and is being dealt with as such' (Hansard (Commons), 25 March 1942).

[2] This was less true in the case of Palestine owing to the existence of an industrial labour force of some size and the agreements to regulate wages according to the cost of living index. Subsidies or unwillingness to increase indirect taxes can therefore be more justified in that country than in the others under review.

that the greater the extent of the price rise the greater would be the profits of local producers and merchants, and, incidentally, the greater would be the sterling balances accumulated. The powerful interests of the great landlords and merchants in Egypt, Iraq and Syria certainly had nothing to lose by the process. Any Government which attempted a really serious anti-inflationary policy in such circumstances could hardly have survived a day. But it is also possible that some Governments were actuated by more altruistic motives than these. It may be that they realized that the inflationary movement was not only in the interests of the wealthier classes but also that it would secure the necessary war contributions without inflicting undue hardships on any very large sections of the community. This brings us to the second main topic which we intend to explore.

We shall now discuss the relationship between the inflationary movements and the relative war efforts, a subject which was broached but not fully explored in Chapter I.

The first point to note is that without a considerable measure of expansion in the volume of money demand there could have been little increase in the volume of national output. In no country during either world war was it possible to secure the necessary expansion of output and diversion of resources to war by the methods of orthodox finance. But the expansion of money demand in the primary producing countries was generally much larger than in Western economies. Can it really be argued that a threefold rise in the Palestine national income was necessary to secure an increase of about one-third in the national output or a decrease in consumption expenditure, at 1939 prices, of 20% between 1939 and 1943? Can it be maintained that a tenfold rise in money supplies in Syria and the Lebanon was necessary to secure the exports of wheat and barley for the rest of the Middle East? It is clear that no single answer about the relative increases of money demand necessary to secure a given increase in national output in primary *vis-à-vis* advanced countries can be given. But even when the traditionally slow pace of development of primary producing countries under normal conditions is remembered it hardly seems possible to argue that the comparatively small increases in output and small proportions of resources diverted to war actually achieved in these countries were only made possible by a large measure of inflation, when the much greater expansion in output in Western economies was achieved without nearly such proportionately large changes in money expenditure. Nevertheless, even when this point is borne in mind, the validity of the general argument that some measure of inflation was necessary to secure the war contribution cannot be questioned.

The next topic we have to consider is whether the upward movement of prices caused any considerable fall in real incomes for large sections of the communities concerned, for it is customary to argue in Western countries that although some expansion of money demand is necessary to develop a war effort, any such movement which is not closely controlled will lead to sharp falls in real income for some classes, which in turn may result in unrest and strikes with consequent hindrance to the war effort. Now we have seen time after time that very often great sections of the agricultural populations of these countries did not suffer sharp falls in real income. Subsistence farmers, clearly, could lose little from price changes, and those mainly dependent on the sales proceeds of their own crops sometimes made substantial gains through the increase in prices, or through the larger volume of crops. Farm labourers working for money wages lost little, as in most cases these rose almost *pari passu* with prices, particularly when the opportunities of working for the military forces are taken into account. If payment was made in kind, the fact that the proportions of crops received by labour, in the Middle East at any rate, were normally fairly rigid, ensured that there was no great fall in real income. In the towns it is not very evident that many wage earners suffered sharp falls in real earnings, for even if wage rates lagged behind prices in the early stages of the war the increased opportunities for more regular employment, and hence the improvements in earnings relatively to wage rates, were often sufficient to compensate for this. The only classes of society which can definitely be identified as being left seriously behind in the chase are the black-coated workers and minor Government officials; but these are not nearly such a large proportion of the community as in Western countries.[1] Nor can it be easily maintained that the falls in real income imposed on the creditor classes by the general rise in prices were very substantial. There is no large section of society entirely dependent on fixed incomes in such countries, for the capital wealth of the community is largely concentrated among a small section of the population which is usually quite able to redeem any losses in unearned income from its current

[1] The converse of the proposition that the Governments of these countries are understaffed and that not many people are suitable for training.

trading activities. On balance, the rise in prices was unquestionably beneficial for countries in which the poorer sections of the population are almost all riddled with heavy debts. Similarly, the stickiness of money rents in both urban and rural areas—though here Egypt is a conspicuous exception—was another source of gain. It is, in a sense, true to say that the greater the inflation of prices the less likely it is that the great mass of the population is suffering from any serious fall in real income. It cannot be maintained both that price changes are difficult to control and that the profit-earning section of the community has very greatly increased its share of the national income, for the extent to which price-inflation proceeds ultimately depends on the amount of redistribution of income from the poorer classes who are likely to spend to those wealthier sections of the community who are likely to save.

Therefore it can be argued that the structure of economic life in these countries is such that the large-scale changes in prices did not imply very widespread falls in real income. Indeed, when the new opportunities of earning high wages in military employment or high prices for grain produced are fully taken into account and weighed against the miserable pittances received by so many millions before the war, the argument is still further reinforced. But, it might well be said, there is abundant evidence of heavy reductions in consumption of staple items such as tea, sugar and cloth in nearly all these countries, and in some even grain supplies were deficient from time to time. Is this not sufficient evidence to show that large-scale inflation imposed undue hardships? In dealing with this point, we must be quite clear that if any war contribution at all was to be levied on these countries then some reduction in basic necessities of this sort was almost inevitable, simply on account of the extremely low levels of national income *per capita*. When the mass of a population lives largely on cereals and vegetables and it is necessary to divert some proportion of the current output of goods and services to war needs (and we have seen that the possibilities of satisfying war requirements by expanding current output or cutting down stocks, etc., were strictly limited), then it is impossible to avoid cutting consumption of cereals and/or vegetables. Therefore, the real point at issue is not whether reductions in current consumption were avoidable or not, but whether the inflationary method of securing them resulted in cuts in 'more basic' rather than 'less basic' goods and whether the poorer classes were mulcted as much as or less than the richer elements. Now it is not difficult to produce good examples of heavy reductions in consumption among the poorest classes of these countries—the very limited quantities of sugar and cloth received by the Egyptian fellaheen are a case in point—and thence jump to the conclusion that the haphazard methods of inflation caused greater hardships than a carefully planned reduction in consumption would have done. But before the jump is taken, three points must be considered. First, the heavy dependence of many primitive economies on imports of some goods—textiles, for instance—was often a much more important factor in determining which items would be reduced in supply than any considerations of internal policy. There would still have been some reductions in cereals consumption in Palestine even if there had been no large changes in prices and incomes. Secondly, the nature of the appropriate comparison must be realized. It is no use arguing in the case of such countries as these that inflation had certain results whereas a carefully planned system would have meant a lesser degree of current hardship. We have seen throughout the course of the detailed chapters how woefully inadequate and inefficient was the administration in so many countries. The real point is not what might have happened in some perfectly organized country, but what was the alternative to large-scale inflation in these countries. Thirdly, it is also important to remember that such current hardships as were incurred were accompanied by other gains which should help to raise the standard of living in the future. The capital wealth of all these countries has been increased not only by the accretion of large sterling balances but also by the many improvements to roads, harbours and communication systems and the new knowledge and skill gained by the personnel who enlisted in the Allied Armies or worked for them in civilian capacities.

On these various grounds, therefore, we have to be careful of the argument that the high degree of inflation hindered the war effort. For some measure of inflation was necessary to develop the war effort; and evidence of resultant widespread falls in real income or reductions in consumption of necessities is not overwhelming. There is, in fact, no very convincing evidence that the large expansion of money demand was directly responsible for limiting output of cultivators. It is not without significance that the two countries in the Middle East where cereal output was best maintained or expanded during the war years were Syria and Iraq, for there prices rose most. Much more important as a determinant of cultivators' willingness to produce more or at least disgorge more of their crops was the supply of consumption goods, and this was associated far more with international questions of physical allocation than with changes in real purchasing power resulting from local movements of prices and incomes.

Can it therefore be said that a large measure of inflation has no disadvantages from the point of view of maximizing the war effort? This might seem to follow from our previous argument, but in reality it would be just as dangerous to accept this line of thought as the doctrine about the unmitigated horrors of inflation. First, even though a large expansion in money demand is necessary to increase the volume of national output, there may be very definite drawbacks in such a policy. The method of recruiting workers to build airfields in India by offering higher wages meant that the airfields were built, but whether this advantage offset the consequent loss of coal and the disruption of other sectors of the economy is somewhat questionable. There can be little doubt that in Palestine the very high profits earned in industry were responsible for general laxity of management and low productivity of labour.[1] If an inflationary process is allowed to develop so far and so fast that there is a general unwillingness to hold the national unit of currency as a capital asset or to meet known contingencies—and, *a fortiori*, if this currency is no longer trusted as a medium for current transactions—then the existence of a war contribution may be impeded. If hoarding not only implies the holding of crops for speculative reasons but also a rush to spend incomes as soon as they are received on consumption goods, then the locking up of real capital in private hands may well reach serious proportions and the economic life of the community be disorganized. The nearest approximations to such a situation were in Bengal in 1943 and in Syria and Iraq in 1941. The consequences in Bengal are too well known to need repetition here and even though the phenomenon was only temporary in the latter two countries, activity was reduced to very low levels at the time.

Secondly, we have argued that severe falls in real income were not extremely common. This does not mean, however, that there was no redistribution of the national income, for the great landlords, merchants, and industrialists absorbed a very large proportion of such increases in the real national income as were achieved. Other classes, particularly the more prosperous peasants, often increased their real incomes too, but the evidence of the detailed chapters is sufficient to

[1] Cf. Nathan, op. cit. p. 490.

show that the increases were largely absorbed by the above categories. And it must not be forgotten that there were both individuals and whole classes who did suffer severe falls in real income, even if they did not form large sections of the population. The outstanding example is the class of black-coated workers and Government officials, but other examples, such as the coal-miners in Bihar, the landless labourers in some parts of India, or some of the peasant farmers in Nigeria are not difficult to find. Thirdly, even though the argument that the reduction in supplies of essential goods was associated with the large measures of inflation cannot be accepted *in toto*, it nevertheless still does not lose all validity and significance.

It seems highly probable that the incentive to work was reduced in some countries for reasons such as these. In some cases this was due to the receipt of high money wages; the labour employed on the American bases in Trinidad is a good example. In the majority, however, it was due to reductions in real income or lack of supplies of necessary goods. The strikes in India and Cyprus in 1942 or in Nigeria in 1945 can hardly be entirely dissociated from the consequences of the inflationary process, even though other factors were also at work.

Finally, we must consider how far an inflationary movement can develop without severe disorganization of the economy. If the expansion in money incomes and prices continues unchecked, then the evils of hyper-inflation of prices eventually appear. Hoarding of goods becomes more prevalent as the currency becomes more suspect; the falls in real income are widespread and severe; and both the volume of national output and the quantity of resources available for war tend to be reduced. Once such a state is reached, the advantages of a large measure of inflation as a policy are more than counterbalanced by the disadvantages. On the whole it cannot be said that any of the countries dealt with in this survey was ever very near the hyper-inflation stage, with the possible exception of Syria and the Lebanon. Nevertheless, some of the symptoms had begun to appear in several countries in 1943, and if a general effort to tighten up controls and restrain the growth of money demand had not been made in that year some of the consequences might have been apparent too.

The scope of this work is really confined to wartime economic problems, but, nevertheless, it would not be right to conclude without applying some of the wartime experiences to the burning questions of the future. It is tempting to make prophecies about the post-war course of prices in these countries and to speculate on the means whereby the high price levels of, for instance, Syria and Egypt, will be brought into line with world prices. This involves many interesting problems, such as the question of whether internal price deflation or external devaluation of the currency should be preferred; the extent to which it will be possible to draw on accumulated foreign balances to pay for current imports, the extent to which tariffs are likely to be used to protect the new industries fostered under the protection of war. But it is certainly impossible to predict events of this nature with any degree of exactitude without access to a large amount of official information and probably impossible even if such access were granted. The tide of events is flowing so quickly that any estimates made here would inevitably be archaic by the time they appear in print. What can be pointed out, however, is that the obstacles to severe falls in prices are far less in primitive economies than in Western countries. First, there are only a few wage earners in these countries, and their Trade Union organizations, if they exist at all, are comparatively new and weak. Therefore the element of rigidity introduced into the price structure of a highly industrialized country by a large wage-earning community, unwilling to see its standards lowered, is mainly lacking. Secondly, the absence of any widespread combinations and associations among producers, and the much nearer approximation to conditions of free competition, means that agreements to restrict output in order to prevent heavy price falls, such as take place in more advanced countries, are not very common. The speculative character of the transactions of many merchants and dealers normally adds impetus to price trends in these countries, and it may therefore be expected that if a downward price movement does start the descent is likely to be fast and furious. Lastly, there is the important point that whilst vast new volumes of internal debt have been incurred by the State at wartime price levels in Great Britain and U.S.A., the general movement in the primary producing countries has been towards a reduction of private indebtedness and, except in India, it is doubtful whether this has been mitigated severely by new State debts. Therefore the same inducement for Governments to bolster up prices does not exist as in this country.

This is all we shall have to say on short-period problems, and we shall now turn to the long period problems of investment in primitive countries. Does the war contain any lessons for those interested in such problems? A very obvious point revealed by wartime experience is the difficulty of increasing the rate of savings in a primitive economy without driving up prices to a high level. Not only is it extremely difficult to persuade small cultivators to hold much wealth in the forms of money or near-money, but the consumption expenditure of the richer classes is also a high proportion of income sometimes. In the Middle East countries particularly, they prefer to lead lives of ostentatious luxury rather than make funds available for capital development, and even those who do make their savings available for new enterprises are more often than not only interested in projects which yield quick returns and high profits. It is true that wartime demands implied a fairly heavy rate of saving,[1] whereas normal development plans would probably not be so exacting, but national income per head is so uniformly low in these countries that the prospects of financing any reasonably large-scale investment without recourse to deficit finance are rather dim unless radical improvements can be made in taxation machinery. In fact, this difficulty is fully recognized by planners,[2] but the usual plea is that deficit finance will not produce a large measure of price-inflation if adequate controls are imposed. But after wartime experiences, who would be bold enough to assert that sufficiently far-reaching controls are really practicable? The fundamental difficulty is to stop the peasant or small cultivator from eating more of his crops when members of his family who have been living off his output leave to start building roads or factories. To carry this out thoroughly will require far more efficient and detailed administration than most of those countries have enjoyed in the past. Therefore the point has to be faced—a larger volume of internal savings can only be secured at the expense of some price-inflation.[3] But is this really so terrible? We have seen that although wartime price-inflation did involve redistribution of incomes and did impose some current hardships, many sections of the population were not badly affected. Provided that an upward movement of prices can be restrained from developing into hyper-inflation there are few real

[1] Net savings in Palestine were running at the rate of about 18% of the national income from 1942 to 1944.

[2] See, for instance, *A Plan of Economic Development for India* (Penguin Ed.).

[3] The proportion of National Income which the Bombay plan proposed should be saved (12%) would almost certainly mean this. A lower figure is assumed by Bonné (*Economic Development of the Middle East*), who anticipates that 6½% of the net product of agriculture and the net income from industry will be available as savings but even this may be too high.

bogies. The most fearsome is most likely to be that of maladjustments between internal money costs and world prices, but that is a by-way we cannot explore here.

But this discussion of financing capital investment from internal sources would be incomplete if we stopped at this point, for it is essential to remember that an important element in the wartime situation was the great reduction in imports. This had several reactions, for it cut off supplies of many staple commodities and weakened the normal incentives encouraging cultivators to produce, but most important of all—and this is another great lesson for the future from wartime experience—it showed how difficult it is to expand the national output, even under the stress of emergency, when external supplies of raw materials and above all machinery are not available in sufficient quantity. The events we have described in India and Nigeria might have been rather different if supplies of electrical and mechanical equipment for the engineering and textile industries had been available to the former or tin-mining machinery to the latter. The obstacles to the building up of an efficient machine-tool industry internally are probably greater than in the case of almost any other single industry, for even if the necessary raw material and basic metal industries can be established nothing can get over the fact that the necessary high degree of skill and technical 'know-how' can only be acquired by the local population after years of laborious experience. Without adequate imports of machinery it is impossible to see how any major increases in national output per head in the course of the next few years can be obtained; with adequate imports—and the finance of these should provide no difficulty for those countries with sterling balances—it should be possible to make some impression on the sluggish economies of these backward countries.

Therefore wartime experience drives home the double importance of adequate imports of capital goods, for they are indispensable if output per head is to be increased, and an increase in output per head is in itself the strongest safeguard against inflationary tendencies due to a higher rate of internal capital investment.

Finally, does wartime experience throw any light on the right priorities in capital development for backward countries? This is obviously a large subject on which several chapters, or, more accurately, several books, could be written, and it would be presumptuous to pretend that a few words written here can be more than pointers to different lines of thought. Nevertheless, it is quite obvious that capital projects *per se* and conceived without reference to the desires or fundamental needs of the local population are not enough. The Colonial Empire may all too easily become a museum of white elephants unless sufficient attention is paid to economic realities. One of the lessons of war experience was the extreme difficulty encountered in most of these countries in increasing the level of output either in the agricultural or the industrial sectors. This was due to many different reasons, some of them, such as the reductions of imports, associated solely with wartime conditions, but even when these are discounted two points seem worthy of notice. First, in some countries, of which perhaps India and Egypt are the best examples, the immediate problem is to arrest the threatened fall in standards of living if present trends continue.[1] The obvious way to do this is to move more of the population into secondary or tertiary industry, for the marginal productivity of labour in agriculture in these countries is so extremely low that such a movement must almost inevitably increase real income per head. Even if the population on the land continues to produce the same amount per head as before and therefore total agricultural output does not increase,[2] the general validity of this standard argument cannot normally be questioned. For the increase in output of manufactured goods will always make it possible to cut down exports of agricultural products, or even secure imports,[3] if such a situation arises. Nevertheless, it must be realized and emphasized repeatedly that if the benefits of industrial development are to be fully harvested, an all-out attack to maintain and increase agricultural output must be made. And in those countries such as Iraq, where the fundamental cause of low productivity is the shifting cultivation employed rather than the pressure of an expanding population on a limited or shrinking area of land, the need

[1] Cf. Keen, op. cit. p. 17; also Worthington, op. cit. *passim*; Royal Institute of International Affairs, *A Food Plan for India*.

[2] Total agricultural output will not decline, unless the number of workers drawn into industry is greater than the increase in the working population.

[3] The argument used by Benham (*Economica*, August 1946, p. 211) that the wartime experience of Trinidad is *prima facie* evidence for preferring agricultural to industrial development in backward countries does not seem valid. There can be little doubt that real *income* (though not *consumption*) per head expanded in Trinidad during the war. And even if there was some reduction in sugar output, etc. it must be remembered that the drain of labour to the bases was very heavy and also that the existence of large estates and a paid agricultural labour force makes analogies with other peasant economies tricky. Another important respect in which the comparison with peacetime conditions in other countries does not hold is that the reduced supply of consumption goods possibly discouraged production.

for measures to increase agricultural output is still urgent, even if the necessity to move greater sections of the population into industry is not so pressing. The most apposite measures to increase agricultural output are obviously a matter for close and detailed study in each country concerned, but as a broad generalization it does not seem far wrong to say that in most of these countries the two greatest obstacles to agricultural progress are first and foremost land tenure and secondly water supply. Without reform of the strip system of farming and without further irrigation and similar measures to increase the area of cultivable land or at least to check the process of soil erosion, there is little chance of much headway being made, even if such improvements as increased use of fertilizers and animal or mechanical power are introduced. It must not be forgotten that the agricultural revolution preceded the industrial in eighteenth-century England, and even though the pressure of population may make industrial expansion an imperative necessity, that is still no argument for reversing this sequence.

Secondly, we have seen time after time how the output of agriculture or of industry was limited by the almost total absence of what are loosely called 'external economies' in Western countries. Methods of marketing, propaganda, publicity, grading and inspection, storage and transport facilities, credit supplies, low standards of health, education and skill among the population are all examples. Whether the best course of future development for an individual country involves a combination of industrial and agricultural development or purely improvement of methods and types of agriculture, it is important to devote some attention to matters such as these.

APPENDICES

APPENDIX I

PRINCIPAL COMPARATIVE STATISTICS

1	2		3	4			5	6
Country	Population 000's		Peak % ratio of labour in Forces or on military work to total population	Net national income £ per head			Peak annual military and defence expenditure (£ per head at 1939 prices)	Net change in sterling assets (+ =increase) 1939–45 (£m.)
	1939	1943		1939	1943	1943 at 1939 prices		
India	380,000	400,000	2·0	4·9	8·5	5·2	0·68	+1350
Palestine	1500	1670	6·1	20	54	24	9·6	+ 100
Egypt	16,500	17,500	1·7	(10)	(22)	(11)	2·6	+ 320
Sudan	5700	6500	0·46	—	—	—	0·67	—
Cyprus	397	420	7·4	—	—	—	5·1	+ 9
Iraq	4000	4500	2·1	—	—	—	2·2	+ (37·5)
Syria and Lebanon	3630	3900	0·9	—	—	—	1·7	—
Nigeria	20,600	22,000	0·6	—	—	—	0·12	—
Trinidad	473	502	6·2	—	—	—	—	+ (19)

	7		8	9	10	11		12	
Country	Wage rates in shillings per week		Wholesale prices in June 1945 (1939=100)	Retail prices in June 1945 (1939=100)	Supply of money (currency and bank deposits) 1945 (1939=100)	Imports in 1943		Exports in 1943	
	1939	1943				Price index (1939=100)	Vol. index (1939=100)	Price index (1939=100)	Vol. index (1939=100)
India	5·4	8·0	241	223	488	195	40	227	54
Palestine	36 13	73 25	330	257	451	325	41	276	(91)
Egypt	12	20	325	290	560	—	—	—	(30)
Sudan	—	—	217	166	425	305	55	133	84
Cyprus	10	26	—	233	(460)	541	46	307	78
Iraq	—	—	488	369	1047	—	(50)	—	(75)
Syria and Lebanon	—	—	961	562	922	296	50	860	13
Nigeria	5·5	10·6	—	176	(253)	222	—	138	(125)
Trinidad	7·9	12·8	—	179	(1790)	197	(86)	130	(110)

NOTES

Column 2. *Population.* Details of sources given in individual chapters. Allied troops temporarily resident excluded. Figures for Syria and the Lebanon are 1942. Trinidad figures include Tobago.

Column 3. *Labour on military work.* Nigeria figure excludes those performing personal services for non-native troops.

Column 4. *Net national income.* Sources given in detailed chapters. Egyptian figures are subject to wide margins of error.

Column 5. *Military expenditure.* Details of constituents are given in individual chapters but all the figures are roughly comparable. Allied and Local Government expenditure added together. Values deflated by cost of living indices except in India where the Economic Adviser's wholesale index was used as this is the only all-India price index available. Nigeria figure is probably less than the peak (see p. 242 n.).

Column 6. *Sterling assets.* Changes are in general from August 1939 to June 1945 except India (March 1939–March 1945). Iraq figures are for Currency Board holdings only. For basis of Trinidad figures see p. 274.

Column 7. *Wage rates.* These comparisons are necessarily very rough as so few wage statistics are available. Typical wage rates in towns have been taken but even this was not possible in some cases. Weekly earnings of coal-miners in India, average rates paid to Jewish labour and Arab labour respectively in Palestine, rates paid to semi-skilled workers in Cyprus, and rates per task paid to sugar estate labourers in Trinidad are used.

Column 10. *Money supply.* See Chapters IX and X for details of incompleteness of statistics on Trinidad and Nigeria.

Column 11. *Imports.* } *Column* 12. *Exports.* } Include civilian Lend-Lease stores but not military or N.A.A.F.I. goods (except Iraq, see p. 201). ( ) indicates estimated and not official figure.

APPENDIX II

WEIGHTS AND MEASURES

India.

13·3 Rs. = £1 sterling.
16 annas = 1 rupee.
12 pies = 1 anna.
1 seer = 2·057 lb.
1 maund = 82 lb. 4 oz.

Palestine.

1000 mils = £1 (P.) or sterling.

Egypt.

100 piastres = £1 (E.). 97·5 piastres = £1 sterling.
1 cantar = 44·9 kg. for cotton (ginned).
1 ardeb = 121·3 kg. for cotton seed and 150 kg. for wheat.
1 oke = 2·75 lb. = 400 dirhems.
1 feddan = 4201 sq. metres = 1·04 acres.

Cyprus.

180 piastres = £1 sterling.

Syria and the Lebanon.

£S.8·83 = £1 sterling.
1 hectare = 2·47 acres.

Trinidad.

4·8 dollars = £1 sterling.

INDEX

Printed in the United States
By Bookmasters